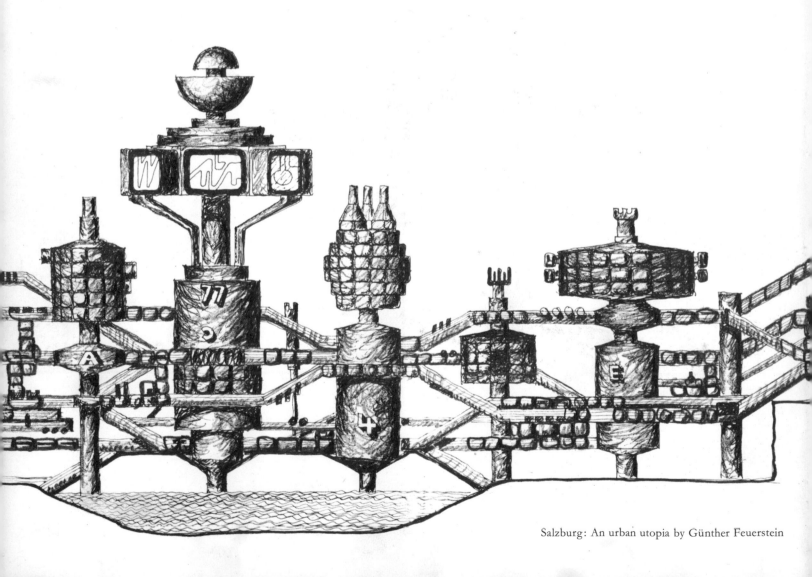

Salzburg: An urban utopia by Günther Feuerstein

Justus Dahinden

Urban Structures for the Future

Translated by Gerald Onn

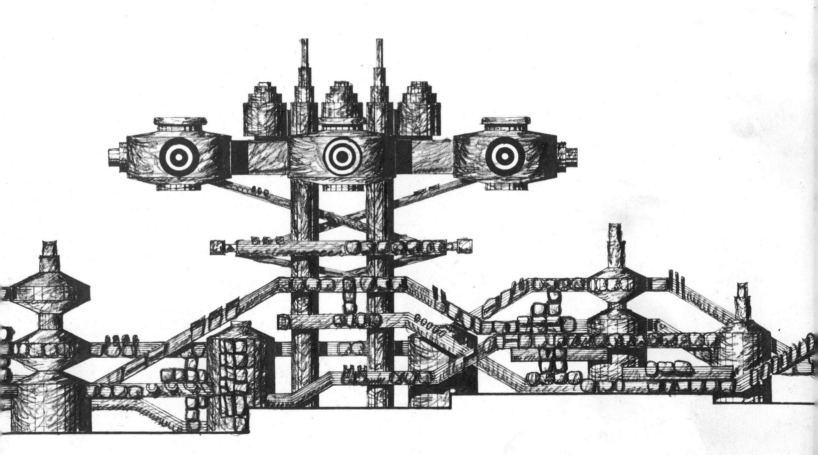

Praeger Publishers

New York · Washington · London

I wish to thank Walter Stahl for com-
piling and arranging the research material incorporated into this book; I also
wish to thank the many architects who
placed their own research material at my
disposal, thus enabling me to present a
wider survey of the present state of
prospective town planning than would
otherwise have been possible.

Contents

'*Today science has merged with technology to form a single composite discipline. As a result, every new idea evolved by our scientists is automatically put into effect. Thanks to our technological and industrial systems, the results of scientific experiments are transformed, within a matter of a few years, into social realities which help to shape the lives of millions of people. Due to this development, we are now able to identify the first characteristic of a qualitative transition; namely, the rapidity of historical change.*'

Georg Picht

Looking into the Future

Because of the scientific and technical revolution that has been the hallmark of our modern era, man will have to adopt a completely new outlook if he is to assume responsibility for the future. This future appears as an artificial, urbanized world that is both the cause and the outcome of social change. But if we are to adopt a satisfactory attitude to this new urbanized world, we have to grasp not only the inevitability, but also the dangers of the changes brought about by current developments. We are living in a period of such rapid technical development that social developments are scarcely able to keep pace. And because of the growing divergence between the effectiveness of our socio-political systems on the one hand and our technical systems on the other we find that our technologists have little understanding of social problems and our politicians little understanding of technological requirements.

Today acceptance of responsibility for the future presupposes total planning, which is inconceivable without a vision of what the future may look like. However, such utopian visions are ultimately prompted by subjective wishes and hopes, and if the future is to be mastered we cannot proceed on the basis of irrational utopian dreams or distorted ideological conceptions, in which one single aspect is artificially isolated and given undue prominence. On the contrary, we have to acquire a prospective view that will enable us to evolve an integral image of the future based on the realities of our present situation and the opportunities that these provide. The creation of such an ideal world will call for protracted endeavours in the political, social and technological spheres. Of the many tasks that will have to be surmounted, the most important are the establishment of supranational systems, the introduction of a comprehensive educational system and comprehensive economic planning, the reorganization of food and energy supplies, the implementation of effective methods of population control, the elimination of any vested interests that oppose progress, the re-definition of the concept of property and the involvement of the public in the planning process.

The Urban Crisis

In view of recent developments, which have led to a considerable loss of urban substance in our towns and are now reducing the whole world to what Robert Jungk has aptly called a 'planet metropolis' by a process of uniform global diffusion, we have to ask ourselves in all seriousness whether towns, conceived as specific concentrations and containers of human activities, really do have a future. This question becomes all the more relevant if we consider that in our society the importance of physical contact is being diminished by the electronics media. In Marshall McLuhan's view the new communications media are gradually turning the world into a 'global village', in which actual participation in the life of the community is being replaced by audio-visual contact and in which information has become more important than participation. And when we further consider that in our modern age, which has also been described as an age of flight and universal movement, densely populated towns have invariably had the effect of bringing all movement to a halt, the question as to whether it would not be better to abolish conventional towns really does become a matter of concern.

Faced with an urban society that has grown insecure due to the present inadequacy of urban design, the town planner must try to provide a range of 'possibilities' designed to cater for every conceivable kind of activity but without imposing a preconceived and authoritarian schema by creating actual 'objects'. The mobile urban forms which have already begun to appear on a modest scale would surely seem to indicate that the traditional town, which reflects conventional bourgeois attitudes and caters for the needs of a static society, is no longer desirable. The Hippy movement is not just a rebellion on the part of modern youth against inhuman societies; it has also promoted the emergence of new urban and social forms, for which inflatable mini accommodations are far more suitable than permanent homes built of bricks and mortar.

In the future decentralization will pose no problems in the industrial sphere. With the establishment of mobile techniques and the abolition of old style factories, with the separation of management and production and the introduction of remote control, it will be possible

1. Our cities are in their death throes—do we still need cities? Street scene in New York City.
2. Our traditional cities are now being called into question in their capacity as social, cultural and economic centres by the global cluster, which will integrate urban and rural life on a massive scale while preserving the personal quality of human existence by means of microzoning. The global cluster foresees the unlimited occupation of space on land, in the air and at sea. Sketch by Justus Dahinden.

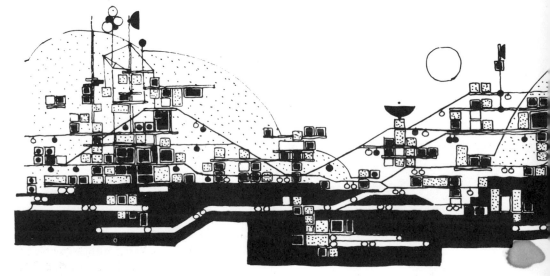

to decentralize working processes without any of the disadvantages encountered today. With the abolition of a centralized working area and the integration of the professional and domestic spheres by means of electronic devices, it will be possible for everybody to work at home, thus removing traffic congestion and rendering the motor car—which has come to be regarded by the present generation of city dwellers more or less as a second skin, as an extension of their ego—completely unnecessary.

If we were to take the model of worldwide 'contemporaneity', which has been sketched here and which obviates the necessity for movement from one place to another, and to translate it into architectural terms, we would have a worldwide cluster incorporating planetary microzoning, which would dispense completely with specific urban concentrations and would also be capable of extension into space. A global cluster of this kind could be terrestrial, subterrestrial, marine, submarine and even extra-terrestrial. In this endless human settlement the artificial and natural environments would be totally integrated, which means that the traditional antithesis between town and country-side, between the structures of urban and rural life, would be resolved.

But although such a prospect is undeniably attractive, the fact of the matter is that our whole conception of higher forms of social life is still intimately bound up with the idea of specific urban concentrations. Our sociologists and psychologists, especially, continue to regard the sense of community which these provide as an important means of achieving a high degree of spontaneity and, consequently, of intellectual stimulus and creativity. Thus, although there may be no functional justification for such concentrations, they are in fact quite irreplaceable. In the final analysis, we are concerned with preserving the complexity of urban life, and it is for this reason that we must retain urban concentrations.

When we come to plan our future urban structures, we must plan them around man; in the interplay of urban structures man must always remain the focal point of interest. Consequently, although I do not doubt that there will be a universal society in the future, I am convinced that this society will be centred on urban concentrations because it is only within such a framework that man can achieve self-realization.

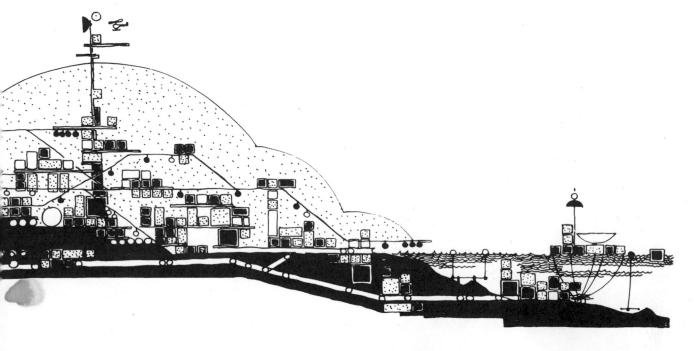

3. The fascination of the big city lies in the complexity of its architectural patterns. View of a commercial district in New York City.
4. Our towns are losing their residential value. A slum in New York City.
5. A traditional rural structure. Rysum, East Friesland.
6. A traditional urban structure. Nürnberg.

Within a few decades the vast majority of people in the industrial countries of the western world will be city dwellers.

Because it concentrates within narrow confines a wide range of highly fascinating human activities and forms of expression, because it provides such an exciting forum for the world at large and has accumulated such a wealth of different values, because of its high degree of sophistication and organization, the modern big city is rightly regarded as man's greatest achievement.

On the other hand, it is equally true that our big cities have become vast reservoirs of poverty and social unrest. Nowhere are overcrowding and lack of hygiene, criminality, physical and psychological hasards, *existenzangst* and aimlessness quite as pronounced as they are in our great conurbations; nowhere are social differences as obvious as they are there.

The image of our cities has been moulded by history and tradition; and in the pluralistic industrial society of our day the problems which have emerged in the course of our long urban development are beginning to assume mammoth proportions. Our cities are now being swept by a wave of dynamism which makes their traditional rigid structures appear more and more anachronistic. What is even more alarming is that none of the remedies applied so far have produced anything like satisfactory living conditions. Political and social programmes have been launched, cautious town planning projects have been initiated, slum areas have been cleared by bulldozers, modern amenities have been provided and functional restructuring has been undertaken. But all have proved ineffectual. On the face of it, this is surprising, for in many cases the conditions have been entirely conducive to successful town-planning. The towns destroyed in the Second World War, for example, were ideal subjects for the planner: who has also had ample opportunity of showing models of new towns at international exhibitions. But, instead of being practically implemented, the new ideas have been talked out of existence in theories and manifestoes. There were many reasons for this lack of initiative. One is the paradoxical state of affairs whereby our highly organized consumer society, which insists on diversification and built-in obsolescence in its commercial undertakings, reveals a marked preference for uniformity, durability and stability when it comes to houses. A further obstacle to real progress in the town-planning sphere has been the static condition of our society. By electing to live in conurbations modern man is still being guided by the authoritarian, hierarchical social forms of the past and turning a blind eye to the new social structures which are now beginning to emerge and which, in Arno Plack's view, will only tolerate a functional hierarchy: 'what we might call a hierarchy of social accomplishments. Instead of having a conical structure with a single peak, a society of this kind would have many such peaks, the exact number depending on the number of different functions fulfilled by its members. The only relationships of subservience that would occur would be based on the social functions fulfilled by the members (as teachers, doctors, craftsmen etc) so that relationships of inferiority and superiority would be firmly based on objective criteria.'[1]

It is difficult to avoid the impression that the principal reason for our society's refusal to embark on an utopian option for the future on any significant scale is that it would necessitate sacrificing too many trusted institutions and making a number of radical changes that would involve incalculable risks.

But the failure of town planning during recent decades was not due solely to social prejudices. The majority of our contemporary architects must also bear their share of the responsibility for

* Notes: see page 215.

having failed to realize that, if they are to acquire a deeper appreciation of the 'disorderly', 'unfinished' and 'impure' quality of developmental architecture, they must renounce the idealistic traditions of the past. Our conception of architecture is too narrow and too encumbered by historical values. Architecture needs to be integrated with all the other disciplines which enter into the general sphere of town planning. Because of its fortuitous character, even 'good' architecture can only temporarily divert attention from the highly unsatisfactory situation in which it is embedded.

New directions in town planning will only emerge when we acquire an integral outlook that takes account of social and political, technical and economic, and instinctual and emotional conditions. For this reason I now propose to discuss a number of factors which play an important part in determining urban structures and which will, I trust, enable me to formulate some of the requirements of future towns.

If we consider the historical development of social life we find two principal forms of organization, namely the agrarian community and the urban community. In the agrarian community social institutions were loosely built up around the individual, the family and the neighbourhood group, while in the urban community, which encompassed a wide variety of activities within a limited area, a large number of special community problems had to be solved within the economic framework of a densely populated environment.

The urban block, which normally consisted of a single building complex surrounded by roads on all four sides, created two architectural areas which, although intimately involved with one another, were none the less completely separated in the physical sense, forming on the one hand the public road and on the other the private dwelling with its enclosed courtyard or garden. The point of contact between these two areas was the façade, which formed a natural link between the individual sphere and the public sphere. This kind of architectural structure, which has largely determined the configuration of urban space, has proved extremely hardy for, although it fails to meet any of the requirements of the contemporary urban community, it has none the less survived right down to the present day.

At the end of the nineteenth and the beginning of the twentieth centuries, when the social and industrial revolutions had reached their peak, there was a far greater diversification of social life. As a result urban architects also introduced greater diversification into their building plans and gradually turned away from the traditional conception of town-planning. This new development received its final sanction in the Athens Charter of C.I.A.M. (1933), which recommended that all future town planning should be based on the segregation of the spheres of social and private life: working, living, entertainment, travel.

What is now needed is a new development which will reintegrate our social and urban structures and reunite the different social groups and activities. Consequently, future town planning must be synthetic; it must establish a new unity between architecture, economics, communications and social contact. For this reason contemporary planners are recommending that megastructures of enormous compactness should be built: instead of being spread out over a wide area the different social spheres will be 'packed' one on top of the other.

But these interlocking structures, which are indispensable if we are to have a healthy urban society and ensure the full development of social activities, are inconceivable unless we are prepared to rethink our urban communications systems.

It is now widely held that the one really viable alternative to the motor car is mass transportation on rails. But, despite the many technical refinements

7

8

7. Houses overlooking a major street—the windows separate the private from the public sphere. Skalitzerstrasse 103/104, Berlin-Kreuzberg.
8. The personal sphere extending into the public sphere. Houses in the Krater district of Matera, Apulia.

9

10

11

12

9. Residential settlement as a social ghetto. Lower middle-class tenements in New York City.

10. Leisure centre as a social ghetto. Playa de las Canteras, Las Palmas, Grand Canary.

11. Old people's home as a social ghetto. Feierabendheim, Waiblingen.

12. University as a social ghetto. Ruhruniversität, Bochum.

that have been introduced, the rail vehicle is essentially a product of the railway age, which is already outmoded. It is capable of transporting large numbers of people but only to a specific destination on a predetermined route. The motor car, on the other hand, provides personal transport and, for this reason, is precisely what the modern urban traveller requires. It is only because motor cars carry so few passengers and because, in our large cities they now appear *en masse,* that they have become such a plague. Consequently, those traffic systems which envisage vehicles structurally similar to the contemporary motor car but capable of carrying the same number of people as the railway, must stand a good chance of being adopted in the future. The METRAN project[2], which was outlined in a study published by the Massachusetts Institute of Technology in 1966, is one of the most interesting conceptions of this kind to have appeared to date. It provides for a differentiated transportation system using individual vehicles controlled by electronic devices.

The original sociological definition of urban processes was based on economic criteria, and the market place was considered to be the most important feature of historic towns. It was regarded both as the source of social dynamism and as the earliest example of a public forum. Hans Paul Bahrdt has accurately described this early attitude: 'A town is a settlement in which all life, including everyday life, tends to be polarized, which means that it takes place either in a public or in a private social collective. Thus, we find a private and a public sphere, which enter into a close reciprocal relationship without ever losing their inherent polarity. Meanwhile, those areas of life which are neither public nor private become less significant. From the sociological point of view, the greater the polarity and the more intense the reciprocal relationship between the public and the private spheres, the more

concentrated the life of the settlement becomes.'[3]

Today the majority of sociologists are more or less agreed as to the value and function of the public sphere. The precise nature of the private sphere, however, is still the subject of lively debate. There are those who consider that the family group should be abandoned in favour of 'communes'. They argue that privacy is tantamount to isolation. In fact, this is not the case: privacy certainly presupposes segregation from the public sphere, but this act of segregation is undertaken in order to create a smaller social unit with its own special properties and its own environment. The important factors in any analysis of privacy are the individual, who wishes to protect himself from external disruptions, interference, controls and so on; the family, which wants to erect barriers against external encroachment on to its specific sphere; and the small group, which does not want to be engulfed in the anonymity of a 'diffuse' public sphere and consequently lays claim, either temporarily or permanently, to specific private areas.

An ideal urban society would never be fully integrated, for it could never permit interference in the affairs of individuals and groups or tolerate the manipulation of private citizens. Here, too, Hans Paul Bahrdt has commented aptly: 'We see, therefore, that those who would restore the security of the family by incorporating it into the security of a neighbourhood, where it would come under public scrutiny, or, to put it in more sober terms, into a fully structured and comprehensive social system, are making a faulty assessment.'[4]

If we consider the history of urban development, we see that the polarity between the private and the public sphere set in at a very early date although it naturally varied in intensity from place to place, depending on the political and social climate of particular towns at particular times. As far as we can tell, the relationship between these two spheres was most balanced in the towns of Greek and Roman antiquity.

Today the two poles are completely isolated by an intolerable geotopographical situation, which precludes all possibility of a natural and productive relationship between them. As a result of urban clearance and rebuilding schemes, vast areas of our towns have been reduced to dormitories, in which the last remaining vestige of a public sphere is the local supermarket, the agora of the 'grass widows', whose time is only partly taken up by the demands of their young families. The concept of 'social temperature'[5], which was coined by Pierre Bertaux to denote the 'exchange activity' of different social groups, provides the best possible assessment of the dormitory town, where such activity is below zero.

But today our town centres have also acquired something of the quality of the outer residential districts. Once the shops have closed, public activity virtually comes to a halt so that evening visitors find little to interest them. Because they make so little allowance either for urban topography or for social requirements, the new traffic zones and traffic regulations appear to be giving an enormous boost to the centrifugal tendencies revealed by urban development of recent years. Today we have reached a point where effective reciprocal relations between the private and public spheres have become quite impossible in the indeterminate confusion of buildings and open spaces and the anonymous stacking of humanity in high-rise blocks with their little used, decorative grass surrounds, which take up so much of our urban space. The provision of modern amenities to improve domestic living and working conditions cannot disguise this socially dangerous fact.

But in trying to restore the duality of the public and private spheres we must be careful not to overreact. Although excessive importance is undoubtedly attached to privacy today, it helps little

to reverse the situation by allowing the public sphere to encroach on all areas of social life. The public sphere acquires its constructive power from its polar relationship to the private sphere. Consequently, these two different spheres must be allowed to develop by reacting harmoniously to one another. This can be done, but only if both are actively promoted as independent entities and then brought into close contact with one another.

It is the fascinating vivacity and the virtually inexhaustible multiplicity of significant impressions that makes the public sphere of a big city such a unique integral experience. Wolf Schneider has spoken in this connection of the 'pleasure of mixing with the crowd' *(Lust am Gedränge)*[6] while Jane Jacobs regards the life and activities of urban streets as a form of dance: 'The ballet of the city sidewalk never repeats itself from place to place, and in any one place is always replete with new improvisations.'[7]

Since it is possible for spontaneous contact to be established for a limited period in predetermined 'places' or on predetermined networks, it is also possible to heighten the appeal of such places and networks by creating 'dramaturgical effects'. In 1965 the E.M.S. (Exploitatie Maatschappij Scheveningen) evolved a project—which, unfortunately, was not carried out—for activating a public place and heightening its emotional impact. Suggestions were submitted by artists from Europe, Japan and the United States for the realization of this large scale *manifestation virtuelle*. Among other things, the E.M.S. proposed to strengthen the aggressive quality of street noises by recording the sound of the sea and broadcasting it through loudspeakers, amplified a thousandfold, in order to rouse the public from its passivity. The whole project was conceived as an immense 'street theatre', using light, sound and movement; and the object of the exercise was to provide *homo ludens* with a new sphere of activity.

13

14

15

16

13. An urban structure as an international stage. Ballet 'Le Teck' enacted on the roof of Le Corbusier's Unité d'Habitation, arranged by Nicolas Schöffer.
14. Urban euphoria. Instant City by Archigram.
15. A memorable shape creates horizons of expectation. 5,600 cubic metre package shown at the fourth Documenta (1968), Kassel, by Christo.
16. The public area is transformed into a street theatre under the direction of *Gestalt* psychologists, communications aesthetes and the occupants themselves. The leisure city of Kiryat Ono by Justus Dahinden.

17

17. Integral activities of a 'static' society. Painting of the market place in Braunschweig by H. van Steenwijk the Elder, 1598.

18

19

18. 'Global Allotments'—an alternative to urban concentrations? A suburb of New York City.
19. A city destroyed by highways and access roads. View of the George Washington Bridge, New York City.
20. Attractive features of a Brasilian slum dwelling—improvization, conversions, anthropomorphism.

20

Georgy Kepes, the Director of the Center for Advanced Visual Studies at the Massachusetts Institute of Technology, tried to stage a similar event in Boston harbour. Kepes claimed that the 'Light-Sound-Wind' sculptures, which he and his collaborators had proposed for this project, would have exerted an influence on the urban scene comparable to that produced by the antique acropolis or the medieval cathedral.[8]

If we take these ideas, which have been successfully propagated in the architectural sphere by the Archigram group ('Instant City'), and carry them one stage further, it becomes apparent that the public streets of a modern town could be orchestrated in such a way as to provide an international stage on which—within a carefully calculated but apparently fortuitous *mise en scène*—everybody would play his part.

When we speak of satisfactory living conditions or values, it is usually in connection with individual apartments and houses. But although it is not generally realized, these concepts are in fact equally applicable to the public areas within our towns. The principal problem in this respect is to ensure that the open spaces between the different buildings help to produce a feeling of security and a recognizable urban atmosphere, for only then will the life of the streets—the chance meetings and fleeting contacts—make any real impression on the people concerned.

It is in this sense that the *Gestalt* of a town—the inner and outer skyline recently discussed by Kevin Lynch—is significant. The *Gestalt* of a town, which is derived from its buildings, light, colour and form, acts as a communal cloak for the inhabitants; sometimes it keeps them warm, sometimes it makes them shiver. There are 'good' and 'bad' towns; some look friendly, others hostile.

In the old towns, which always had well defined features and which were surrounded by natural or artificial borders,

it was possible to 'find one's way around', proceeding from one point to another throughout the whole of the urban area. Today this is seldom possible. It is also interesting to note that in historic towns the 'external' space invariably created a sense of security and that, although the urban structures followed the irregularities of the terrain, they never gave the inhabitants the feeling that they were ensnared in a labyrinth. This was due largely to the contrast between the natural landscape and the artificial environment, which was very pronounced from certain vantage points.

With the centrifugal expansion of our towns the demands made on the town centres, which have had to supply virtually all the needs of the increased population, have become excessive, and their value as residential districts has been greatly reduced by insensitive development projects. The new suburbs, which have sprouted up like malignant growths, are completely faceless and rootless. They are like crippled limbs attached to the otherwise healthy body of the town centre.

The present attitude to architectural requirements, both in the suburban districts and in the town centres, is one of indifference. Nobody seems to care about the habitational value of our urban environment. As for the buildings within which people live and work, these have degenerated into purely functional areas, which do not even function very well. Any irrational features in environmental design are immediately suspect because they yield no tangible profit.

One of the principal factors leading to the degeneration of the public sphere in our modern towns has been the need to provide new roads capable of carrying mechanized transport. In order to lay these roads, wide channels have been cut through built-up areas with the result that many historic buildings have been demolished. The effect on the urban environment has been similar to that produced by the amputation of a human limb.

While our middle income groups have been acquiring a higher standard of living, housing conditions for the less well off have worsened. This has led to the emergence of slum districts in our major cities which have become a symbol for the exploitation of a specific class: the have-nots. Slum districts are self-contained functional entities. But, although they have very definite dis-advantages—they are dirty, unhygienic and badly neglected—they also possess one great advantage as far as the public sphere is concerned. This advantage, which stems from the need for improvisa-tion, lies in the impermanence and the adaptability of such districts, which are reminiscent in this respect of modern 'disposable architecture' and so are better suited to the changing needs and customs of a consumer society than perfectionist architecture. It goes without saying that this should not blind us to the inhuman conditions obtaining in these districts.

Today town planning is acquiring a new dimension: macrostructures or spatial towns. The relationship of 'historically' orientated man to macrostructures is essentially the same as his relationship to the microcosm. The only difference is that while he was able to relate to the microcosm organically by passing through a protracted 'acclimatization period', in the case of the new macro-structures he will have to make a sudden leap and adopt a completely different attitude immediately. It is all too easy to get the scale wrong, especially if one insists on looking for formal analogies between micro- and macrostructures. The mere fact that a particular structure has proved itself on a small scale is no reason for assuming that it can be reproduced on a large scale.
And so, if our macrostructures are to be habitable, we must acquire a new sense of scale values. Otherwise the sheer size of these structures will prove intolerable. This presupposes a new aesthetic and new priorities for the planner. But it does not necessarily follow that we have to go

as far as René Sarger, who argues that in our spatial towns all rectangular forms should be replaced by diagonals.
One effective way of humanizing macro-structures is by means of microzoning. This relies on opposition and confronta-tion rather than fusion and subordination, and it produces architectural units based on a human scale to which man will be able to relate. This process might best be described as the 'democratization' of planning by means of 'inner' proportions.
In dealing with the problem of scale we must also consider the problem of uniformity which arises as a result of objectivization. The megastructures proposed by the Japanese Metabolists, the endless spatial grids and the cellular agglomerates all suffer from this defect. The process of objectivization that underlies our purpose-built structures places man in an impersonal relationship to the object world. He finds himself in a rationalized environment, forced to come to grips with problems that grow more and more complex and abstract. Consequently, instead of stimulating him, the environment exerts a repressive effect. This trend can only be reversed when we stop regarding man as just one more object in an object world and return to the anthropological conception of a subject-object relationship, which will enable man to interact with his en-vironment on the basis of 'visual thought' and 'kinaesthetic experience'. As Kevin Lynch has pointed out in his investiga-tion of man's relationship to his town[9], it is the appreciation and experience of urban space that enable us to grasp what is happening in the world around us. Our sense of urban space depends primarily on the information provided by the townscape.
Alexander Tzonis has pointed out that all traditional architecture is based on a system of 'visual order', whose principal categories—duration and perfection—have little relevance for the flexible architecture of the future.[10] According to Henry van Lier our future environment

21

21. An inhuman high-rise complex. Le Corbusier's Plan Voisin, 1925.

22

23

22, 23. Two examples of successful urban microzoning—the scale of the environment is entirely human. Florence under the Medici, woodcut reproduced from *Supplementum Chronicarum,* 1490 (22) and Habitat '67, Montreal by Moshe Safdie (23).
24. A nightmare vision of the urban scene. A child's drawing entered in the competi-tion held by the Städtebauinstitut Nürnberg 'Kinder sehen ihre Siedlung' (How Children see their Settlement).

24

25

26

25, 26. Two historic towns, compact and functionally integrated. Münster in Westphalia (25) and Mexcaltitan, Nayarit, Mexico (26).

27. Activity area in Joseph Pierre Weber's Zehnminutenstadt (Ten Minute City).

will be composed of a synergetic network of structures, which means that the traditional link with 'containers' will be replaced by an 'operations' link, thus establishing a completely new kind of architectural order.[11]

The growth of urban forms has two distinct aspects. On the one hand it is a case of simple expansion, while on the other it involves a process of metabolic regeneration.

The size of medieval towns was prescribed by fixed boundaries in the form of outer walls, defence works, moats or natural features. Thus, the growth of medieval towns was effected by increasing the density of the existing urban area, a process that could be controlled to any desired extent. Consequently, since they were unable to stretch outwards into the countryside, the structures of our medieval towns agglomerated within the urban nucleus. The effect of this 'inward expansion' on urban ecology was far less pernicious than that produced by the endless 'outward growth' that has been such a marked feature of twentieth-century urban development. Inward urban growth is similar to natural growth. In both cases we find a programmed structure which, after passing through its prescribed period of external growth, concentrates on the renewal of its 'metabolism' with the result that it never becomes unbalanced.

In order to master the problems of urban growth, the model of the linear town was developed. This consists of an unlimited ribbon development, which is really an enlarged version of a *Strassendorf* ('street village'—a village in which farms and buildings are set out on either side of the street). The central branch of this skeletal formation, which is also the major traffic route, develops into a series of lively public spaces. From this 'heartline' with its urban centres for cultural, educational, commercial, financial and political activities, lateral roads run out to the residential districts. The spaces between these lateral roads are used for green areas, which extend from the central traffic route right out into the open country.

But the risk of uncontrolled growth is not completely averted by linear towns, not even if growth is restricted, in accordance with Joseph Pierre Weber's recommendation, to selected areas whose maximum size is determined in advance.

There is probably only one satisfactory solution to the problem of urban growth: large units which can be multiplied at will, which have completed their primary growth phase (macrostructure) and which, like our medieval towns, are capable of spontaneous internal renewal.

The principle of 'controlled growth' in town planning takes account of man's desire for orderly systems, comprehensible dimensions, properly evaluated scales and relations.

The need for adaptability, compatibility and multi-purpose functionalism, and for improvisation and architectural spontaneity in the public sphere has become particularly urgent. Any new town-planning installations in this sphere

27

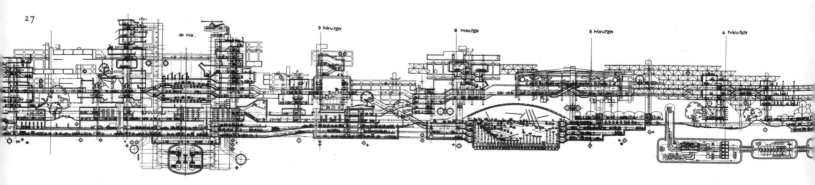

should reflect the transitory nature of our rapidly changing consumer society. Instead of 'growing' in the traditional sense, our urban areas would then undergo a process of constant change. The technical problems posed by this type of development have already been solved by the conception of an 'architectureless' townscape with mobile structures. In combination with a controlled microclimate, lightweight building materials could be used, which would give almost unlimited freedom and provide optimum working conditions. True, the industrial techniques that would have to be employed for the creation of 'consumer architecture' in such a climatically controlled multi-functional urban area would necessitate serial production. But that does not mean that the area would have to be unimaginative or monotonous.

Having tackled the question of urban growth, we must now consider the problem of land ownership. The social and economic importance of the land can hardly be overestimated. Ownership of the land gives effective control of agricultural and industrial production, of mining operations and inland waterways and of the whole housing policy of the country concerned.
Since the French Revolution, the laws governing land tenure in the countries of western Europe have been interpreted both in socio-economic theory and in socio-political practice in favour of private ownership. Moreover, landed property is now regarded in the same way as goods and chattels with the result that it is becoming more and more scarce. Not surprisingly, this has made effective town-planning extremely difficult, if not completely impossible.

In drawing up a new system of land tenure, we would have to start from the basic postulate that since land cannot be increased at will, any land gained as a result of planning operations carried out without the participation of the landowner should become public property. Moreover, if we are to improve the present state of land tenure, we must get away from the traditional system on which conventional town-planning is still based of dividing urban land up into lots; it creates so many obstacles that every urban redevelopment programme is hampered from the outset. New laws should be passed to strengthen the powers of the local authorities. Among other things, the community should be empowered to erect megastructures above existing cities. In this way the land market could be completely re-organized and there would be a spontaneous movement away from our present static system of land legislation towards a more flexible form of legislation for the utilization of space. We could then go on to consider the possibility of a completely new kind of communal ownership.

The examples set out in a later chapter of this book include a number of experimental town planning projects which open up a wide sphere of development.

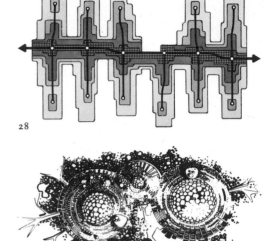

28

29

28. Diagram showing linear development for urban areas: Open-line City by Cesar Pelli.
29. Dynapolis. Radio City by Justus Dahinden.

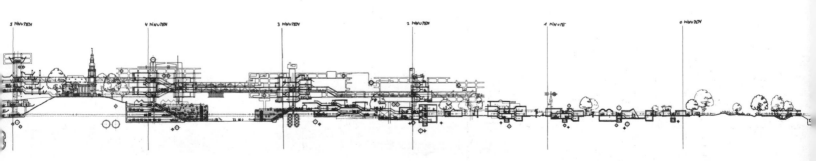

It is now becoming apparent that, instead of regarding a 'town as an "object" which we plan in our capacity as "subjects", we must learn to look on it as a complex socio-technical system which is caught up in a process of constant change and which consists on the one hand of people (socio) and on the other hand of means (technical); and we must bear in mind that the component elements of this system (which may themselves be systems) are able to enter into a reciprocal relationship with, and influence one another.' (Eugen Bruno). The complexity of town planning requirements calls for a concerted interdisciplinary effort, in which the architect will have to act as coordinator. 'Among academicians the architects are the only group who still exercise a comprehensive function, for they are the only group who have to collate different objects and different areas of knowledge in the course of their professional activities . . .'[12]

In considering the implications of a sudden transition to a new epoch of urban culture, we must bear in mind that man's inherent ability to adapt to the new 'massed existence' that will be the crucial feature of urban life in the future is limited. Alexander Mitscherlich has dealt with the question of human adaptability in his symposium *Über das beschädigte Leben*[13] (On Stunted Life) where, among other things, he asks the rhetorical question: 'When are we at one with ourselves and when

are we beside ourselves?' Mitscherlich reaches the conclusion that, although man adapts relatively quickly to new environments and the demands they make on him, inwardly he continues to cling to his old familiar milieu. From this it would follow that there are two distinct kinds of adaptation, which proceed at very different rates. Consequently, if man is to adapt to a new environment in the real inner sense, we shall have to exercise great caution when we introduce new urban structures. So-called original systems, whose advocates merely sing the praises of a particular principle of town-planning without considering the practical implications of that principle, will serve no useful purpose.

One crucial problem posed by future urban developments is the problem of density. There are two important factors which will have to be reconciled. On the one hand the domesticity of the private sphere calls for contact with nature and the introduction of microzoning to make life tolerable for the individual, while on the other hand the multiple social activities of the public sphere call for powerful concentrations of people in large communities. The increasing density of a megalopolis must inevitably create tensions and exert a restrictive effect on individual activities and freedoms. But human behaviour cannot, and must not be completely predetermined if our towns are to survive as centres of human encounter.

30. Inward-looking communal area in a leisure city: total mobility is vouchsafed by the use of hydraulic floors, removable spectator terraces etc. Kiryat Ono by Justus Dahinden.

30

Urban Structures for the Future

Having dealt with the social and anthropological aspects of modern conurbations in the first part of this study, I now propose to concentrate on the architectonic features of urban structures.

The relationship between urban structures and social forms is reciprocal; a change in one of these spheres automatically produces a reaction in the other. Thus, the critical reader might well ask whether the modular composition of microstructures, which liberalizes building processes, will not also promote social disintegration as a result of their cellular formation, whether the need for disposable architecture does not spring from our inability to free architecture from its present static condition as a first step in the development of total flexibility, or whether the mobility of what Robert Jungk has called a 'society in flight' is not due to the inadequate organization of living space rather than to some inner human need.

In view of the complex nature of this facet of town planning, I have been obliged to adopt a somewhat discursive approach, which has produced a list of concepts as heterogeneous as the material under review.

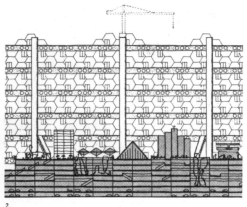

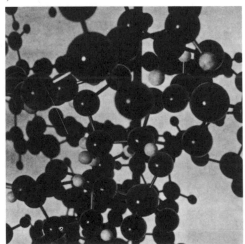

Cellular Agglomerates

Cellular agglomerates are composite structures consisting of integrated modular units. Consequently, they are not divided into primary and secondary structures, for the outer shell of the individual components serves both as a load-bearing element and as a space divider. Additional units can be added horizontally and, provided the cells are adequately reinforced, vertically. In the latter event the composite building might be described as a rigid macro- or spatial structure.

In the case of vertical agglomerates the micro-units must be strong enough to support the weight of the entire spatial structure in optimum conditions of stress or combinations of different stresses. Moreover, in the majority of cases it will be necessary for the individual units to be equipped with their own service and waste disposal systems. From a structural point of view cellular agglomerates are, of course, an ideal form of architecture. They would be even more attractive, however, if they were composed of autonomous, i. e. self-servicing cellular units. In this particular sphere modern architecture has merely reached the threshold of a progressive development which, if successfully pursued, could lead to a large-scale liberalization of spatial urban systems. Space travel has already provided an example of the kind of achievements that are possible with its projects for interplanetary stations, which will be constructed by coupling autonomous cells.

One of the problems posed by cellular structures made of lightweight materials is that of acoustics. Because of their integral composition every single sound is carried from cell to cell. Another problem is that of spatial dilation (expansion and contraction due to temperature fluctuations); this sets up macro-structural tensions which may produce secondary forces and so damage the cells and weaken the couplings.

1. Honeycomb.
2. Hexagonal residential cells by Herbert Prader, Franz Fehringer and Erich Ott.
3. Stacked cells in an orthogonal system by Wolfgang Döring.
4. Autonomous cellular units coupled together for a space station.
5. Model of a molecular agglomerate.

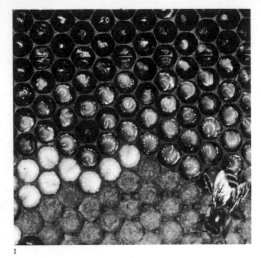

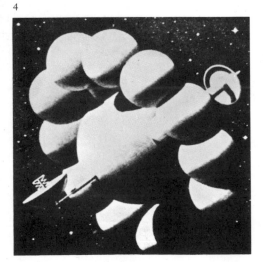

Since, on the horizontal plane at least, there is no limit to the possible growth of cellular agglomerates, there is a danger of excessive outward expansion which would be harmful from a town-planning point of view. The growth of cellular agglomerates has often been compared to natural growth. But this comparison is inappropriate since, in the vegetable world, growth leads to an ultimate condition of maturity.

Cellular units can also be added to existing rigid structures in order to increase the available living space. Mixed projects of this kind have been suggested by Chanéac, the Häusermann brothers and the Hausrucker-Co.,

whose 'Pneumacosm' was designed with the express purpose of providing flexible secondary rooms in existing high density urban areas.

The interior of cellular units can be fitted out without using permanent fixtures. Friedrich St. Florian has proposed that, instead of constructing rigid partitions to provide individual areas for different habitational purposes, 'activity elements' should be introduced which could be rearranged at will. This would, of course, be a form of microzoning but one capable of almost infinite variation. He has described this kind of procedure as 'imaginary architecture' and speaks of 'creating imaginary space'.

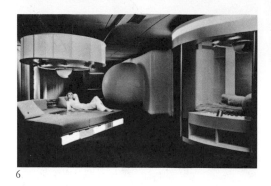

6

6. Microzoning of a multi-purpose residential cell by means of individual functional units. Visiona by Joe Cesare Colombo.
7. Expansion of a static urban area by means of dynamic cellular structures. Pneumacosm by Hausrucker-Co.

7

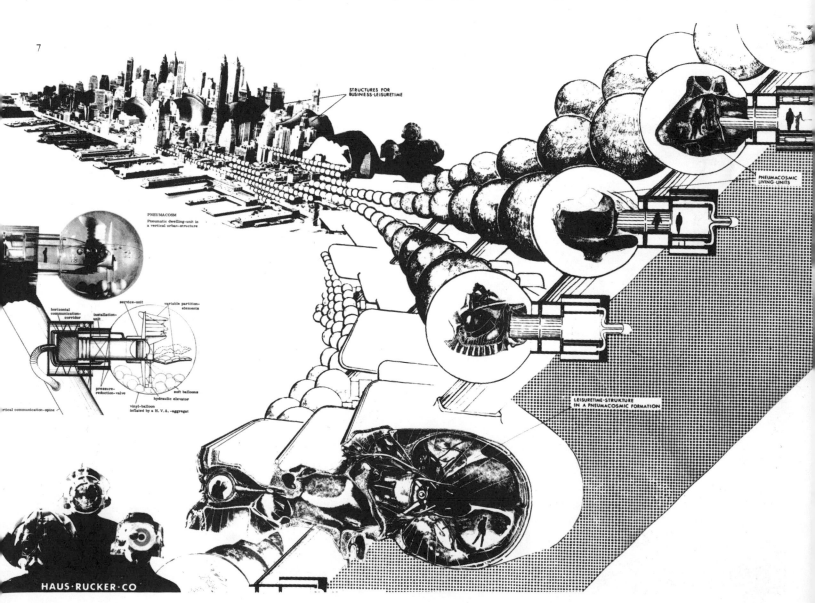

8

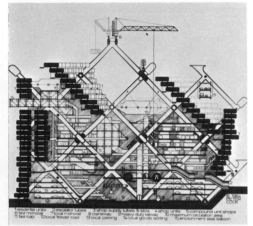

9

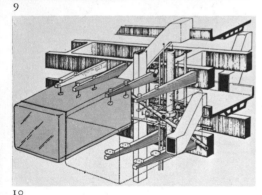

10

Clip-on, Plug-in

In Clip-on or Plug-in architecture, buildings are designed on the basis of a primary system (which is concerned with the load-bearing parts) and a secondary system (which is concerned with the infillings). Thus, instead of separate functions, we have separate elements, which then produce a plurality of functions. This plurality is reflected by the three building components: load-bearing frame, infillings and services. The more independent of one another these components are, the more variable the total system will be. Ideally, it should be possible to extend, exchange or remove any individual parts of a building at any time without affecting the stability of the total structure.
This kind of component construction takes due account of the aging of individual parts of buildings and makes regeneration entirely feasible; it also makes for economic construction. From this it would follow that the aging of a complete urban structure could be controlled so as to reflect changes in social patterns. The most important representatives of Plug-in or Clip-on architecture are the Metabolists and the Archigram group. While the Metabolists are intent on developing a philosophical system based on the concept of cyclical change, the Archigram group proceeds on a purely pragmatic basis and simply regards the use of separate components as the logical conclusion of the Athens Charter. The members of this group are fascinated by the technical possibilities and the multi-functional and consumer character of this kind of architecture (or anti-architecture). Commenting on the development of Clip-on in England, Reyner Banham wrote: 'The epitome of the clip-on concept at that time (1961) was the outboard motor, whose consequences for the theory of design intrigued many of us at that time, in the following terms: given an Evinrude or a Johnson Seahorse, you can convert practically any floating object into a navigable vessel. A small concentrating package of machinery converts an undifferentiated structure into something having function and purpose. But, equally, the undifferentiated object might be a paper cup full of raw black coffee, and the clip-on could be the packets of sugar and cream and the stirring stick which convert to the particular cup of coffee that suits your taste.'[14]
Because of this insistence on technology, 'technical equipment', which has always played a subsidiary part in traditional architectural design, has become a structural element in its own right. As a result of this new development, 'components' and 'mechanisms' are now such an important feature of urban structures that we are fully justified in speaking of 'urban machines'.
The capacity of macro- and micro-structures for growth and change varies

8. Urban macrostructure with load-bearing frames distinct from the infillings. Cluster in the Air by Arata Isozaki.
9. Plug-in City by Peter Cook.
10. Ultratechnoid structure (clip-on) by Shigeo Tanaka.
11. Structural additive. An urban utopia for Salzburg by Günther Feuerstein.

11

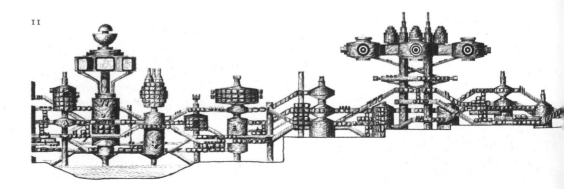

in accordance with the different functions which they fulfil. The primary (load-bearing) system has to provide a general infrastructure. Consequently, if present methods are used, the final form of every individual element must be kept in mind from the outset, which means that a preliminary study has to be made (maximization process), which may or may not be fully utilized. The secondary (infilling) system, on the other hand, can be extended or altered at any time, which means that no such preliminary study needs to be made (minimization process).

The fact that individual parts of the microstructure which fail to meet the demands made on them at a later date are exchangeable has been particularly emphasized by the Metabolists. The concept of 'metabolic regeneration' prompts a comparison with the processes of natural growth. In nature the tree—which helped to inspire Clip-on architecture—is divided into a trunk, branches and leaves; and each of these sections develops in accordance with its own inner rhythm of growth and re-generation.

By extending the metabolic principle, Alan Boutwell has arrived at his conception of a variable 'container-house' consisting, like the motor car, of a chassis and a body. All the technical equipment in this house is incorporated into a special cell. Boutwell's idea is that these mobile units should be raised by

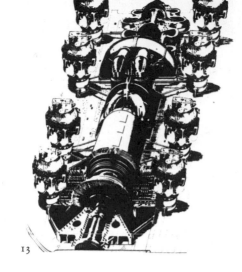

12. Petrol Engine.
13. A mechanical urban structure inspired by the exchangeability of modern spare parts. Congress Centre for Vienna by M. Shimazu.
14. The division of structures in nature. Branch and leaves.
15. Multi-purpose design in an orthogonal space frame composed of modular elements by Eckhard Schulze-Fielitz.

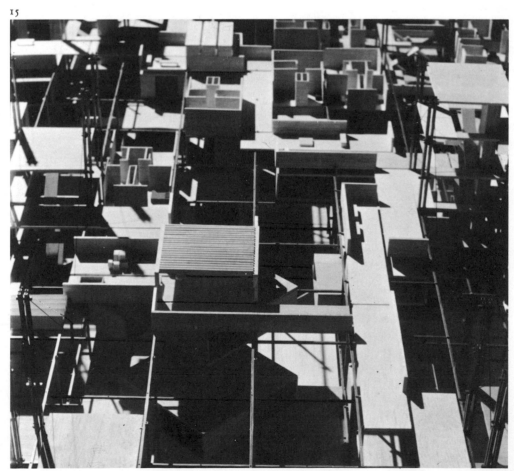

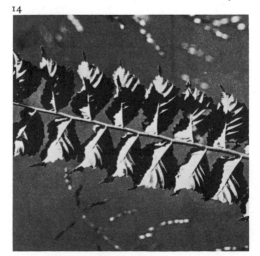

16. Mobile container homes in a neutral space frame by Alan Boutwell.

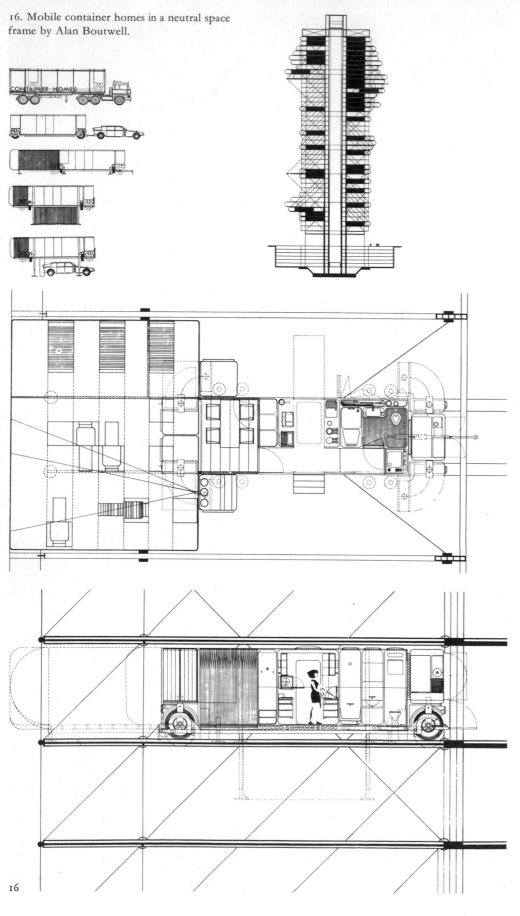

hoists and plugged in on high-rise structures on specially prepared sites. Once it has been placed in position, the chassis with its cellular service unit can be bolted into place, and the basic cell can then be extended as desired. This is done by inflating membranes made of translucent nylon by means of compressed air. The membranes are placed, and then held in position by vertical guide rails.

Where microstructures are concerned, ease of handling and erection are of major importance. Small containers can be mass-produced using fine materials, which cut down weight considerably so that the finished containers can be lifted and plugged in by hoists sited on top of the macrostructures. The hoists would not be incorporated into the structures but left clearly visible, a fact emphasized by the Archigram group, which attaches considerable importance to such devices as visual symbols of social change.

One important question that has to be considered, in view of the lightweight materials that would be used for spatial cells, is that of fire precautions. In this respect it would be desirable, and entirely feasible, to fit sprinkler installations throughout the whole of the megastructure. Moreover, where the load-bearing members are made of steel, the hollow sections could also be filled with water as an additional precaution.

In order to ensure that the total structure functions properly, the service systems would have to be extremely adaptable. Water, waste and soil pipes, cables, refuse shoots and central heating ducts could either flank the structural framework or be integrated into it. In the latter case, however, design problems would be posed by the fact that service pipes would have to pass through load-bearing structures; and it would also be more difficult to exchange individual components at a later date. Thus, the flanking systems would seem to be more suitable. Completely autonomous micro-units would, of course, be the ideal solution. As I have already mentioned in the section on cellular agglomerates, these would not only provide all their own services but would also dispose of all waste products, thus removing the necessity for rubbish shoots and waste pipes.

Future dwellings will be fitted out to the same high standards as present-day space capsules. Commenting on this development Richard Buckminster Fuller wrote: 'The man-residing-in-space-problem is: to reduce the dimensions of the ecological energy exchange pattern of the man process of input-output, energy-matter-energy transformations and exchanges from a multi-mile diameter tree-air-earth-worm-bird-bee-rain-wind, etc., relay system to a three-foot diameter closed circuit system of less than 500 pounds total—a thermo-electro-chemical process by which man—employing approximately invisible gadgets and with the almost subconscious grace and effort of blowing his nose quietly into a kerchief and without any offensive odors or other visible, audible signs—will be able to sustain high health for twelve months without either 'garbage' or 'sewerage' disposal or without further supply input from sources external to his sky house other than the sun radiation income.'[15]

Clip-on and Plug-in architecture lend themselves particularly well to the kind of mass production methods used in the motor car industry. It seems probable, therefore, that we shall see a symbiosis between architecture and industrial technology.

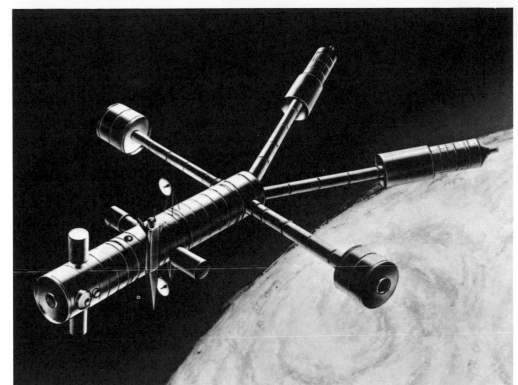

17

18

19

17. An example of structural autonomy in a self-servicing system. Fifty-Man Space Base by the McDonnell Douglas Astronautics Corporation.
18, 19. Serial production of cellular frames. Volkswagen assembly (18) and a cellular structure by Chanéac (19).

20

20. Wolkenbügel (Cloud Props) by El Lissitzky, 1925.
21. A high-rise apartment building on *pilotis*. Unité d'Habitation by Le Corbusier, 1945.
22. Service masts with interconnecting bridges. Administration and health centre for Tokyo by Arata Isozaki.

21

22

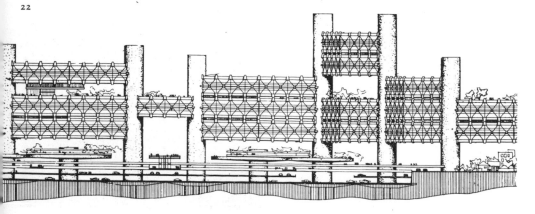

Bridge Structures

Bridge structures are spatial urban structures built up on bridge-like supports. Where these span long distances they have the advantage of enabling macrostructures to be developed independently of local topographical features; they can also be used to span existing towns. Although bridge structures, which are ultimately based on the town-planning precepts set out in the Athens Charter of C.I.A.M., must inevitably segregate the spatial town from the earth, thus exerting a polarizing effect, within their own purely spatial sphere they have the opposite effect of integrating all forms of social activity.

The two major prototypes for this new conception were the houses on *pilotis* evolved by Le Corbusier and the high-rise buildings with vertical access which have been built in the United States from the turn of the century onwards, and which will doubtless have inspired El Lissitzky to design his 'Wolkenbügel' in 1924.

In 1960 Kenzo Tange and Arata Isozaki designed new bridge structures for use as administrative centres, which consisted of single storey units supported on long spans by individual access towers. At about the same time Yona Friedman, Constant, Eckhard Schulze-Fielitz and others began to experiment with three dimensional spatial grids; apart from metabolist considerations (which had become the focal point of interest in progressive town-planning circles in Japan), these European architects were also concerned with the spatial integration of urban structures and consequently of urban activities.

From the point of view of building construction, the most interesting aspect of these designs is the steel frame specification, which would make it possible for a box frame type of construction to be employed, using standardized units for both structural and infilling purposes (steel sections, connectors, cells). This type of construction, which involves a vertical development of the single storey units used for bridge structures, was employed by Kenzo Tange in a number of designs for new buildings in Skopje, Yugoslavia. The principal static characteristic of this and similar types of 'vector-active' systems (systems incorporating both tension and compression members) is the fact that the connectors are hinged and so are thus unaffected by movement. Consequently, all the jointing in the structural frame can be made by either bolts or rivets. Such constructions are very economical. Although capable of supporting heavy loads, they are none the less sparing of materials. Today, of course, buildings have to be high if they are to be economical, and it is their stability at relatively great heights that provides the necessary basis for the use of plug-in units in spatial towns. According to the investigations carried out by Eckhard Schulze-Fielitz, spatial grids provide optimum accommodation in orthogonal constructional systems and optimum stability in combinations of tetragonal and octagonal systems. From this it would presumably follow that a synthesis of all three systems would be the most satisfactory all-round solution. The so-called 'minimized diagonal', which involves a kind of spatially rigid quoin, constitutes one attempt to achieve just such a synthesis. The orthogonal system can also be made more economical by changing the direction of the tension in the cellular infilling from one storey to the next.

If they are to achieve optimum stability, space frames must do more than discharge forces by means of non-continous compression and/or tension elements or non-continuous compression elements and continuous tension elements. Both types of element must be continuous in Richard Buckminster Fuller's Tensegrity-Mast. Continuity in the space frames also makes for economy in the production of individual parts of the building. Thus, the stability achieved by the repeated triangulation of the frames

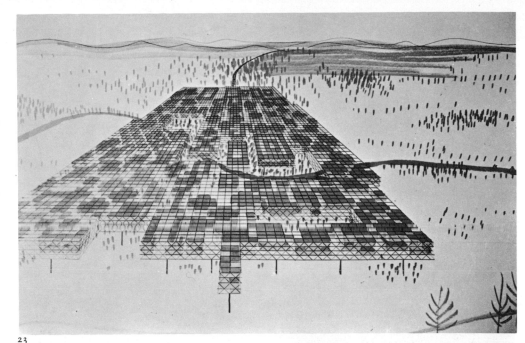

23

24

25

23, 24. Primary structures for integrated urban systems in the form of spatial grids. Spatial cities by Yona Friedman (23) and Eckhard Schulze-Fielitz (24).
25. 'Vector-active' space frame composed of modular building elements. The Mero System.

27

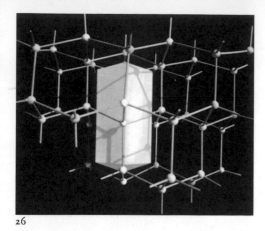

26. Structural grid derived from the molecular axial structure of diamonds and incorporating a spatial cell by J. Marogg and A. Huonder.

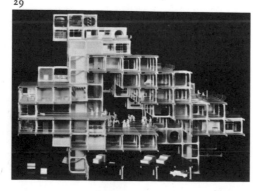

27, 28. Idealized 'mass-active' space frame in an orthogonal system by Frei Otto (27) and in the Takara-'Beautilion' by Noriaki Kurokawa, International Exhibition, Osaka, 1970 (28).
29. A flexible space frame designed for large spans. Metastadt by Richard J. Dietrich.

makes it possible to incorporate multi-storeyed cellular infillings (maisonnettes) into the spatial structure.

Space frames, which are constructed to take a three-dimensional load (wind, live load, strain, shear forces), have a highly restrictive effect on both utility and mobility. Although it is perfectly true that, because of its dependence on standardized components, structural design must invariably reduce the architect's freedom of action, in this particular case it has such an inhibiting effect that, according to Günther Domenig and Eilfried Huth, it leaves virtually no freedom at all.

To complete the picture I must now refer briefly to a number of individual spatial grid structures. The first of these is the 'Triodetic System', which is built up from steel sections and can be used for either plane or space frames. This system is suitable for the construction of primary structures such as domes, roof spans and so on.

Richard Buckminster Fuller's 'Eight Piece Grid', is a combination of tetragonal and octagonal structures composed of tubular sections.

J. Marogg and A. Huonder were prompted primarily by economic considerations to investigate the molecular structure of diamonds. From their study of the molecular axial system which they found in these hard crystals, they were able to evolve a sectional structure with hinged connectors which was extremely stable in all directions. In this structure the load forces are discharged diametrically via three compression and three tension components from each of the axial sections of the tetragon. In their works J. G. Helmcke and Frei Otto have used 'mass-active' frames derived from the cellular structures observed in diatoms. Unlike 'vector-active' frames, these have rigid connectors. Just as plants strengthen those parts of their organism which have to meet heavy demands and consequently become centres of tension by transferring foodstuffs to them from less heavily taxed parts, so too in 'mass-active' frames the architect can relieve tension concentrations by modifying the cross sections.

In order to avoid the preliminary structural work necessitated by the separation of the load-bearing frame from the infilling, the Planungsgruppe Berlin 61 (Georg Kohlmaier, Barna von Sartory and Stefan Polonyi) evolved a modified form of bridge structure. This involves prefabricated units (cellular components) which are bolted together and then covered by a flexible skin. By varying the number of storeys, the stability of the frame is ensured automatically despite the changing load.

From a town-planning point of view, we have to consider the social and design problems posed by large bridge superstructures where these span existing 'organic' towns and deprive them of air and light. The radical way in which Yona Friedman proposes to span the historic city of Paris with a spatial grid system only thirty metres above the ground is positively alarming. After all, there is nothing that can replace man's loss of 'contact with the earth'. The 'spatial greenery' proposed for such structures is not an adequate solution. If we wish to assess the urban value of a bridge complex, we have to consider the overall economy of the super- and substructure, the growth potential of the infrastructure and the degree of freedom provided by the microzoning within the spatial grid; and in order to assess its social value we have to consider the residential quality of its private areas, the density of social integration and the way in which the terrestrial and non-terrestrial spheres of activity are polarized.

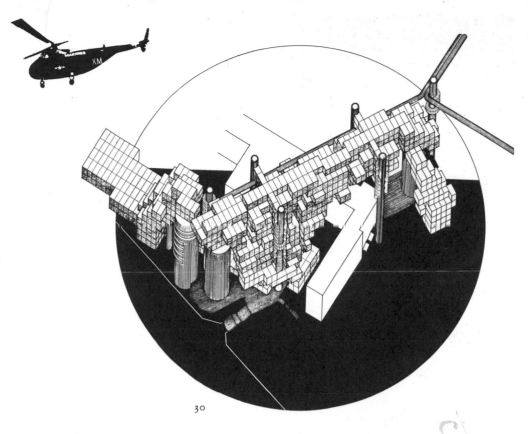

30

30. Spatial structure composed of rigidly interlocking cells. Project for the Technische Universität Berlin, by Georg Kohlmaier, Barna von Sartory and Stefan Polonyi.
31. Urban area beneath a spatial grid. Project for Paris by Yona Friedman.

31

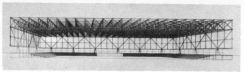

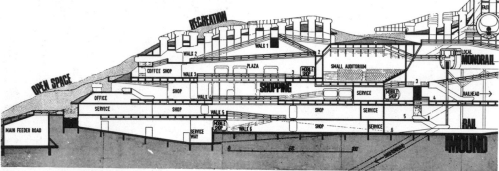

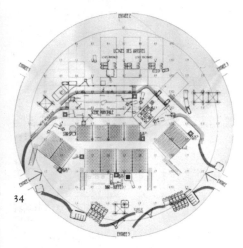

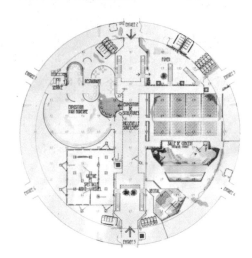

32. Container architecture by Ludwig Mies van
der Rohe. Convention Hall for Chicago, 1953.
33. An inward-looking, multi-use container.
City Mound Project by Peter Cook.
34. A multi-purpose container providing
total mobility for communal activities.
Features Monte Carlo by Archigram.
35. A visionary form of mobility. Mammoth
containers capable of independent movement. Walking Cities by Ron Herron.

35

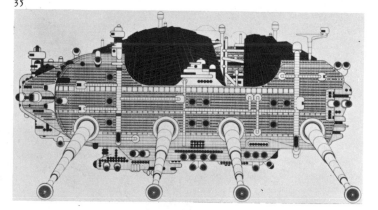

Containers

If architecture is regarded as a means of
structuring space, then those elements
which actually create space and those
mechanisms which produce a 'living
environment' are clearly its most important
facet. The concept of 'neutral' space was
formulated in order to achieve flexibility
in the utilization of space; by means of
an outer shell or container an undefined
and as yet unutilized volume is produced; variable 'inner' conditions are
then created which cater for a whole
range of uses. Günther Feuerstein has
found an apt definition of such volumes.
He calls them 'manipulative'.[16] There are
no basic postulates in container architecture, although functional restrictions
may occur in certain circumstances.
Containers can be of any size, from a
small cell to a large hall, although
ideally—as in the case of pneumatic
constructions such as hot air and air
cushion containers—they should be able
to expand and contract.
But in every case the really crucial
consideration is the microclimate. This
must meet modern requirements and be
capable of adapting to changing conditions, which calls for a highly sophisticated air-conditioning system.
One of the earliest forms of multi-purpose
containers was the antique basilica, which
served as a market place, assembly
room, money market and courtroom.
More recent examples of containers are:
Francis Fowke's Albert Hall in London
(6,000 square metres; 1867–71),
Friedrich von Thiersch's Festhalle in
Frankfurt/Main (1907); Max Berg's
Jahrhunderthalle in Breslau (5,000
square metres; 1912–13); and the
multi-functional halls of Mies van der
Rohe.
In our own period we have Peter Cook's
'Mound' project (1964) and the Archigram design for a Leisure and Amusement Centre in Monte Carlo (1970).
Containers of this kind, in which all the
fittings are mobile, are not unlike
television studios: the automated

mechanisms combine with special lighting and sound effects in a sort of 'mixed media', thus creating a constantly changing environment and heightening the emotional tension. We also have contemporary containers on an urban scale, such as the 'Walking Cities' developed by the Archigram group and the domes designed by Richard Buckminster Fuller and Frei Otto. These are intended to enclose whole architectural landscapes, which would have a controlled mesoclimate. When large containers of this kind are actually built, it will be possible to revitalize the activities of urban communities so that they more closely resemble what Werner Ruhnau has called the 'great game'. The constant temperature and the protection from the elements provided by domes will eliminate the harmful effects of the natural environment and so enhance the habitational value of the public sphere. The regulation of the climate is, of course, no easy matter. Completely new systems will have to be evolved such as radiation systems for maintaining the temperature and displacement systems for ventilation.

In this connection it is worth noting that Holger Lueder has recently investigated the effect of environmental influences on the vegetative nervous system in man.[17] It seems that unless climatic conditions remain relatively constant, malfunctioning of the vegetative nervous system occurs, which then produces physical illnesses. From this it would follow that architects concerned with the regulation of microclimates will need to have a working knowledge of physiology and bioclimatology.

Every urban container must have adequate service and disposal systems. But we have already seen in earlier sections that this will necessarily restrict the utilization of space. For this reason there is now a growing movement in favour of autonomous service and disposal systems, which would necessitate the incorporation of mechanical,

36

37

38

36–39. Free architectural landscaping under large spatial 'skins': German Pavilion by Frei Otto (36, 37) and American Pavilion by Richard Buckminster Fuller (38, 39) at the Expo '67, Montreal.

39

40

41

chemical and electronic units within the container, where they would form a closed circuit. At present, however, such developments are still extremely rudimentary.

One intriguing idea for a self-service system has been put forward by John E. Starbuck and Richard F. Brox, who. designed a 'Town on the Moon' in 1968. They wanted to create a terrestrial type of vegetation in climatically controlled containers on the moon, thus setting up a biological chain. The light needed for purposes of photosynthesis was to be provided by a gas such as helium, which would be stored between the double membrane of the containers and made incandescent by means of laser beams.

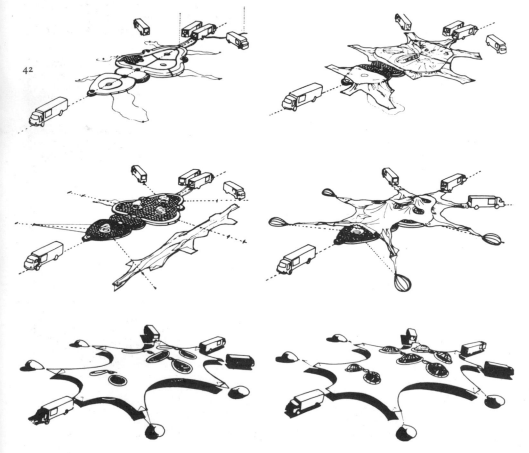

42

40, 41. Lightweight architecture with highly efficient communications systems. Radio City by Justus Dahinden.
42. Large mobile container with additional apparatus. Travelling Hall by A. Stinco.
43. Controllable crypto-climate. Space suit.

43

Marine Structures

Marine structures are better able to reflect the changing nature of our society than fixed structures on dry land; unlike motorways, waterways do not need special sites. Moreover, for coastal towns which suffer from a shortage of building land (such as Tokyo, Hongkong, New York and Monaco) building on the water reduces the pressure on the urban land market. Finally, transportable floating towns offer our highly mobile society the means of living in a state of permanent movement; they provide a kind of 'total tourism', thus enabling people to live in different places in different seasons.

Floating on water is a dynamic condition and one that produces a feeling of weightlessness. Consequently, new kinds of forces will come to the fore—such as buoyancy, tidal flow and heeling and trimming movements—which means that our planners will have to rethink their role if they are to build urban structures on water. Shipbuilding methods could be applied in this field to a certain extent: floating containers could be built in dry docks and subsequently coupled together. The floating town of Unabara, which was designed by the Japanese architect Kiyonori Kikutake, is an example of this kind of project.

The exterritoriality of floating towns would create a new property concept. Unlike our sorely overtaxed mainland areas, oceans are not yet in short supply; consequently, instead of buying plots, householders would only have to pay anchorage and transit fees.

Marine structures would also enjoy considerable climatic advantages: the weather at sea is less subject to sudden shifts; there is also more sunshine than on dry land; and because of the high atmospheric pressure, any harmful concentrations of mist would disperse more rapidly.

With the establishment of marine civilizations, man would also be able to draw on vast new reservoirs of energy

44

44. Floating town in Kowloon, Hongkong.
45. Multi-purpose floating units for urban activities by Justus Dahinden. The individual units can be coupled together.
46. Hydrogenetic Biotecture by Rudolf Doernach.
47. New Venice by Eckhard Schulze-Fielitz.

45

46

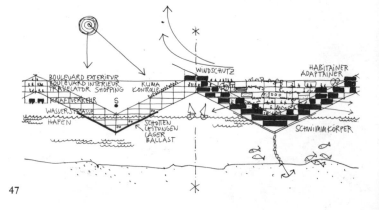

47

33

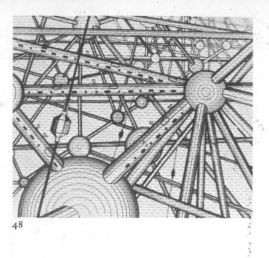

48

48. Underwater City by Warren Chalk.
49. Underwater urban structures by Hidezo Kobayashi.

49

and raw materials. In this connection Hidezo Kobayashi has advanced some interesting ideas for a *buoyant future*. Apart from exploiting the deposits of minerals, oil and natural gas stored beneath the seabed, he has suggested that energy could be generated by harnessing the movement of the waves and the rise and fall of the tide. The sophisticated container system evolved by Kobayashi for his structures on the seabed envisages a combination of different structures, some fixed, others floating. The communications networks for these towns, which would be fully or partially submerged, would involve primary, secondary and tertiary systems. Monorails would be erected just above the surface of the water so that the lower half of the carriages would be sub-

merged. Pipe lines with fully automatic, computer-controlled 'torpedoes' would also be installed for goods and passenger transport.

Marine civilizations will have to contend with one important social problem: isolation. This will be particularly acute in those cases where the floating towns are both relatively small and completely cut off from the mainland.

The Diagonal in Space

In European architecture the façade always played a dominant role because it answered the needs of an ostentatious society. It was not until the 1950s, when three-dimensional urban structures began to emerge, that our architects made the crucial breakthrough which enabled them to introduce the diagonal into town planning.

The great historical examples of terraced architecture were the cult buildings of the Assyrians, Egyptians and Aztecs, which were a product of cosmically orientated religions in non-European countries.

Although a few terraced gardens were laid out during the Baroque and Rococo periods, it was not until the turn of the century that terraced structures were really seriously considered in Europe.

In 1901, however, Tony Garnier designed a housing project for the harbour district of Lyons in which the houses were to have been set out in terrace formation on the hillside behind the quays, and in 1910 Le Corbusier designed a school of arts and crafts in the shape of a pyramid, in which every studio was to be provided with its own terrace for open-air work. Shortly afterwards, in 1912–13, Henri Sauvage, the as yet relatively unknown Art Nouveau architect, built his first 'immeuble à gradins' on the Rue Vavin in Paris. Finally, in 1920–1, Hans Poelzig designed a new Festival Hall for the city of Salzburg in the Hellbrunner Park in the form of a terraced cone.

This development was continued by Alvar Aalto, who designed a small estate of four terraced houses for a steep hill in Kauttua, Finland in 1937. The first of these houses was built between 1938 and 1940. Eventually, in the 1950s, the idea of building terraced houses on hillsides was taken up in Switzerland and Scandinavia and, later, in other countries.

In 1967, when the 'residential hill' designed for the city of Marl by the architects Peter Faller, Roland Frey,

50

51

52

50. Stepped buildings in Mexico. An Aztec settlement in Teotihuacán.

51. Forerunner of the residential hill. Stepped house on the Rue Vavin in Paris by Henri Sauvage, 1912–13.

52. Stepped buildings on a natural hillside in Umiken, Switzerland, by the 'Team 2000' (Scherer, Strickler and Weber).

53. Residential hill in Marl by Peter Faller, Roland Frey, Hermann Schröder and Claus Schmidt.

54. Residential hill in Celerina, Switzerland, by Justus Dahinden.

53

54

55

56

57

58

55. Structural patterning with diagonal partitions. Skyline of a stepped town by Merete Mattern.
56, 57. 'Active' front façade and 'inactive' rear façade of a microzoned, stepped urban structure. Habitat '67, Montreal, by Moshe Safdie.
58. Stepped urban structure which serves both as a support for a climatic 'skin' and as a container for spatial cells. Detail of Kiryat Ono by Justus Dahinden.
59. Braced spatial load-bearing structures with stepped microstructures. Suspension type construction on water by Frei Otto.

Hermann Schröder and Claus Schmidt was completed, the potential of terraced houses on level sites again came up for discussion. By way of a variant on the Marl project, a design for 'half-a-hill' was evolved which was similar in all essential respects to the hospital design produced by Marcel Breuer for the town of Wuppertal-Elberfeld in 1928. Because of the staggered layout of the storeys, each private area in a terraced block can be allocated its own individual terrace. Consequently, this type of construction offers a genuine alternative to the traditional family house and one that is relatively economical in its use of land. But, if terraced houses erected on hillsides are more economical than traditional family houses, free-standing terraced structures are more economical still; for, since they cast little or no shadow, they can be sited much closer together.

Terraces combine the economic advantages of the tenement block with the individuality of the family house; they also permit the close integration of the private and the public spheres. While the open area on the top of the terrace is utilized for private purposes, the enclosed area beneath it can be used for public activities. Beneath the diagonal supports which carry the residential area, public installations can be sited to provide consumer and transport facilities, meeting places, leisure and recreational centres. The polarity between

59

the private and public sphere created by
such a terraced project would provide the
best possible basis for decent living
conditions in modern conurbations.
The terraced projects that have been
carried out to date have all been relatively
small and, because so few dwellings
were involved, virtually no public
amenities were provided. Consequently,
we find an 'active' private sphere in con-
junction with an 'inactive' public sphere,
a development that could turn out to be
every bit as pernicious as the courtyards
of the metropolitan tenement blocks
erected in the late nineteenth century.
But, at least, the active frontal areas—
which Hans Hollein has aptly described
as 'buildings you can walk on and which
do away with barriers'—give some idea
of the way in which this particular type of
structure could help to transform the
present urban scene with its massive,
closed-in buildings and repellent 'façades'
into a much more human place.
Terraced structures can be erected in
very different ways. The best known
forms are quite simple geometrical
designs involving either rectilinear or
crescent-shaped areas. But more complex
forms have been proposed based on
funnel and culot shapes and hyperbolic
and parabolic figures.
Terraces are 'receptive' forms; they are
open to the sunshine and the light. In a
number of utopian designs, this aspect
has been stressed to such an extent that
we are confronted with what are virtually
'cosmoforms'.

60

61

62

63

60. Wohntrichter (Residential Funnels) by
Walter Jonas.
61. Ville cosmique by Yannis Xenakis.
62. 'Receptive' forms in mushrooms.
63. 'Receptive' forms in urban architecture.
Residential shells for San Sebastian by Jan
Lubicz-Nicz.

64

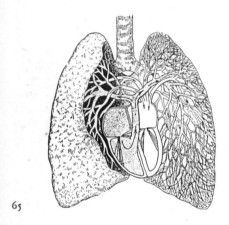

65

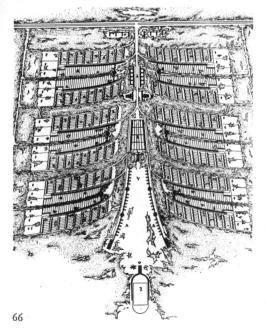

66

64. Symbolic organic forms in Art Nouveau: Entrance to the Paris Metro by Hector Guimard, about 1900.
65. Human lung.
66. Residential town by Hans Bernhard Reichow, 1939.

Biostructures

As far as the problems of urban civilization are concerned, biology is regarded either as a romantic antithesis to Arthur Miller's 'air-conditioned nightmare', or as offering a possible means of reproducing natural processes in our man-made environment. In so far as it reflects opposition to the perversions of modern life and the harmful effects which these exert on our physical and mental health and social relationships, the antithetical view is understandable. However, it is also unproductive since it involves a preoccupation with past values which can never be revived. The alternative view is much more to the point. To try to use our knowledge of the biological processes of origination, growth, cyclical change, decline and death in order to free architecture from its traditionally static role, thus enabling it to adapt more adequately to the processes of modern social life, must be regarded as an entirely legitimate means of overcoming our present problems. By combining the science of living matter (biology) with the science of architectonics (structures), we have been able to establish a synthetic science of living structures, which we call bio-structures. This synthesis embraces all urban structures—buildings, organs and control systems—which are now regarded as interdependent.

It is perfectly true that our biostructures, like the contemporary 'back to nature' movement, have their roots in Romanticism and, more particularly, in Art Nouveau. For the artists of Art Nouveau nature guaranteed immediacy and originality, and so they sought refuge in nature from the problems posed by the onset of science and technology. The morbid sensualism, whose advocates regarded natural forms as symbols of the human soul, was the dialectical antithesis to the newly emerging rationalism. In the architectural sphere, this antithesis was probably best expressed by Antoni Gaudí, who combined mysticism

and constructive ingenuity in the most fascinating way.

The theoretical premises of 'organic architecture'—a byproduct of Art Nouveau—are clearly demonstrated in the town planning ideas evolved by Hans Bernhard Reichow, who used natural structures in a completely arbitrary and quite impermissible manner to depict the organizational forms of contemporary society. It may well be that societies with a firm hierarchical organization can be compared to the circulatory system of the blood or the structure of a tree. But our pluralistic society with its great wealth of interrelating phenomena most certainly cannot. The only kinds of structural systems that could possibly do justice to such complexity would be those based on articulating networks. Christopher Alexander has drawn attention to this problem: 'The tree—though so neat and beautiful as a mental device, though it offers such a simple and clear way of dividing a complex entity into units—does not describe correctly the actual structure of naturally occurring cities, and does not describe the structure of the cities which we need. Now, why is it that so many designers have conceived cities as trees . . .? Have they done so deliberately, in the belief that a tree structure will serve the people of the city better? Or have they done it because . . . they cannot encompass the complexity . . . in any convenient mental form . . .?'[18] It is to be assumed that this simple image of the tree was prompted by a longing for a less complex social order. The fact that such ideas were particularly virulent after the First World War, during the painful transition from the old class society to our modern mass society, is no accident. Hans Paul Bahrdt refers to such biological derivations as 'negative concepts'.[19]

Today we find two distinct processes at work. On the one hand a sort of Art Nouveau revival, and on the other hand a movement towards a deeper appreciation of the structural and functional correlation between nature and architecture.

Paolo Soleri is the leading representative of the new Art Nouveau trend. His speculative, expressionistic work is based on a highly differentiated ecological system which reflects 'arcological' factors and which has preserved him from the biologistic formalism to which others—John Osajimas for example—have succumbed.

The other trend, which is determined by technological and rational criteria, derives its structures from the geometrical forms found in the crystalline world and from vegetable and animal cell formations. Here the interest in biological phenomena was prompted by the search for new building structures combining low cost with high strength. Richard Buckminster Fuller, David Georges Emmerich and Frei Otto are representative of this trend. The ideas evolved by Frei Otto are particularly interesting. He has suggested that diotamaceous growth processes could be applied to spatial structures.

In the functional sphere attempts are now being made to incorporate the cybernetics of natural processes into man-made structures by programming the building materials to effect subsequent modifications similar to those produced by the chemical processes of dissolution and regeneration.

William Katavolos has described 'organics', which are able to regulate growth by promoting expansion or contraction, to meet man's changing needs.

Rudolf Doernach's 'hydrogenetic biotectures' are also based on processes of growth and change observed in biological systems. Doernach maintains that towns live and die, like people; he considers that urban structures and mechanisms form a natural counterpart to the ecto-, meso- and endoderm. Consequently, he has suggested that walls and windows should be 'provided with genetic information' so that they can adapt to changes in the weather in the same way as the human skin.

Erwin Mühlestein has conceived the

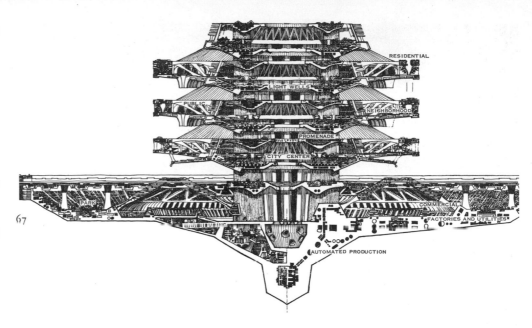

67

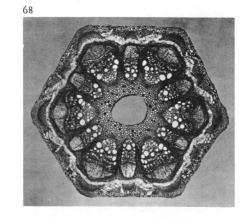

68

67. Expressionistic-speculative biostructure. Babel II B by Paolo Soleri.
68. Natural form with highly developed structural and functional characteristics. Section of plant.
69. Biologic formalism: Congress centre for Vienna by John Osajimas.

69

70

71

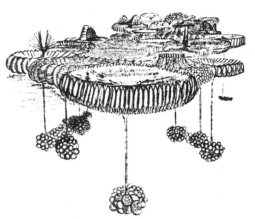

idea of 'a town with windowless windows'. This involves the use of a medium between the panes of glass whose molecular structure can be regulated in such a way that it is possible to see out but not in.

In so far as they produce variable environments, pneumatic and hydraulic structures are also based on biostructural principles. With their mechanical installations, which provide them with air, they are in fact biostructural 'machines to live in'.

Biologically-based construction presupposes the elimination of our present-day makeshift technology and the complete chemical, physical and biological symbiosis of man with his environment.

70. Biotectonically programmed apertures. Fensterlose Fensterstadt (Town with Windowless Windows) by Erwin Mühlestein.
71. 'Breathing' organism of a pneumatic residential structure. 'Wolke' (Cloud) by the Bau-Cooperative Himmelblau (Prix, Holzer and Swiezinsky).
72, 73. The cybernetics of natural processes reproduced in synthetic structures. Organics by William Katavolos (72) and Hydropolis by Rudolf Doernach (73).

72

73

WOLKE ·· HIMMELBLAU ·· GRUPPENDYNAMISCHER WOHNORGANISMUS ·

① PROMOTER ② BLITZ (hydraul. Arm) ③ METAMORPHE TRAG · VERSORGUNGSSTRUKTUR ④ PN EUMOLANDSCHAFT ⑤ SCHWEBENDE KLIMAHAUT ⑥ FAHRGESTELL ⑦ SPRUNGNETZ ⑧ SCHWIM M · TAUCHGARTEN ⑨ NAHRUNGS - AUTOMATEN ⑩ SONNENDECK ⑪ SANITÄRBLOCK

Alfred Neumann and Zvi Hecker

Apartment block in Ramat Gan, 1960

Ramat Gan is a northern suburb of Tel Aviv. The building is located on a steep hill (**1,2**) and affords a fine view of the Mediterranean. Its basic shape is an elongated hexagon, which results from the combination within a spatial framework of hexagonal prisms (**4**). The first three storeys follow the ascending line of the terrain, while the three upper storeys project outwards in overhanging layers (**5**). The interior is like a terraced piazza with small-scale landscaping effects. It has its own microclimate, which protects the occupants from the summer sun and the winter's cold.

A typical floor contains two or more apartments, which are designed in correspondence with the hexagonal system used for the main structure (**3**). The principal feature of these apartments is provided by the large polygonal terraces (**6**), whose hollow prismatic forms are in striking contrast to the enclosed sections of the block.

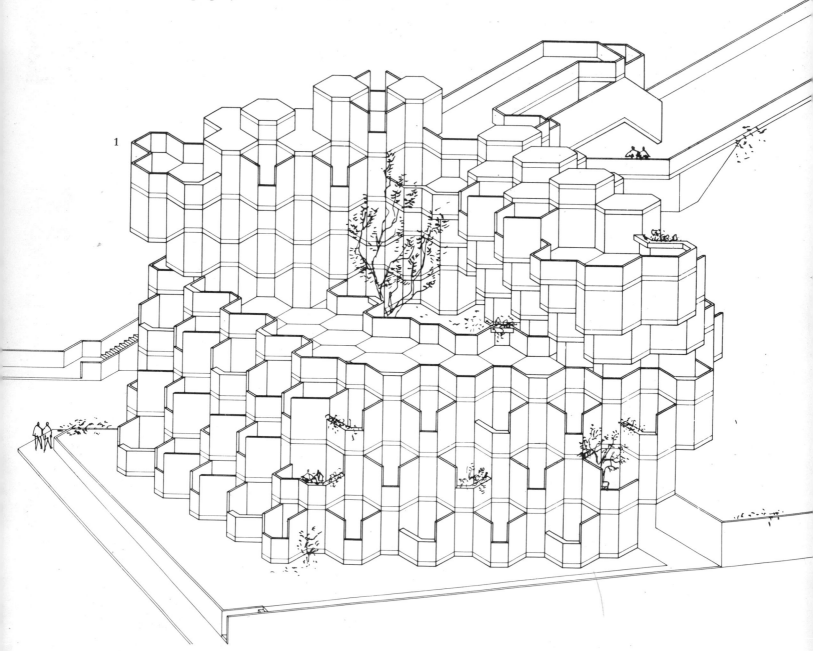

1

2

3

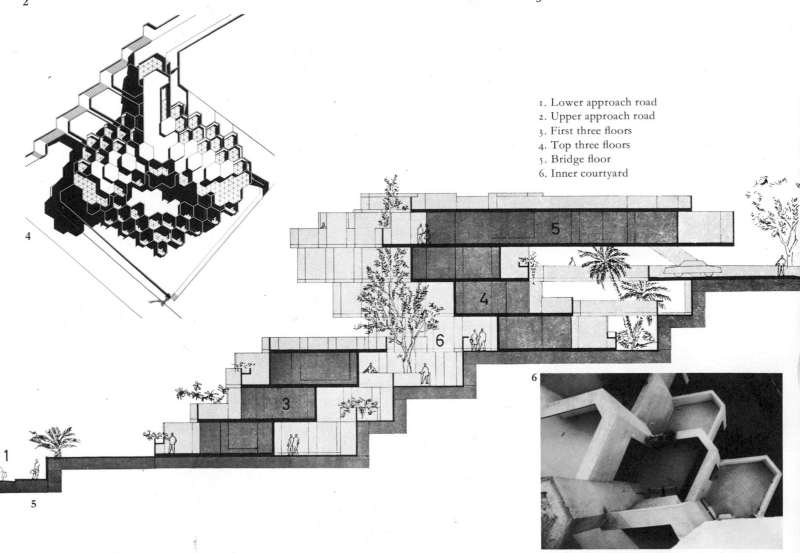

4

1. Lower approach road
2. Upper approach road
3. First three floors
4. Top three floors
5. Bridge floor
6. Inner courtyard

5

1

6

Cellular Agglomerates

Moshe Safdie

Habitat '67, Montreal, 1967
Habitat Puerto Rico, 1968

Although Habitat '67 (**1–8**) was built for the Montreal Expo' in 1967, Safdie had already started work on this project several years before and published plans for it in 1964. The original project provided for two complementary structures, but in the event only the first of these, which contains 158 residential units (**1, 4–8**), was actually built.

This structure is composed of 354 modular units (**6, 8**), whose structural members were made from precast concrete. These units are 3.05 metres high, 5.33 metres wide and 11.73 metres long; they weigh approximately 90 tons. They were cast on the building site and subsequently connected to one another by a post-tensioning system (involving high tension rods and cables), thus creating a continuous structure in a zigzag line. Access—and additional structural support—are provided by the lift and staircase towers and by the covered bridges which link them. For the projected complementary complex (**2, 3**), to contain one thousand units, Safdie modified his structural systems. In this design the residential units are set out in a terraced formation between pairs of box girders inclined at acute angles (**2**), and thus, in contrast to the first scheme, and as a result of the 'saw-edged' grouping, lessen the confrontation of the units.

Safdie followed Habitat '67 with a whole series of similar projects. These include his Habitat Puerto Rico which is illustrated here (**9–12**). In longitudinal section the residential cells in this project resemble flattened hexagons (**11**). They are 3.96 metres wide and weigh 22 tons, which means that they can be transported on motorways (**10**). The irregular alignment of the cells in Habitat Puerto Rico produces a most attractive spatial composition.

1

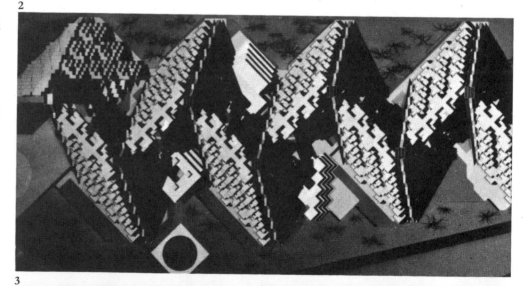

2

3

Cellular Agglomerates

4

5

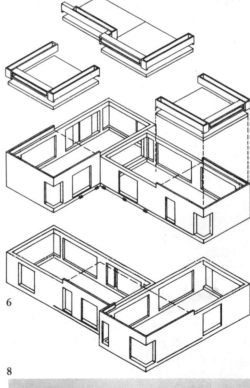

6

7

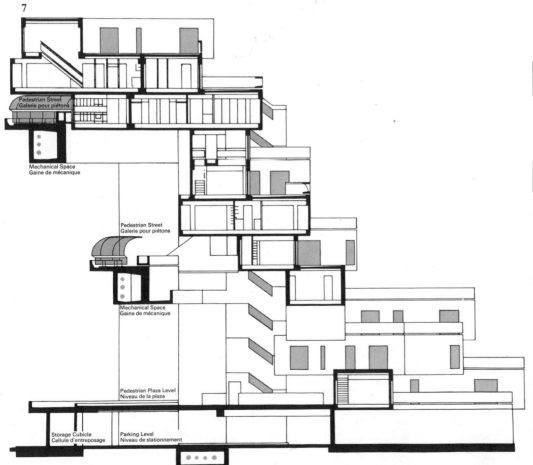

Pedestrian Street
Galerie pour piétons

Mechanical Space
Gaine de mécanique

Pedestrian Street
Galerie pour piétons

Mechanical Space
Gaine de mécanique

Pedestrian Plaza Level
Niveau de la plaza

Storage Cubicle
Cellule d'entreposage

Parking Level
Niveau de stationnement

8

Cellular Agglomerates

9

10

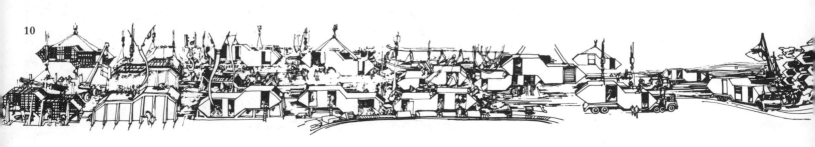

Cellular Agglomerates

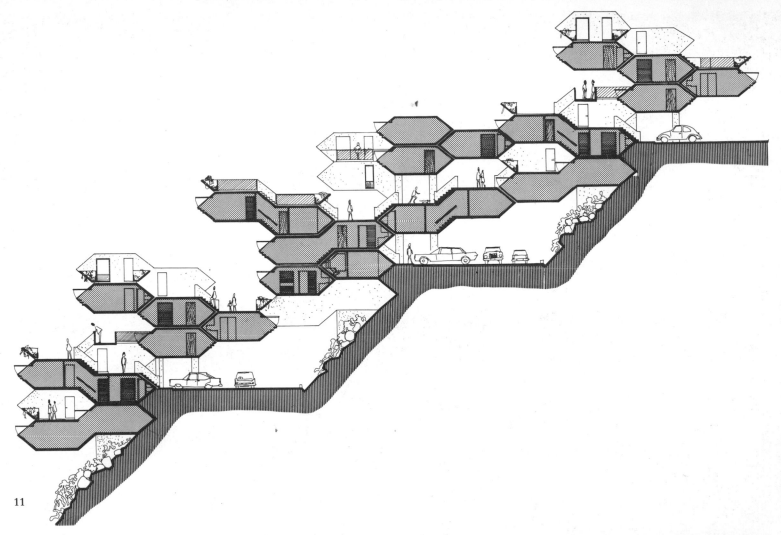

11

12

Justus Dahinden

Trigonic spatial cells, 1965

The trigonic cell is an equilateral triangle with 10.35 metre sides. It can be subdivided into a secondary system of equilateral triangles with 3.45 metre sides by means of mobile partitions (3). The technical apparatus is incorporated into the hollow sections of the load-bearing structure and is distributed along the outside walls in horizontal conduits, where it is readily accessible at all times. The fixed corners are used for cupboards or sanitary installations. The floor area of each unit is 50 square metres; the floor area of the basement, including the staircase and entrance hall, is 23 square metres; the cellar area is also 23 square metres.

Trigonic cells can be executed in heavy materials—as in the Trigondorf (Trigonic village) Doldertal in Zürich (1)—or in lightweight materials (2). They are also suitable for larger agglomerates (4, 5). A macrostructure can be devised consisting of stacked elongated platforms which also serve as pedestrian ways.

The cells can also be incorporated into a suspended structure. In a design of that kind (6, 7), two steel cables were attached to hilltops on either side of a valley and carried a series of suspenders, which were anchored in the valley below. Flexible platforms were then introduced into this stable structure, where they provided a foundation for the trigonic cells. The service installations were suspended from the platforms. Access was provided on both sides of the valley by inclined lifts, and pedestrian corridors passed through the 'settlement' from end to end.

1

2

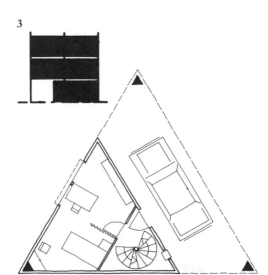

3

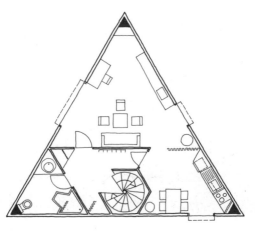

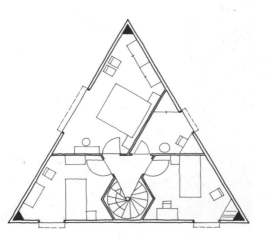

Cellular Agglomerates

Cellular Agglomerates

6

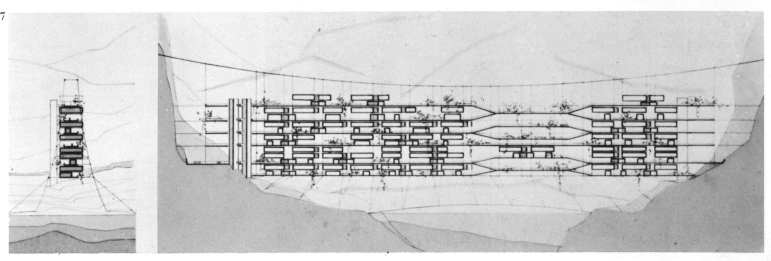

7

Cellular Agglomera

1

2

3

Herbert Prader, Franz Fehringer and Erich Ott

Composite linear city with hexagonal residential cells, 1969

This team of architects has produced a design for a linear city, in which a central public area is flanked by two disc-shaped superstructures for the private sphere (**1–3**) which can grow in either direction.

The most striking feature of the design is the careful and detailed treatment of the hexagonal residential cells. Although these cells are distributed over a large number of storeys, the team has decided to dispense with a load-bearing frame. By spotwelding 2.5 millimetre gauge sections of sheet steel (**6**), the cells could be made strong enough for them to be stacked in a self-supporting beehive formation between ten and fourteen storeys high. The empty spaces in this formation, which may be equivalent to several cells (**4**), can be fitted with 'residential landscapes' prefabricated from lightweight synthetic material and fitted out with floors, galleries, partition walls and so on (**5–7**). In static terms the corners of the hexagons act as joints; when the cells are stacked, high strength Y-sections made of synthetic material are inserted between the edges of neighbouring cells, thus creating an interlocking structure. Because of this arrangement the sides of the cells are not quite contiguous, which also makes for better sound-proofing. The walls of the cells act as compression members, the ribs in the floors and the front panels as tension members. Access to the cellular structures is provided by free-standing towers and arcades, which are attached to the towers and which each serve three storeys (**3, 8**).

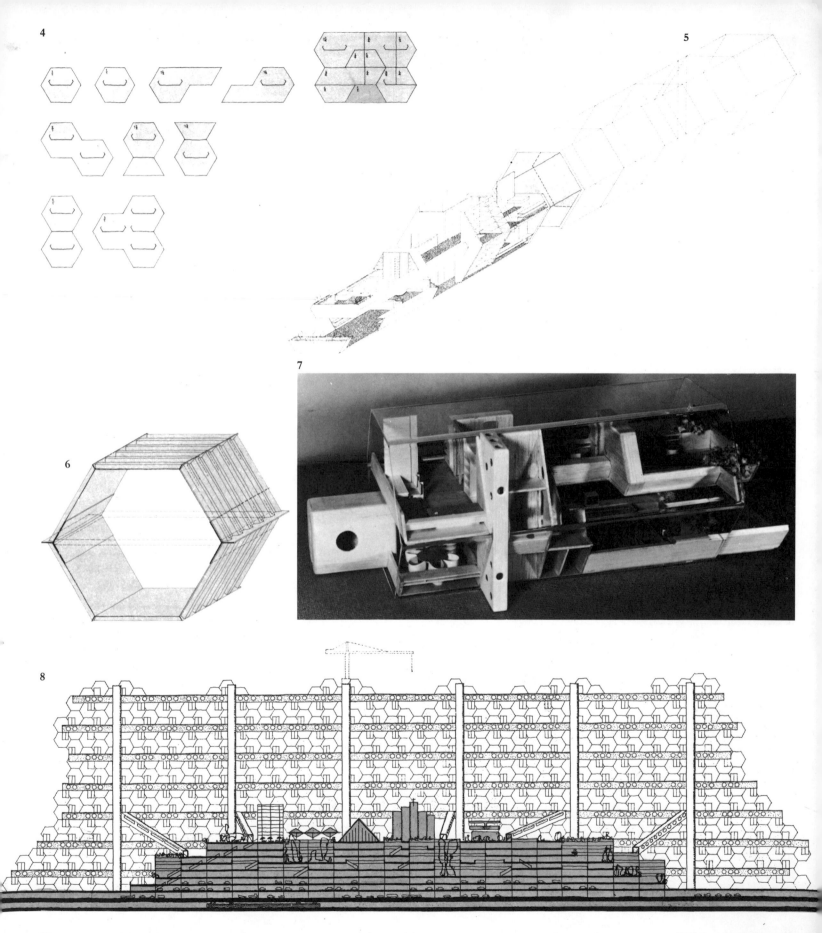

David Georges Emmerich

Jeux de construction (Construction games), 1966

Emmerich is one of the leading exponents of 'constructive geometry' in France. Between 1967 and 1969 he gave courses in constructive geometry at various French Academies and in 1970 published a book on the subject[20] which testifies to his wide ranging interests.

The building system illustrated here depends on a small number of prefabricated components, which can be combined in different ways to produce a wide range of spatial designs.

The basic component is a square panel measuring 80 cm × 80 cm (1), which is made of sheet steel lined with synthetic material. The ends of the panel are Z-shaped, which means that simple, bolted joints can be used (3), and it is insulated on the inside against heat loss. This square panel is supplemented by triangular panels, which means that, in addition to simple cubes, Emmerich is able to produce octahedra, rhombohedra and so on (4). He is also able to produce combinations of cubes and octahedra, of cubes and rhombohedra and of cubes, octahedra and rhombohedra ... (5). Emmerich's residential units can be stacked without additional structural support up to a maximum of three storeys (2, 7). Beyond that a steel skeleton is needed (6).

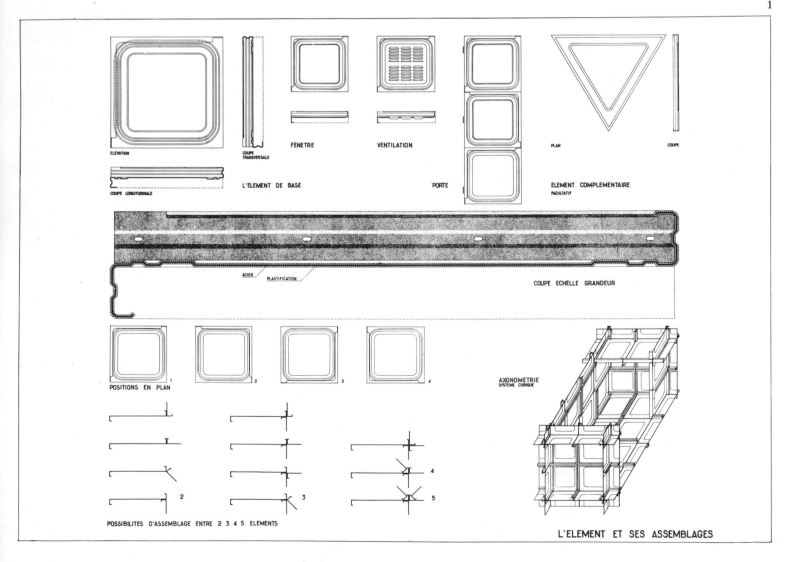

ELEVATION
COUPE TRANSVERSALE
COUPE LONGITUDINALE
FENETRE
VENTILATION
PLAN
COUPE
L'ELEMENT DE BASE
PORTE
ELEMENT COMPLEMENTAIRE
FACULTATIF

ACIER
PLASTIFICATION
COUPE ECHELLE GRANDEUR

POSITIONS EN PLAN
AXONOMETRIE
SYSTEME CUBIQUE

POSSIBILITES D'ASSEMBLAGE ENTRE 2 3 4 5 ELEMENTS

L'ELEMENT ET SES ASSEMBLAGES

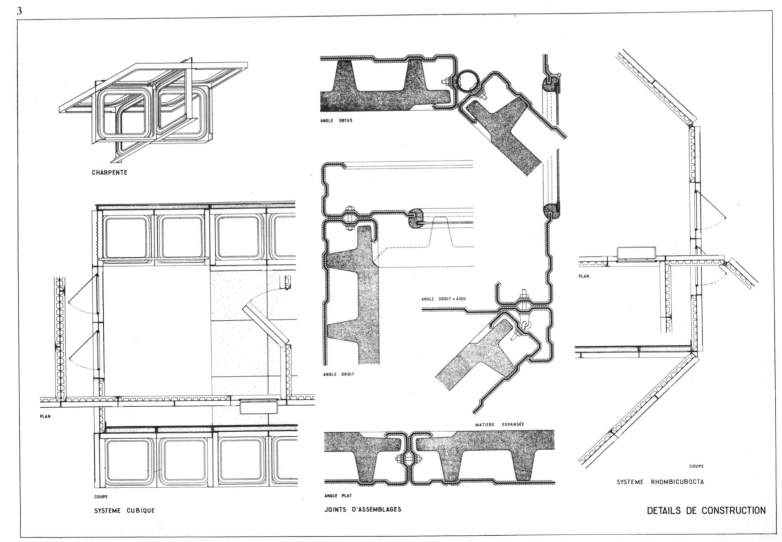

2

CHARPENTE

ANGLE OBTUS

ANGLE DROIT + AIGU

PLAN

ANGLE DROIT

MATIERE EXPANSÉE

PLAN

COUPE

ANGLE PLAT

COUPE

SYSTEME RHOMBICUBOCTA

COUPE

SYSTEME CUBIQUE

JOINTS D'ASSEMBLAGES

DETAILS DE CONSTRUCTION

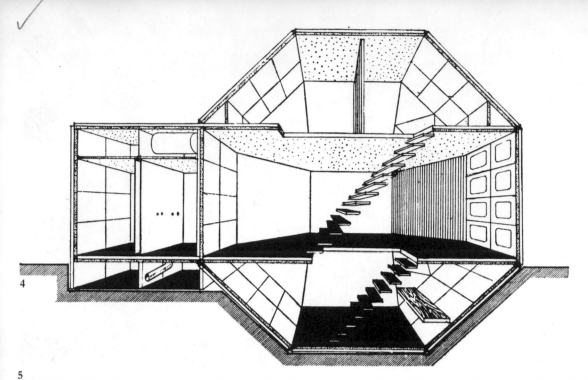

4

5

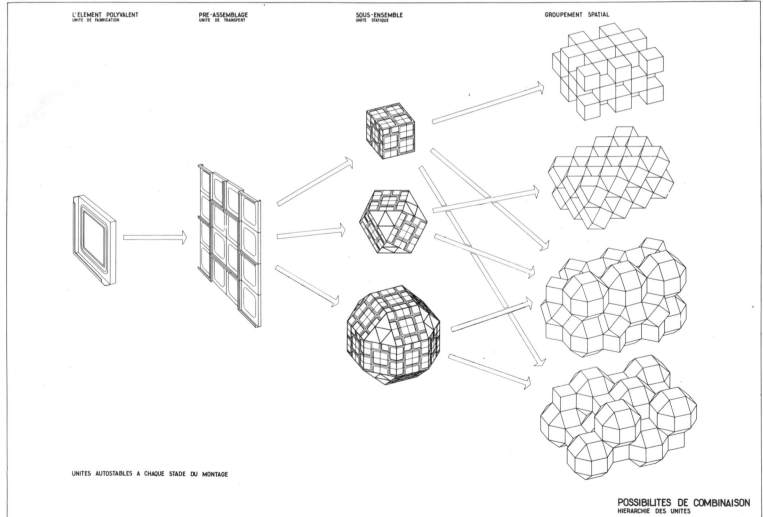

L'ELEMENT POLYVALENT
UNITE DE FABRICATION

PRE-ASSEMBLAGE
UNITE DE TRANSFERT

SOUS-ENSEMBLE
UNITE STATIQUE

GROUPEMENT SPATIAL

UNITES AUTOSTABLES A CHAQUE STADE DU MONTAGE

POSSIBILITES DE COMBINAISON
HIERARCHIE DES UNITES

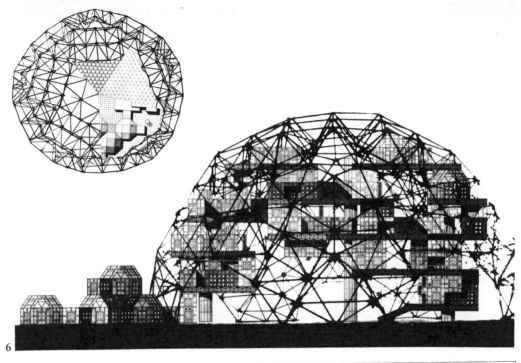

6

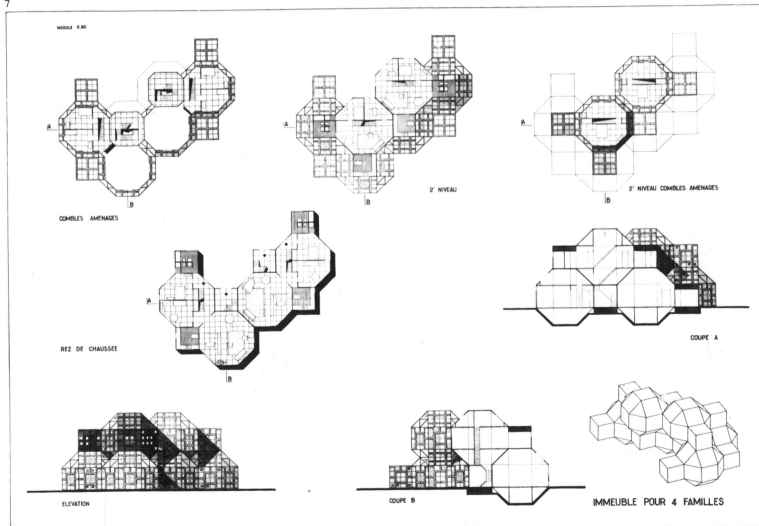

MODULE 0.80

COMBLES AMENAGES

2' NIVEAU

2' NIVEAU COMBLES AMENAGES

REZ DE CHAUSSEE

COUPE A

ELEVATION

COUPE B

IMMEUBLE POUR 4 FAMILLES

7

Paul Maymont

Maison 'Diamant' (Polyhedral house), 1967

Maymont's Maison Diamant consists of polyhedral cells with an external diameter of approximately 8.50 metres and an interior height of between 2.10 and 2.60 metres. Because of their folding surfaces, the cells have suitable rigidity and so no additional buttressing members are needed. The triangular wall panels are 7 centimetres thick, they are coated with phenol resin on the inside and covered with an outer skin of stainless steel. These panels are separated from one another by sections of synthetic material which provide insulation against heat loss and prevent the transmission of vibrations from one cell to another. Each residential unit is composed of four standard cells, a garage cell and a terrace cell (which is half the size of a standard cell). The cells can be stacked (1–3), although for the present composite free-standing structures are limited to two storeys. For structures of more than two storeys a space frame has to be used (5). Maymont has specified the dimensions of the structural members of such space frames: 0.55 metres in diameter and 28 metres in length.

The polygonal ground plan (4) of the cells must necessarily restrict the utilization of their interior space. They would make suitable holiday or leisure apartments, and it seems likely that Maymont's project will be used for such purposes.

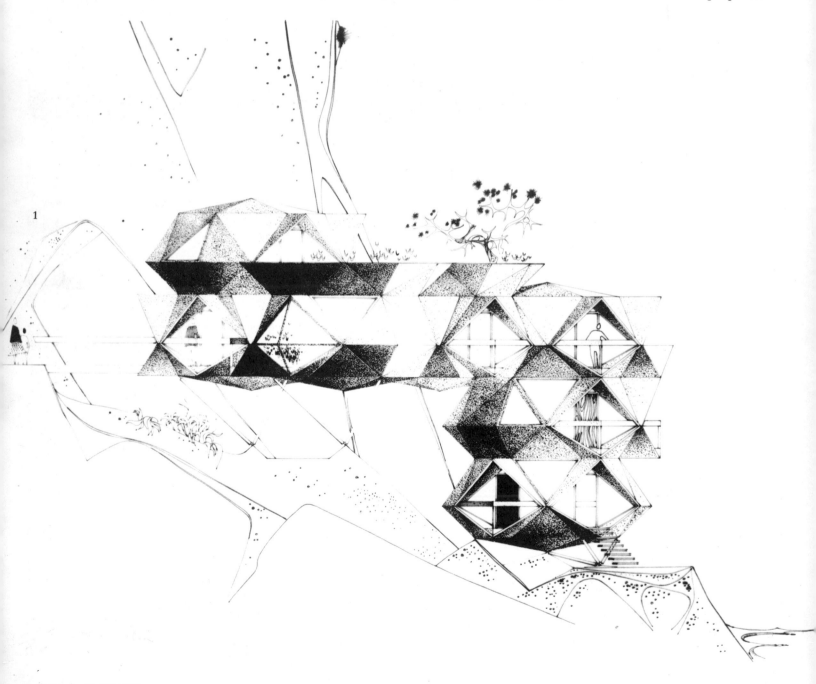

1

2

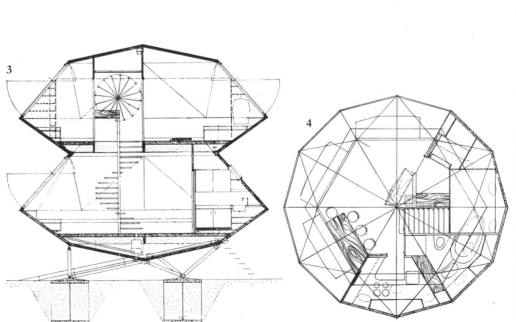

3

4

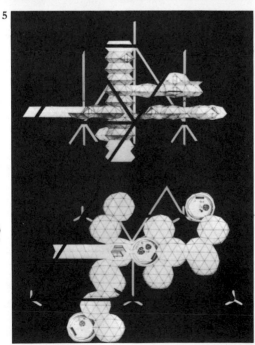

5

Cellular Agglomerates

Chanéac

Cellules polyvalentes (Multi-functional cells), 1960

For over ten years now Chanéac has been investigating the technical and town-planning problems posed by cellular structures. His favourite material is polyester reinforced with fibre glass (**1**).

In many of his projects, the mass-produced modular units are simply placed side by side or stacked one on top of the other (**2, 3**), but he has also produced designs featuring primary and secondary structures. His 'Alligator Cities' are representative of this composite style: in these designs the cells are hung on a load-bearing skeleton, which also provides access to the cells (**4**).

Another proposal put forward by Chanéac is for 'parasite cells', which could be added on to conventional buildings to extend their floor space (**5**). This particular style of building, in which the architect is constantly required to adapt to new and unforeseen needs, Chanéac calls *architecture insurrectionnelle*.

Of course, mass-produced low-cost cells made of synthetic material are throw-away articles and, as such, they would aggravate the problem of waste disposal which is one of the less desirable by-products of our industrial civilization. However, Eastman Kodak have initiated a hopeful development in this field with the discovery of a new process by which synthetic materials are pulverized by exposure to ultraviolet rays. The powder can be assimilated by bacteria.

1

2

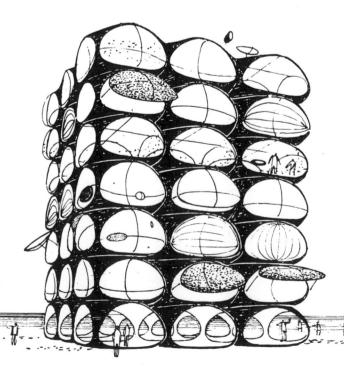

3

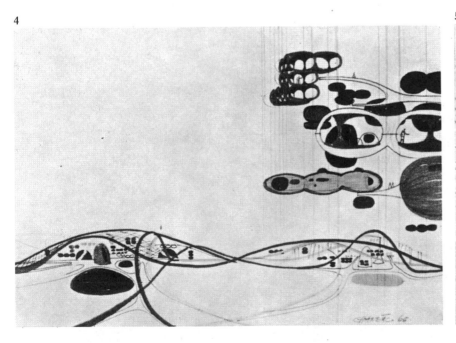

4

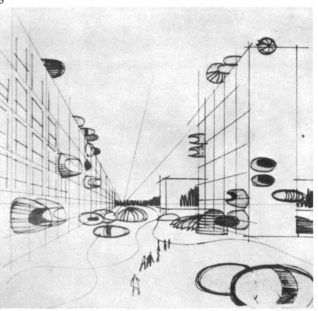

5

Cellular Agglomerates

Claude and Pascal Häusermann

Outil 'Habitation' (Implement 'Dwelling'), 1969

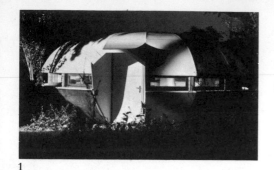

1

The *maison individuelle* designed by these two French architects was prompted by a general interest in town-planning problems. They believe that the 'demographic-urbanistic' evolution now taking place will lead to the formation, within the post-industrial leisure society, of an 'intellectual and cultural urban community'. At present, however, they feel that this process of change is being inhibited by the actions of the authorities and, more particularly, by the great welter of regulations which the building industry is required to observe. In their view, the only way of breaking out of this impasse is by developing a highly efficient building industry capable of flooding the market with enormous quantities of low-cost residential cellular structures (1), thus creating a state of such utter chaos that it would leave the authorities quite powerless to intervene (2). This 'pirate architecture' (Chanéac) would provide 'residential implements', which would be in keeping with the life style of the emerging 'intellectual and cultural community' and would eliminate all possibility of urban monotony.

The Häusermanns recommend that an 'air column' should be provided as a standard accessory with each residential unit so that people could form their own spatial agglomerates, if they so desired (3, 4). The height of these agglomerates would be limited by the length of the columns.) They also suggest that 'imaginary' sites should be provided, by which they mean unoccupied sites, so that the 'spatial resident' would be able to extend or convert his property without disturbing his neighbours.

All these ideas depend for their realization on the existence of 'friendly relations' leading to mutual assistance between all sections of the community. The Häusermanns have given no thought to the formation of the public sphere, presumably because they have been too preoccupied with their individualistic (and extremely naïve) schemes for urban development.

2

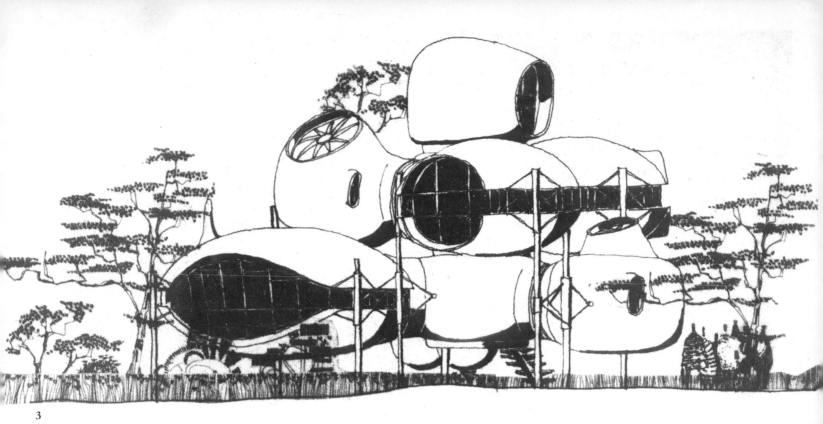

3

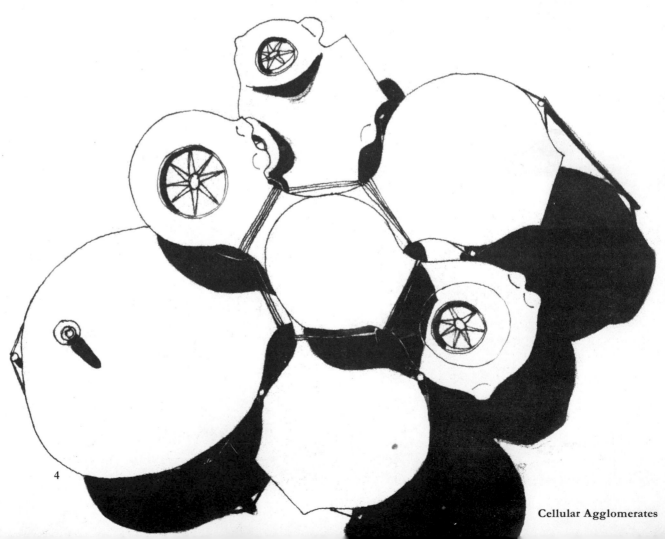

4

Cellular Agglomerates

Wolfgang Döring

System of variable spatial elements made up of synthetic materials, 1965

This design emerged as a result of the experience acquired during the development and production of spatial elements for a building firm working with prefabricated components.

In Döring's other design (see page 66) the load-bearing structure and the infillings are largely independent of one another with the result that the individual cells are readily exchangeable. Here, however, the load-bearing structure and the infillings are completely integrated. The vertical force exerted by the cells—which consist of double shells made of polyester resin—is contained by an integrated steel structure (**3**). Lateral forces are contained by braces attached to the exterior of the cells (**2**). The maximum height of the structure is limited to twelve storeys.

It is also possible to contain part of the lateral force by means of braces, which would allow the upper cells to project beyond the limits of the building site, thus effecting a useful economy (**1**). No information has been provided about the projected service systems.

1

2

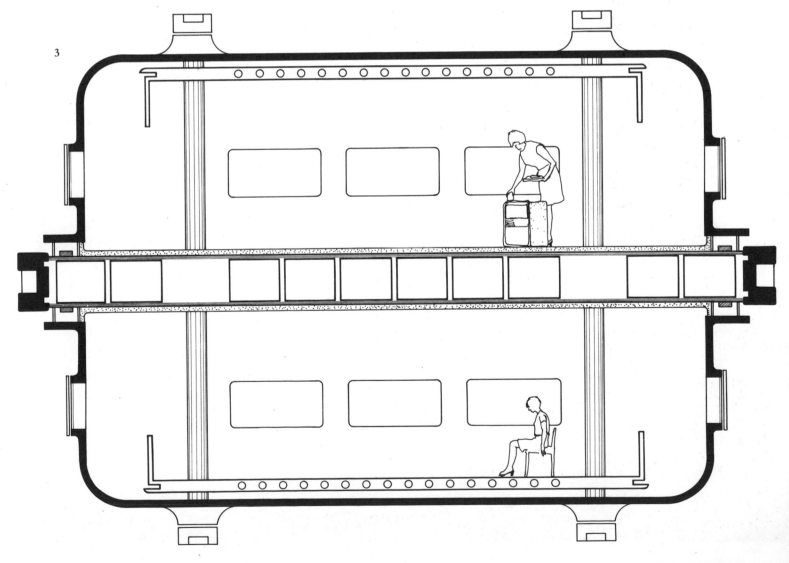

3

Wolfgang Döring

Stapelhaus (House of stacked units), 1964

Although Döring was concerned primarily with the solution of constructive problems while he was working on this project, he none the less contrived to produce a design of great linear and formal beauty (**1**). The building consists of a steel skeleton stiffened with wire bracing and containing a series of prefabricated, standardized cells, which are made from pressings (**2, 3**). These cells are stacked one above the other (Duplex method) on either side of a central core, which houses the service and disposal systems (**4**).

1

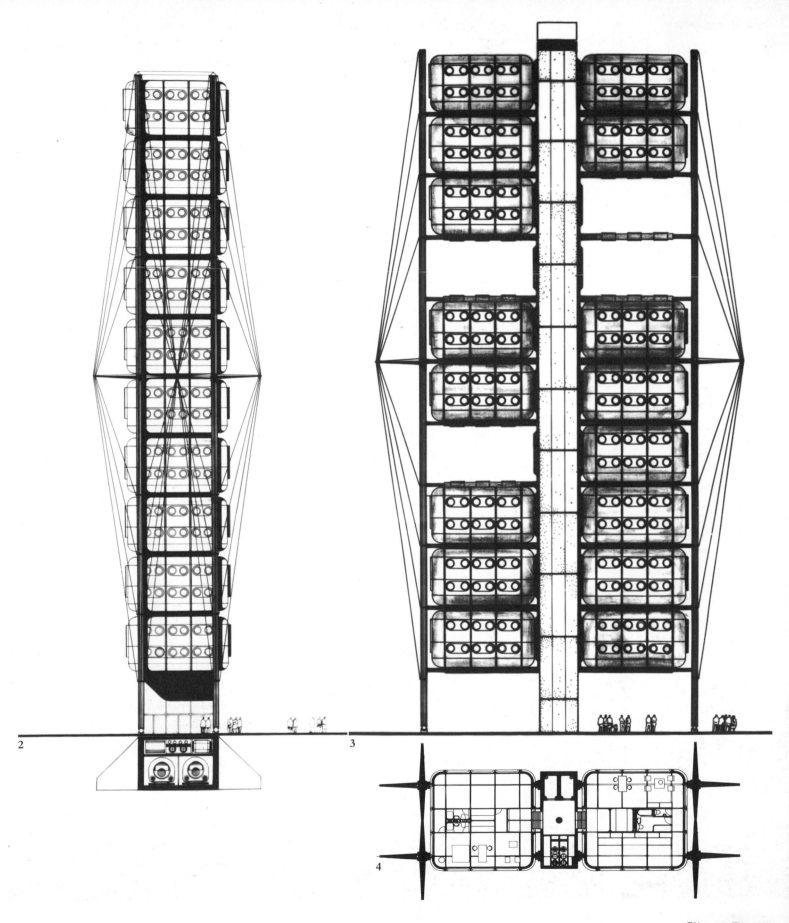

2

3

4

Clip-on, Plug-in

Arthur Quarmby

Corn on the Cob, 1963

Quarmby envisages the erection at various places throughout the continent of Europe of load-bearing masts equipped with service and waste disposal systems that would provide sites for clip-on residential cells (**2**). These sites would be rented to private individuals who had bought their own living units.

The 160 metres high mast designed by Arthur Quarmby is made up of concrete sections, which are post-tensioned together on the ground before being hoisted into place. These sections, each of which has two massive arms, are assembled one above the other, the arms spiralling round at thirty degrees (**1**).

The living units are suspended from special suspension points on the tips of the concrete arms and are placed in position by a large twin-jib crane located immediately beneath the uppermost section of the structure, which contains water storage tanks, a restaurant, a laundry and shops.

Each living unit is fitted with a flexible service tube which is clipped on to the central core. In the living units certain sections of the walls have been made transparent—and in the living rooms sections of the floor and ceiling as well—so as to give occupants the impression of suspension in space.

1

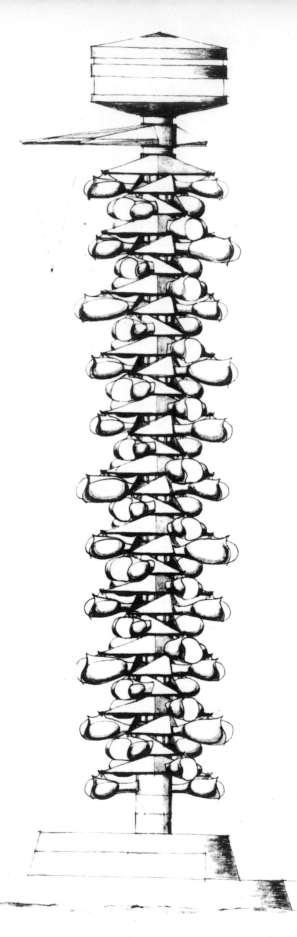

2

Warren Chalk

Capsule Unit Tower, 1964

Warren Chalk's Capsule Unit Tower consists of a central shaft, which houses the lifts, staircases and service and disposal units, and residential cells, which are hung on the core to form circular storeys (**1, 4**). These residential cells (**2, 3**), which are trapezoidal on account of the radial layout, are ablc to expand and contract within the relatively narrow limits imposed by this strict system. Interchangeable secondary cells for bathrooms and partition walls, which can be rolled back to create more space, provide a certain degree of flexibility, which means that these apartments can be adapted to meet different needs. In this they resemble the cells designed for the project Living 1990 (see page 112). The residential units are connected by hydraulic lifts (**2**), which create something of the character of a maisonnette.

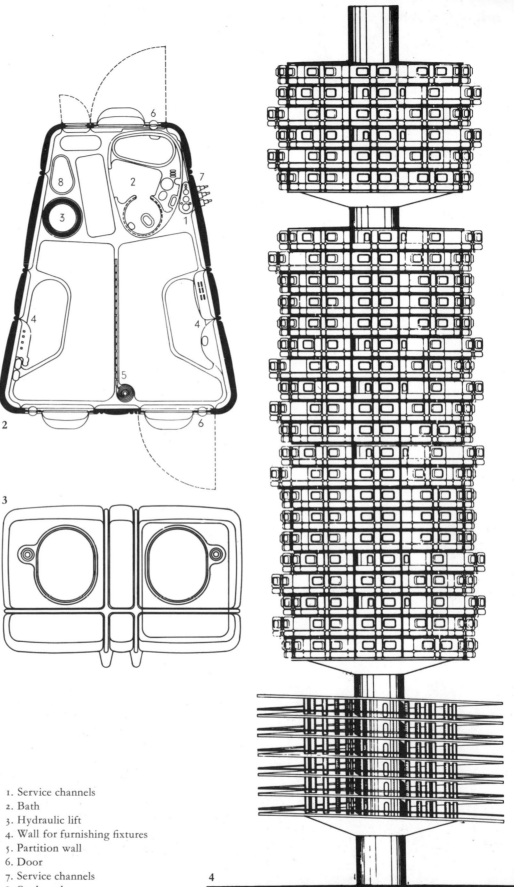

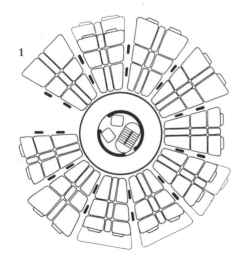

1. Service channels
2. Bath
3. Hydraulic lift
4. Wall for furnishing fixtures
5. Partition wall
6. Door
7. Service channels
8. Cupboard

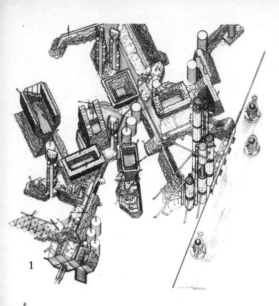

1

Peter Cook

Plug-in City, 1964

Plug-in City is undoubtedly the most impressive design produced by the Archigram group. But, although the structural systems incorporated into this project are most intriguing and are based on a whole series of new ideas, it is not at all easy to assess their true significance. This is due, not so much to the utopian dimensions of the project, as to the lack of detail and precision in its presentation. Moreover—unlike the Metabolists, who attach great importance to theory—the members of the Archigram group have established virtually no theoretical or philosophical premises for their design programme. Nor have they tried to coordinate their projected constructions by placing them in specified settings. In fact, their urban designs are so free as to be almost an-

archic. In pursuing this open plan policy and refusing to establish predetermined schemes, they were motivated by the desire to leave the greatest possible scope for growth and regeneration.

The dominant feature of the Plug-in City is the lattice-shaped frame (3). This consists of intersecting tubes, half of which are used for service and supply systems and half for escalators. Prefabricated cells are then hung on the infrastructure in line with the component tubes. These cells are raised into position by a crane installed at the very top of the frame, which is also used to feed goods into the tube system (5). Further features of the Plug-in City are the Stopover Apartments (2, 4), which resemble Warren Chalk's Capsule-Unit Towers, the Car Silos, which are partially integrated into the lattice structure (2), and the Movable Buildings, which are a development of the hovercraft (1, 4). The public areas, which are embedded in

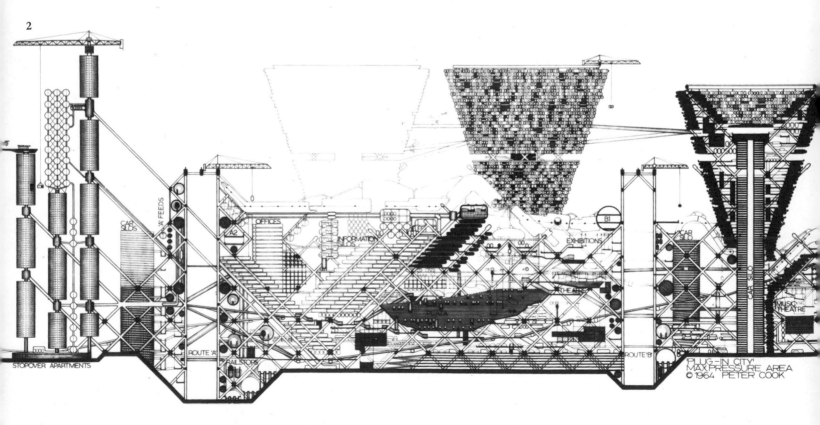

2

the urban structure in a variety of places, are covered by inflatable skins, which afford protection from the elements (**4**). In both the micro- and macro-spheres spatial relations are highly differentiated. The bizarre and extremely angular alignment of many of the buildings is strongly reminiscent of medieval and even of antique urban composition (**1**). This sortie into living plasticity makes a welcome change from the rigidity of strictly geometrical design.

The Plug-in City is a living structure and, as such, has no definitive form; every part of this structure is capable of either further development or contraction. Moreover, a Plug-in City can be erected alongside totally different existing structures without striking a too discordant note. Very few urban renewal projects succeed in integrating the old with the new and, in view of this, the Archigram group has made an important contribution to this difficult problem.

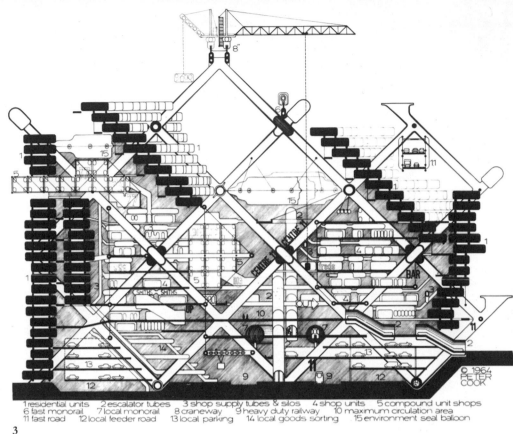

1 residential units   2 escalator tubes   3 shop supply tubes & silos   4 shop units   5 compound unit shops
6 fast monorail   7 local monorail   8 craneway   9 heavy duty railway   10 maximum circulation area
11 fast road   12 local feeder road   13 local parking   14 local goods sorting   15 environment seal balloon

3

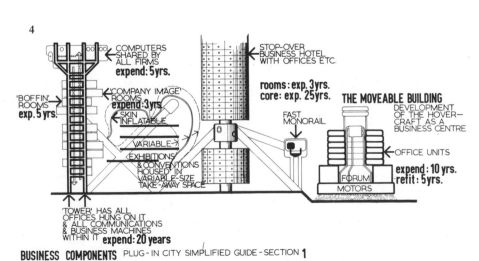

BUSINESS COMPONENTS PLUG-IN CITY SIMPLIFIED GUIDE - SECTION **1**

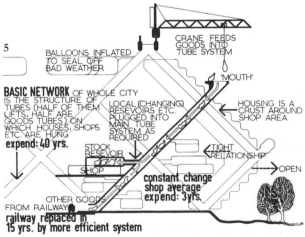

SUSTENANCE COMPONENTS   PLUG-IN CITY SIMPLIFIED GUIDE - SECTION **2**

Clip-on, Plug-in

Arata Isozaki

Cluster in the Air

These structures, which Isozaki proposes to erect above existing towns, are faintly reminiscent of Japanese temples and pagodas (**1**). They consist of a load-bearing access core with projecting arms, from which residential cells are suspended (**2, 3**).

Isozaki has not explained how the structural problems raised by this design would be resolved. Nor has he given any detailed information about the internal organization of the internal core or the residential units. Consequently, it is not possible to give an accurate assessment of his project. In general terms, although the relatively small site needed for such structures would make it fairly easy to fit them into existing towns, it would also increase the sense of isolation which is such a marked feature of urban life.

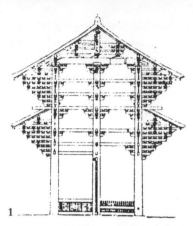

1

2

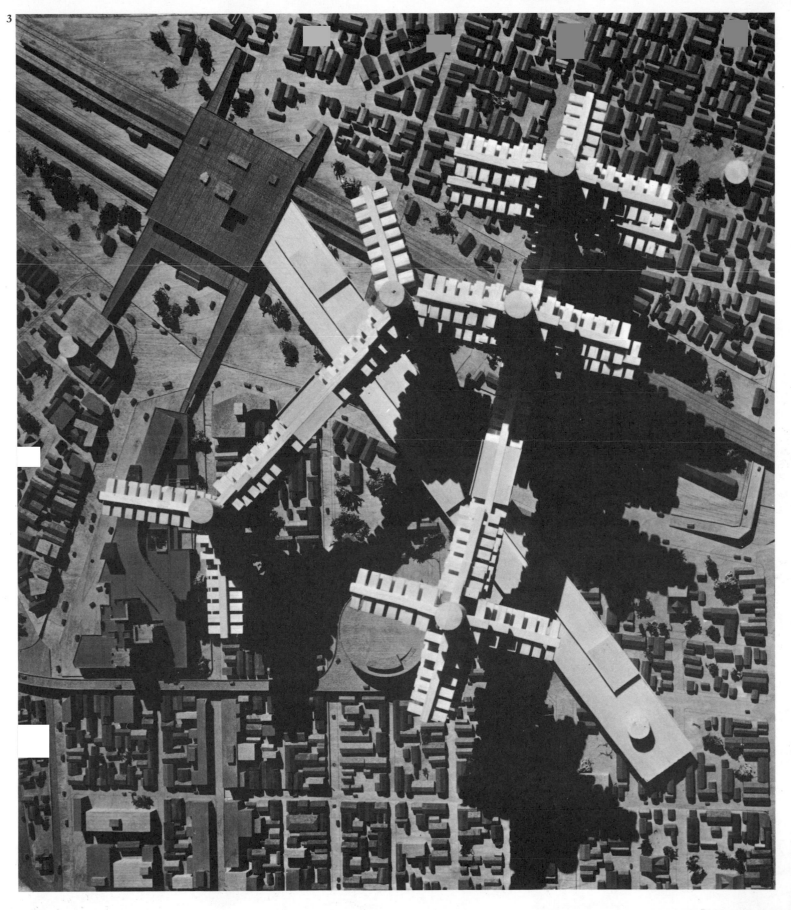

Clip-on, Plug-in

Noriaki Kurokawa

Town Plan for Tokyo, 1961

Kurokawa, one of Kenzo Tange's associates when Tange was working on the redevelopment of Tokyo (see p. 124), has also developed his own plan, which incorporates both a horizontal and a vertical infrastructure.

The horizontal infrastructure—built thirty-one metres above ground level (this being the maximum permitted height for new buildings in Tokyo in 1959)—would provide an entirely new level connecting all areas of the city. This upper level would be reserved for pedestrians. All vehicular traffic would be carried by an underground road network, while helicopters and aircraft would also be available for air travel.

For his vertical infrastructure Kurokawa has developed two alternative systems: the 'bamboo type', and the 'tree type'. The 'bamboo type' (5) involves the use of a gigantic hollow cylinder divided into a number of equal sections, rather like a bamboo cane. Small airports would be built on the circular inner platforms constructed round the edges of these sections and the aircraft would leave the cylinder at the top, which would be completely open. Apartments would be erected on the outer face of the cylinder. In the 'tree type' infrastructure (6) the central core would be used for service and waste disposal systems, while projecting arms attached to its outer face would support flat circular discs, growing smaller towards the top of the 'tree'. These discs would provide terraced macrostructural building sites for public

1

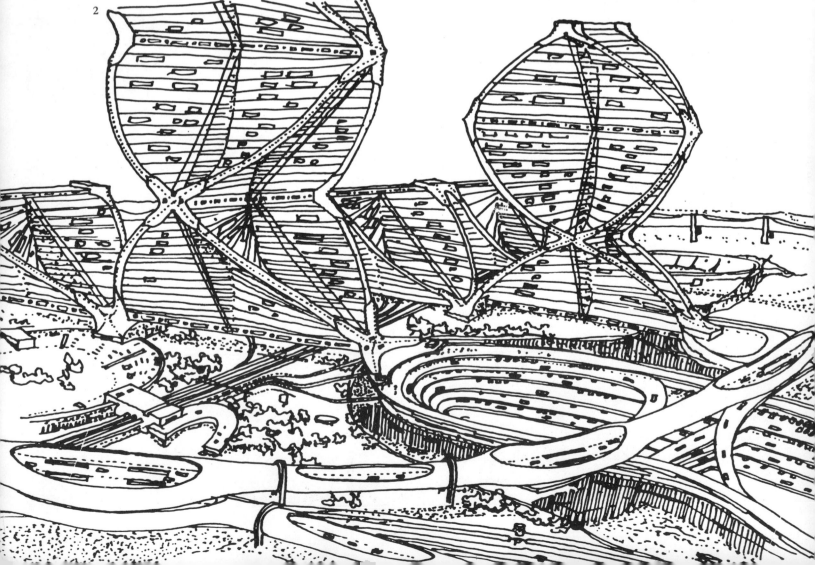

2

buildings, recreational areas and residential cells. The different levels of the terraces would be so far removed from one another that even the inner living areas would receive adequate amounts of sun and light. For the Ginza district, Kurokawa has evolved a special scheme that takes account of the higher density levels. The horizontal infrastructure would involve a 'cyclical' traffic system (3, 4) built on a cellular basis, extendable at any time and in any direction, which would complement the network of expressways now under construction. For his vertical infrastructure in the Ginza district Kurokawa proposes to build 'helicoidal' towers (1, 2). These structures, composed of elements arranged in spiral formations, would link up at every tenth floor, thus forming a complex network of orthogonal and diagonal passages.

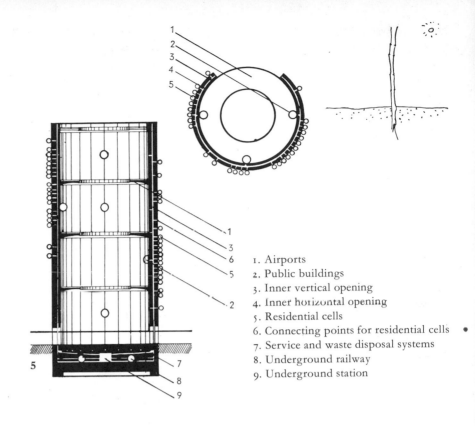

1. Airports
2. Public buildings
3. Inner vertical opening
4. Inner horizontal opening
5. Residential cells
6. Connecting points for residential cells
7. Service and waste disposal systems
8. Underground railway
9. Underground station

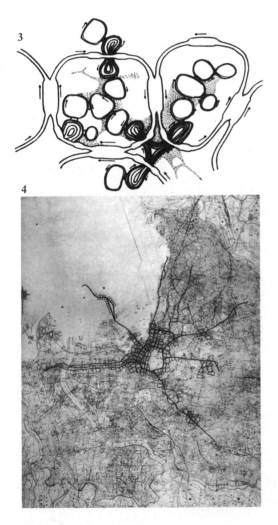

1. Inner vertical opening
2. Workshops
3. Inner horizontal opening
4. Schools
5. Residential cells
6. Public buildings
7. Green area
8. Airport
9. Ventilation shaft
10. Underground railway
11. Underground station
12. Service and waste disposal systems

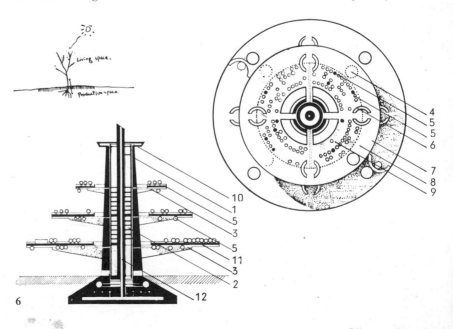

Kuniaki Suda, Hiroshi Toyomura and Yoshiyuki Haruta

Design for the competition held in 1967 under the auspices of the magazine *The Japan Architect:* 'Urban Residences for a High-Density Society'

Like many of the entries in the competition, this project envisages a composite urban structure consisting of a multi-storeyed base section for commercial facilities on the one hand and residential towers on the other (**1–3**).
Although little information has been provided about the commercial sphere, the residential towers have been described in some detail. The central core of these towers consists of four individual shafts, which bear the weight of the entire structure and also provide access to the maisonnette type apartments, which are grouped around the shafts, twelve to each twin storey (**5–7**). The upper sections of the maisonnettes, which contain the living areas and terraces, are slotted into place between the decks, while the lower sections, which provide sleeping accommodation and consist of cellular units assembled from component parts, are suspended beneath them (**4**). The area between the four shafts houses a waiting-room for lift passengers at the bottom and a dining room and lounge at the top. These facilities would be used by all the residents in the tower, for no kitchens would be provided in the individual apartments. The different towers are linked by bridge structures about half way up. These would contain Kindergartens, Post Offices, nurseries, banks and similar facilities (**2, 3**).

Key to Ill. 1:
1. Shopping street
2. Monorail
3. Stadium
4. Commercial area
5. Residential tower
6. School

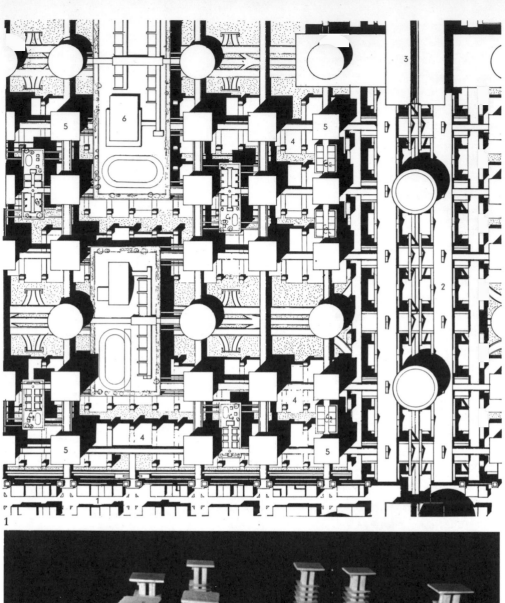

1

2

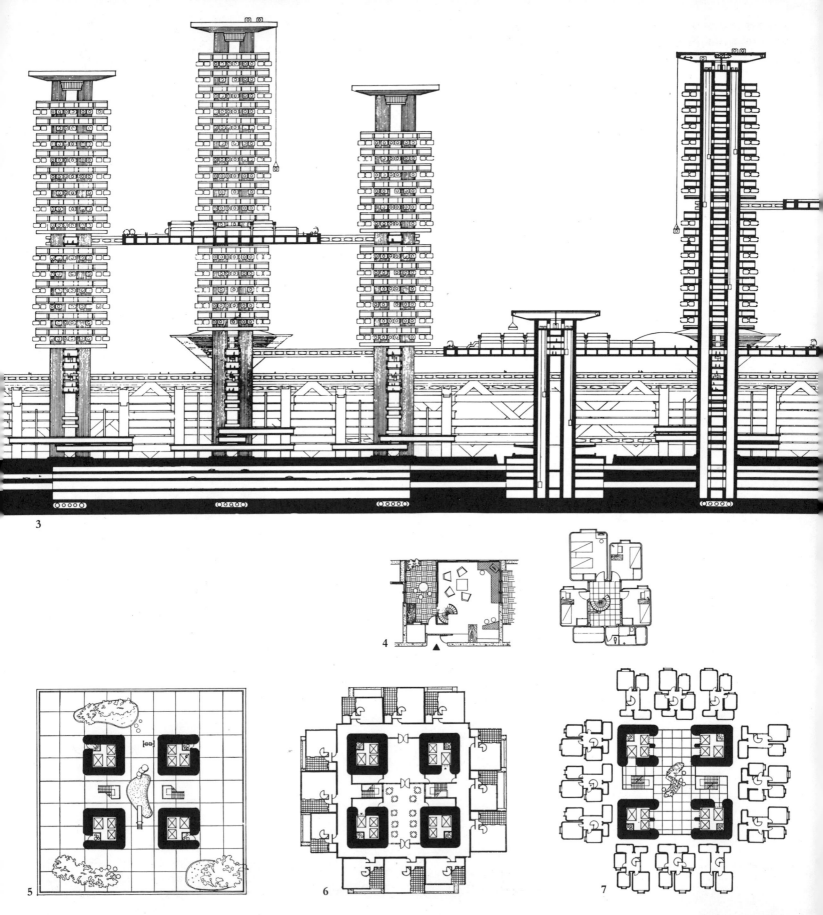

3

4

5

6

7

Clip-on, Plug-in

**Tadaaki Anzai, Masao Otani, Shingo
Takamizawa, Kunitsugu Takuri and
Shokyo Nishihara**

Design for the competion held in 1967
by the magazine *The Japan Architect*:
'Urban Residences for a High-Density
Society'

These structures are composed of
closely aligned circular towers (**5**) which
rise up from a rectangular base that is
braced with triangular frames and houses
communal facilities (**4**). Each of the
towers is made up of eight access shafts
arranged in a circular formation, which
are the main load-bearing members; of
rings, which provide circular galleries;
and of vertical discs broken down into
sixteen segments, which support the
residential units (**6, 7**). In most Japanese
projects of this kind only the bedrooms
are exchangeable. But in this project the
living-rooms have also been designed as
exchange units (**1–3**). Since most of
the larger apartments are twin-storeyed,
the circular galleries have been grouped
together in pairs (**4**), the lower gallery
in each pair serving as a meeting place
for the local residents. Since they would
be required to fulfil this communal function, these galleries have been generously
proportioned and planted with shrubs
and bushes, which means that the
apartments would be set in an attractive
environment. In order to reduce the
open area inside the rows of apartments
to acceptable proportions, it would be
blocked off at regular intervals by circular
decks.

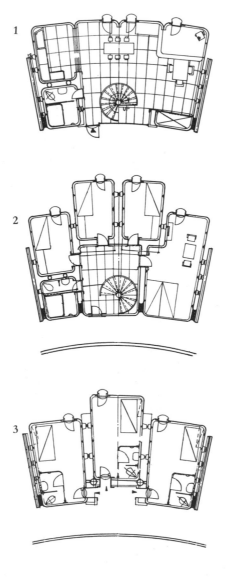

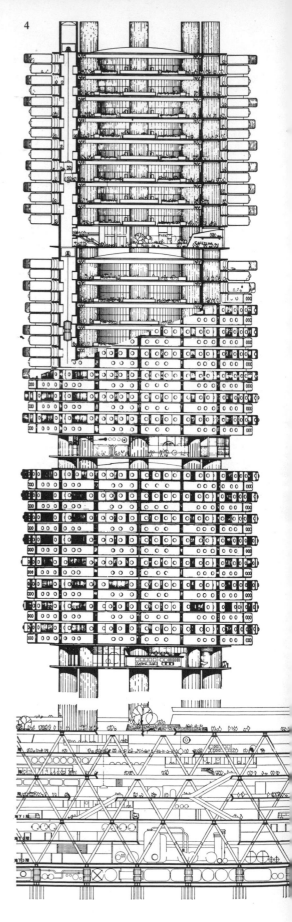

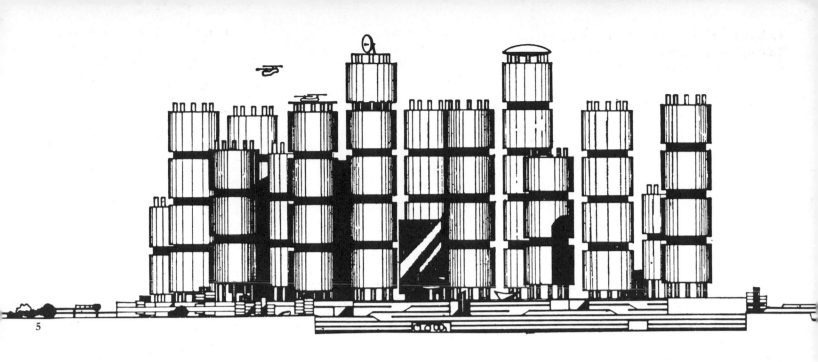

5

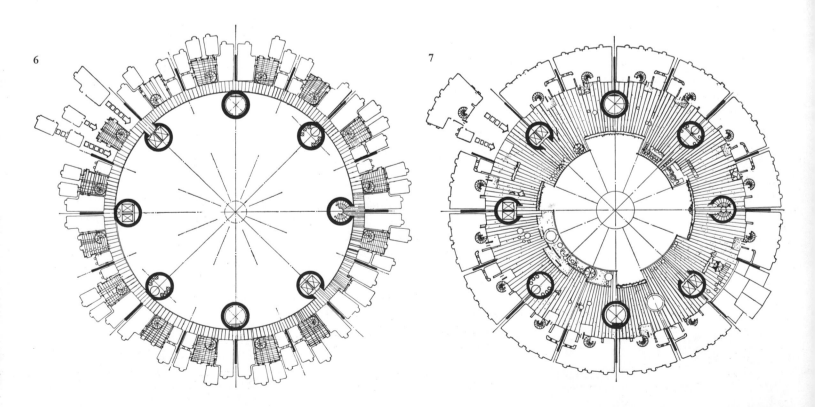

6

7

Clip-on, Plug-in

Tetsuya Akiyama, Iwao Kawakami, Norio Sato, Yuji Shiraishi and Yoshiaki Koyama

1. Living-room
2. Entrance to the children's rooms
3. Entrance to the parents' rooms
4. Children's room
5. Parents' bedroom
6. Parents' living-room

Design for the competition held in 1966 under the auspices of the magazine *The Japan Architect:* 'Urban Residences and their Connective Systems'

The loosening of family ties, which has become such a marked feature of our industrial civilization and which was vaguely reflected in the preceding project, forms the whole basis of this present design.

The residential towers, which look more like oil refineries than apartment buildings (3), are composed of residential sections stacked one above the other, each of which accommodates sixteen 'team units' (4–6). Each team unit contains apartments for twelve families and a generously proportioned communal area for fifty people (7, 8). This communal area (or team space) is surrounded by twelve tubes, each of which houses a family residential unit (1, 2) consisting of a general living area, which is integrated into the structure, and individual cellular units (for children's and parents' rooms), which are incorporated as required. Separate entrances are provided to the different living areas within each residential unit (resulting in a multiplicity of tubular corridors).

Although the family and team areas are specified in considerable detail in this project, there is no mention at all of larger communal areas. This is not surprising, for the architects consider that social activities should be restricted to small groups.

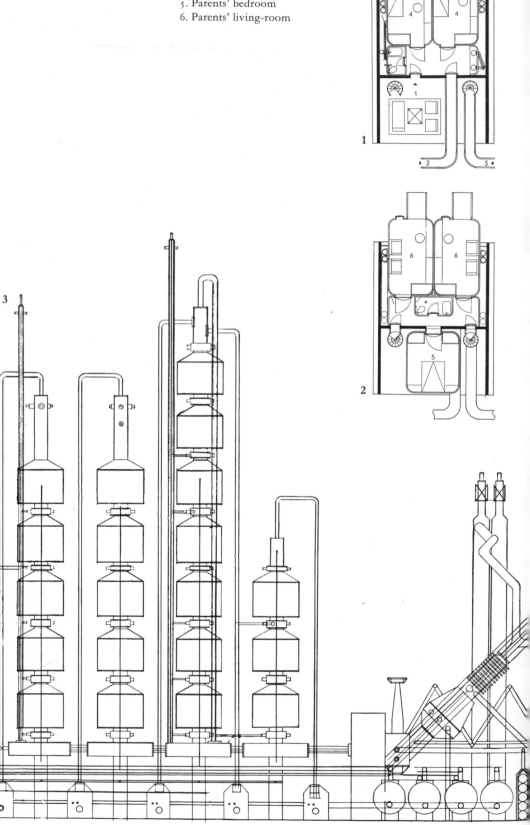

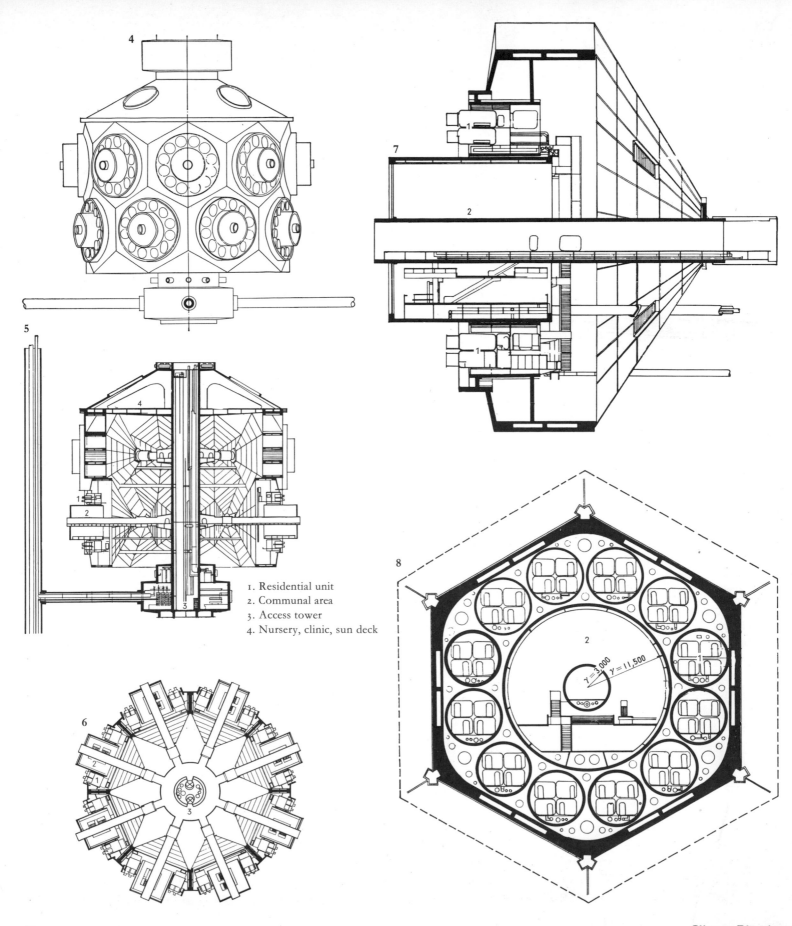

1. Residential unit
2. Communal area
3. Access tower
4. Nursery, clinic, sun deck

**V. Kalinine with Y. Ivanov,
P. Kovaliov, V. Maguidov and
V. Tarassévitch**

Redevelopment of the city centre in
Moscow, 1966

This proposal for the restructuring and
restoration of the central district of
Moscow was one of the entries in a town-
planning competition. Moscow is now
faced with the same problem as the major
cities of the West. The 'tertiary sector'
has expanded to such an extent in the
central districts of the city that the local
residents are being driven out to the
outer suburbs. The Russians have come
to realize that by building new districts
on the outskirts of Moscow, they are
simply creating an intolerable commuter
problem and overburdening their
transportation system. And so in this
project for the restructuring of the city
centre, Kalinine and his associates have
sought a spatial solution which would
have the effect of reintegrating the working and residential spheres.
Three ring roads are already being
constructed in Moscow and the project
envisages the construction of two
further ring roads inside these. The
redevelopment scheme is concerned with
tne area embraced by the second of these
ring roads—the B-ring.
The proposed population density would
be between eighty and one hundred and
fifty persons per acre. Instead of clearing
the whole district with bulldozers—a
method frequently employed in urban
redevelopment schemes—the Kalinine

team is seeking to preserve the existing
urban structure as far as possible. Thus,
the Kremlin would remain the focal
centre of the city (**1**). The A-ring, which
links the urban nucleus with the first
'shell', has been designed as a spacious,
two-storeyed complex. Service industries
would be housed on the first floor, while
the ground floor would be given over to
traffic routes and parking areas. The vast

bridge structures would radiate outwards from this ring; they would be
raised high above the ground, which
would virtually eliminate the 'dead
zones' normally created by high rise
buildings. The old urban zone would be
broken up by the introduction of green
areas. In all other respects, however, it
would retain its original character.
Monorails would be fitted beneath the

2

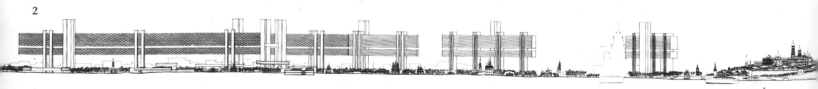

1

bridge structures to carry passengers to and from the A-ring.

With their long clear spans, the bridge elements would be both visually and psychologically less oppressive (2) for the inhabitants of the old urban areas over which they pass than other high density megastructures, such as Yona Friedman's spatial grid, which is intended to spread out over Paris like a vast carpet.

Nor would the occupants of the apartments in the bridge structures feel hemmed in, thanks to the very considerable distances which separate these structures. Moreover, because their apartments would be so high up, they would not have the sensation—one that is quite common amongst the residents of traditional high-rise buildings—that they were half in the air and half on the ground,

for this sensation disappears above fifty metres. These bridge structures would also be advantageous in that their occupants would only have to go down in a lift to be able to step out into the public sphere of the city centre. Thus, although the private and communal spheres are not fully integrated, movement between the two is relatively easy, facilitating the creation of an integrated community.

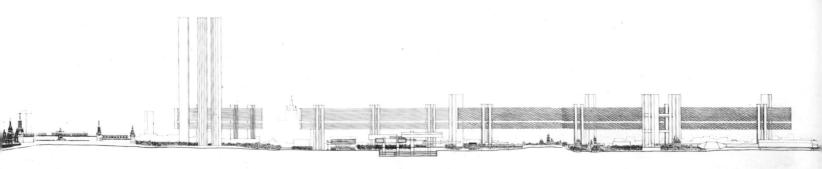

Fabrizio Carola (Architect)
Ettore Minervini and Luciano
Boscotrecase (Engineers)

Girder building, 1966

In this design vertical access is provided
by towers, which also house the service
and waste disposal systems. Viewed in
cross section, the towers are seen to
possess three 'centrifugal arms' (**1**).

These contain a groove running from
top to bottom, which houses the supports
for the bridge elements.
The 40 metres long and 13 metres wide
girders, which are made in three different
versions from prefabricated tubular
elements (**4,5**), are divided down the
middle by a narrow corridor. These
pretensioned hollow sections are connected by hinged joints throughout the
entire length of the bridge structures.

Because of the triangular disposition of
the towers, it is possible to arrange the
structures in a wide variety of architectural compositions, making due allowance for local topographical features
(**2,3**). Carola and his associates maintain
that their girder buildings could be used
not only for apartments, but also for
communal installations (**1**), but it seems
doubtful whether the system would be
flexible enough for this.

1. Apartment
2. Hotel
3. School

2

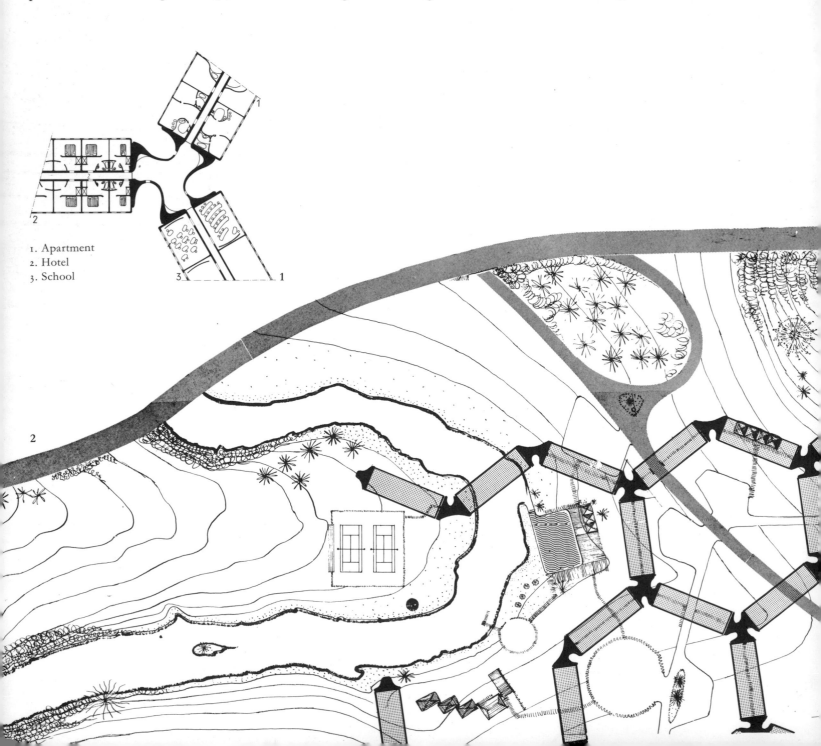

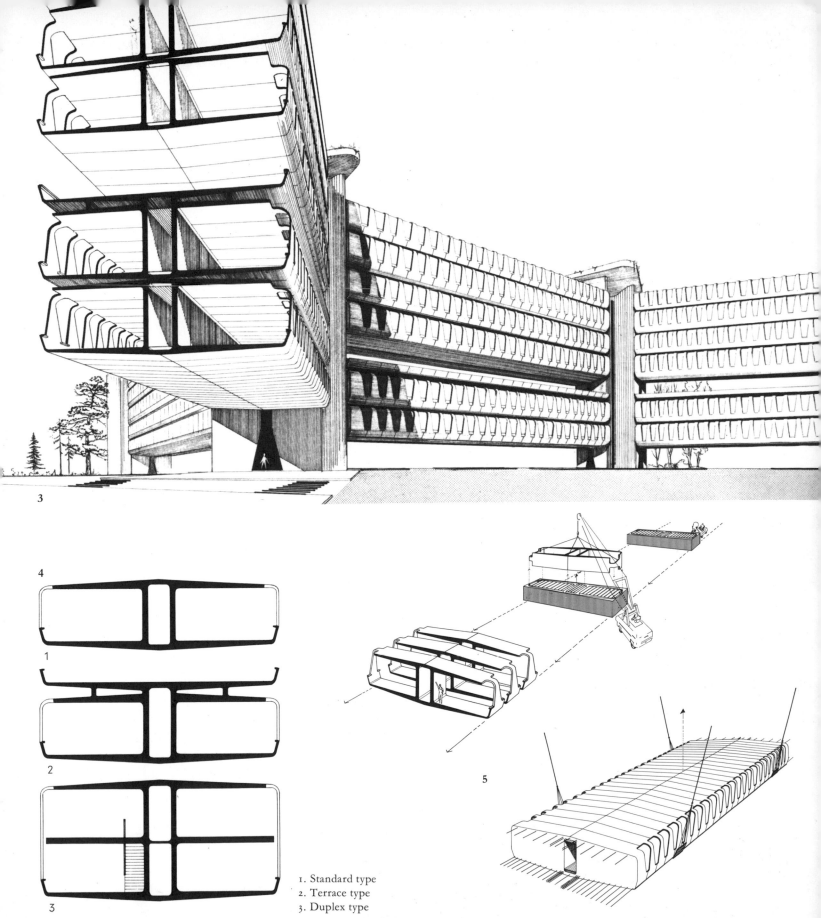

3

4

1

2

3

1. Standard type
2. Terrace type
3. Duplex type

5

85   **Bridge Structures**

André Birò and Jean-Jacques Fernier

Ville en X (City with X-shaped load-bearing structure)

This is a project for a linear city capable of unlimited growth in any direction (**5**). Terraced areas are supported by large X-shaped frames (**2**, **4**), producing an urban formation which might best be described as a pseudo bridge structure and which is reminiscent of the linear cities on *pilotis* designed by Le Corbusier for Algiers and Rio de Janeiro in the thirties. Unlike other urban bridge structures, the Ville en X is designed to cater for traffic on a really large scale and to replace existing motorways. The production and service installations, which are sited beneath the point of intersection of the X-shaped frames, do not appear to have been thought out in any great detail.

The gardens laid out above the tubular installation for road and rail traffic are flanked on either side by shops, educational institutes and leisure centres (**1**, **3**). It is here that the communal life of the linear city would develop and, since the terraced residential apartments are situated on either side of this communal area, their occupants would inevitably be disturbed to some extent. The stepped rows of apartments, which occupy the whole of the upper half of the bridge structure, are designed in the customary way with inward sloping rear façades (**2**). The ideal alignment for such a structure is north to south and when this alignment is altered, in other words when the structure branches out or changes course, there are difficulties with sunlight.

In sociological terms, this kind of linear city is not an urban centre but simply a traffic route flanked by urban complexes.

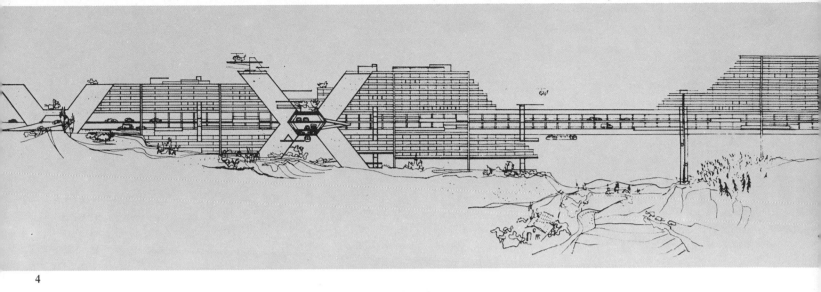

4

5

Bridge Structures

Yves Salier, Adrien Courtois and Pierre Lajus

Ville Tripode (Town with tripod structures), 1966

This building system is based on the idea that high density urban structures should have the least possible contact with the ground. The tripods (2) are set out in a broad hexagonal framework (1) and are built up from tubular components which provide support for clip-on living units. Further tripods can be erected on top of those resting on the ground and, by building upwards in this way, it is possible to create an open and 'transparent' urban structure. These three architects attach particular importance to the visual aspect of their design and in this connection it must be said that this optical extension of urban space is a distinct advantage.

The internal communications systems (inclined lifts and staircases) are housed in the tubular members of the skeletal frame, which provide direct access to the living units; traffic junctions are sited at the intersections of the tubes. The lower units are raised sufficiently above the ground to allow traffic to pass unimpeded. No detailed specifications have been given for the communal centres in the public area, but one third of the area between the support piers for the superstructure (which are situated about one hundred metres apart) will be reserved for communications links and large open and covered parking lots, one third will be set aside for public buildings and one third will be used to provide green areas (3). The living units will be attached to the diagonal tubes of the main structure, and thus form a stepped composition. Some units will be completely enclosed within the main struc-

ture (those situated beneath a further tripod), but others will face outwards and so will receive natural warmth and light. The fact that certain residential spheres will be completely cut off from the natural environment is one of the disadvantages of this system, which also suffers from an imbalance between built-up and open areas. With only two thousand living units per square mile, the structural density of the complex is rather low. The projecting secondary constructions, which are needed for the assembly of the cells, are not very economical either. On the other hand, the transparent character and the human scale of these buildings are very welcome features. Of course, living in this kind of megastructure would be rather like living in a tree: Any occupant who wanted to participate in social activities would have to leave his lofty retreat and come down to earth.

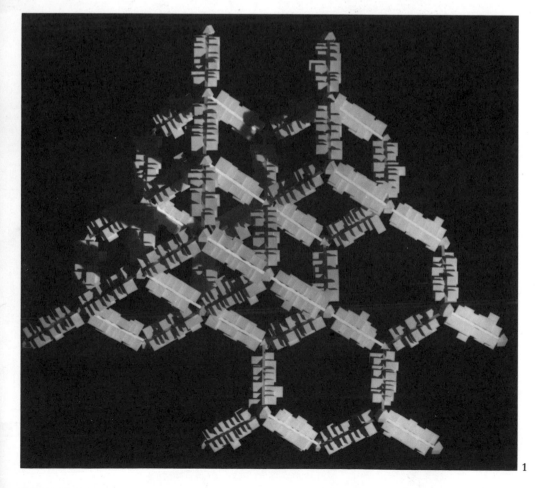

1

2

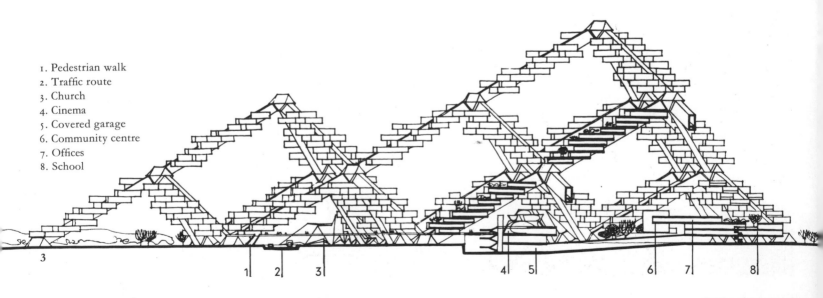

1. Pedestrian walk
2. Traffic route
3. Church
4. Cinema
5. Covered garage
6. Community centre
7. Offices
8. School

3

1   2   3   4   5   6   7   8

Bridge Structures

Arata Isozaki

Spatial Structure, 1960

In this project Isozaki has designed an urban cluster consisting of vertical service and access masts twelve metres in diameter, erected on a modular grid and linked by multi-storeyed bridge structures (**5, 6**). The module for the grid is eighty metres. The masts can be arranged in any desired pattern (**1–4**). Parking areas and service installations are situated at ground level underneath the traffic routes, while cultural and communal facilities are provided on elevated circular decks.

Thus, the surface of the terrain is reserved largely for functional and technical purposes, while residential and communal facilities are provided in a spatial setting.

On this particular grid Isozaki's structural system can be extended in any direction. His vital design is like a chain of molecules reproduced on an urban scale.

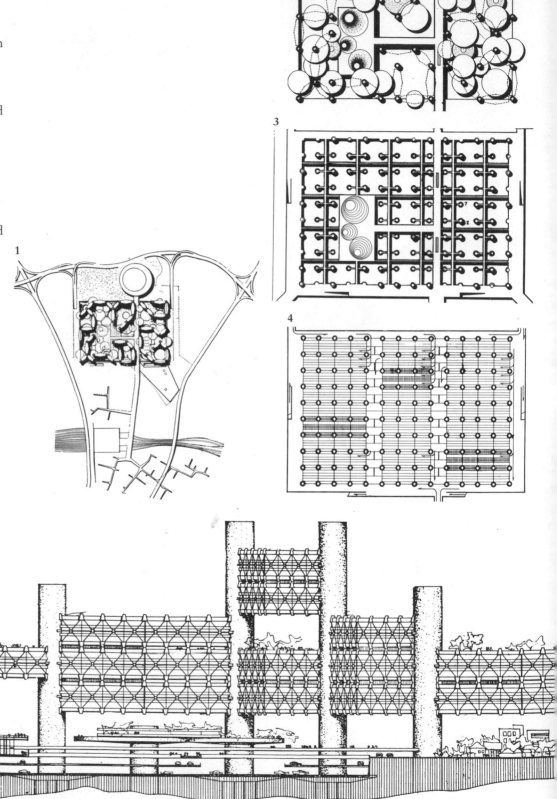

Akira Shibuya, with Kinji Nakamura, Hideo Shimizu, Kikuo Kawasumi, Susumu Abukawa, Yoshio Yamamori and Kazunori Odahara

Design for the competition held in 1966 under the auspices of the magazine *The Japan Architect:* 'Urban Residences and their Connective Systems'

The metabolic features of this design are more pronounced than those in Isozaki's project (p. 90). The bridge structures are essentially the same as those developed by Kenzo Tange for his 'Project for Tokyo' (p. 124) but would produce a much higher density. These bridge elements would be supported by towers up to two hundred metres in height

1

(1, 2) and would contain apartments distributed over three levels. The entrance to the bridge elements would be at the pedestrian level, which would provide access to the individual apartments. The whole of the residential area would form an integrated part of the bridge structures. In accordance with the metabolic principle of constant change, the strictly functional living areas—such as bedrooms, bathrooms and halls—would consist of cellular units made of synthetic material which could be suspended from the bridge structures as and when required (3–7). The public transportation systems—highways, monorails and so on—would be situated on different levels at the bottom of the megastructures, where they would give direct access to various communal centres.

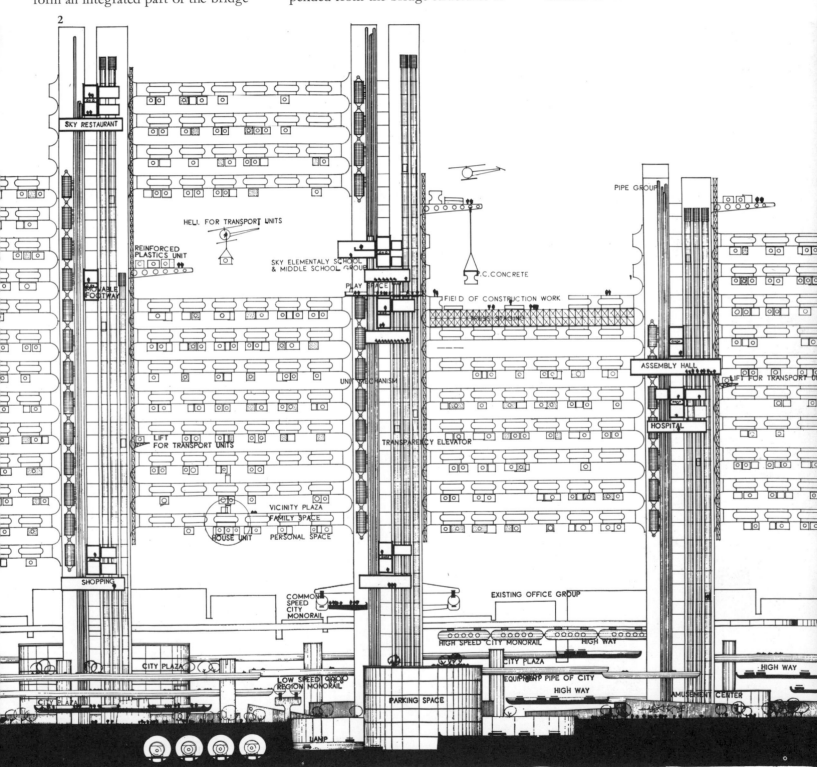

2

SKY RESTAURANT

HELI. FOR TRANSPORT UNITS

REINFORCED PLASTICS UNIT

MOVABLE FOOTWAY

SKY ELEMENTARY SCHOOL & MIDDLE SCHOOL GROUP

PLAY SPACE

PIPE GROUP

P.C.CONCRETE

FIELD OF CONSTRUCTION WORK

UNIT MECHANISM

ASSEMBLY HALL

LIFT FOR TRANSPORT UNITS

TRANSPARENCY ELEVATOR

HOSPITAL

LIFT FOR TRANSPORT UNITS

VICINITY PLAZA
FAMILY SPACE
HOUSE UNIT   PERSONAL SPACE

SHOPPING

COMMON SPEED CITY MONORAIL

EXISTING OFFICE GROUP

HIGH SPEED CITY MONORAIL   HIGH WAY

CITY PLAZA

CITY PLAZA

HIGH WAY

LOW SPEED REGION MONORAIL

EQUIPMENT PIPE OF CITY
HIGH WAY

CITY PLAZA

PARKING SPACE

AMUSEMENT CENTER

UANP

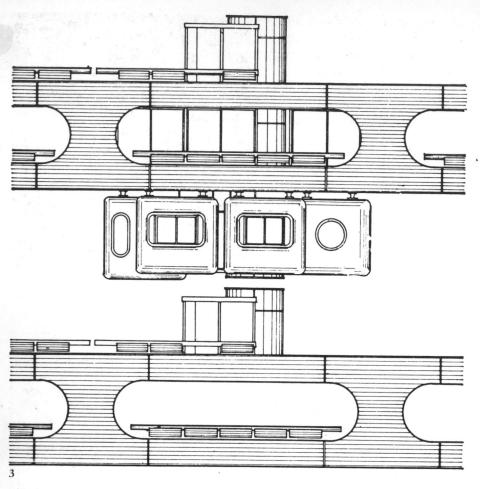

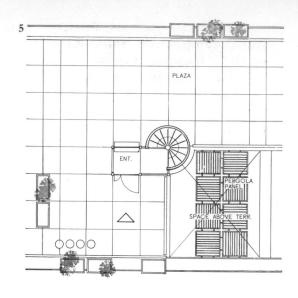

5

PLAZA

ENT.

PERGOLA PANEL

SPACE ABOVE TERR.

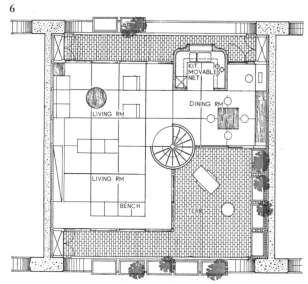

6

KIT. MOVABLE NET

DINING RM

LIVING RM

LIVING RM

BENCH

TERR.

3

4

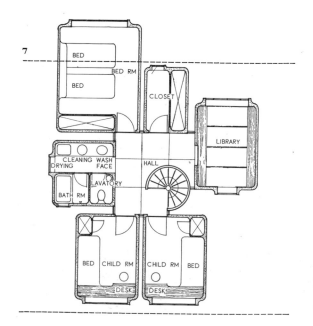

7

BED

BED RM

BED

CLOSET

LIBRARY

CLEANING WASH FACE

DRYING

HALL

BATH RM

LAVATORY

BED CHILD RM CHILD RM BED

DESK DESK

**Hiroshi Inagaki, Mitsunobu Ueno,
Yaeko Kawabe, Hiroshi Shimamura,
Masakatsu Nishio, So Nishikawa,
Hakuji Hoshino, Munehisa Miyazaki,
Kenzo Yoshikawa and Fumie Innan**

Design for the competition held in 1967
under the auspices of the magazine *The
Japan Architect:* 'Urban Residences for a
High-Density Society'

In this project the central cores of the
bridge structures are no longer conceived as enclosed tubes but as groups of
free-standing columns (**1**). In the internal
area formed by each group of columns
communal installations—such as schools,
restaurants and shops—can be suspended
as required. The areas between the
groups of columns, i. e. between the
central cores, are occupied by space
frames containing residential cells (**2**).
In each of these structures there is a
central area which provides public
facilities for the immediate neighbourhood and is served by lifts. The individual
apartments are constructed from cellular
components coupled together in line,
which can be extended in one direction,
if required (**3**).

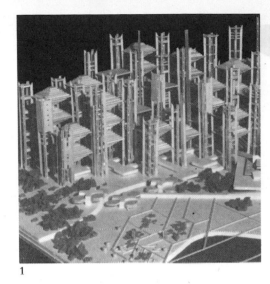

1

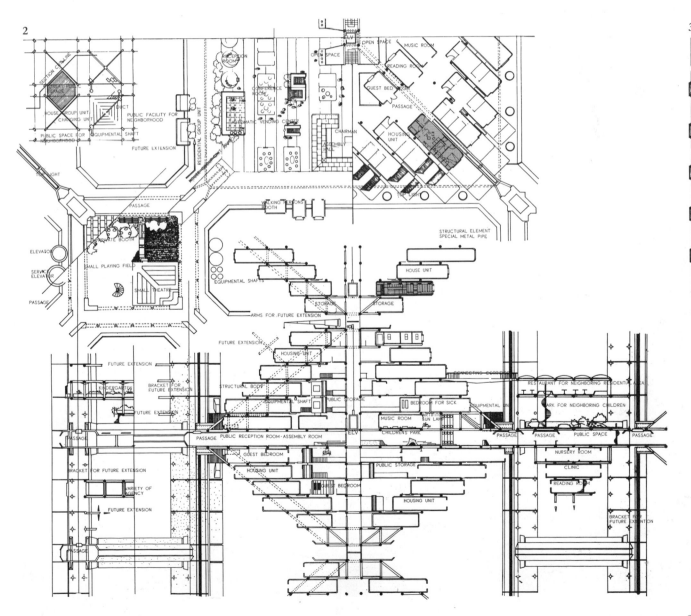

2

3

Kunihiko Hayakawa, Mikiro Takaki, Tsutomu Kimura and Katsuhiko Akimitsu

Design for the competition held in 1967 under the auspices of the magazine *The Japan Architect:* 'Urban Residences for a High-Density Society'

This project differs fundamentally from the three preceding projects because it proposes radical changes in the existing structure of society. Basically, this team of architects wants to dissolve the family unit as we know it: children are to be taken from their parents at a very early age and brought up in 'dormitories'; special living areas are to be provided within a cellular residential system for the members of different social groups—children, bachelors, young married couples and so on. This would call for the creation of an elaborate bureaucratic machine, for every change in family status would have to be recorded and arrangements made for people to change their accommodation accordingly.

The component units of this high density project (**1, 2**) would consist of cylinders surrounded on all four sides by terraced structures (**3**) set out in a grid formation. The terraces would contain individual cells resembling Pullman car compartments, while the cylinders would provide very large communal areas to compensate for the restricted space in these private spheres.

The tops of the cylinders would open out to form cone-shaped platforms, which could be used as helicopter pads. This would be the basic design. However, in addition, Hayakawa and his associates have evolved residential bridge structures which—like those developed by Shibuya—are reminiscent of the commercial centre in Kenzo Tange's 'Project for Tokyo' (p. 124).

1

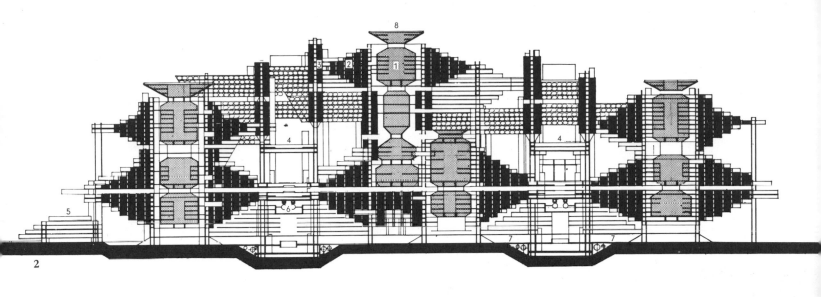

2

1. Communal area
2. Stepped single and double residential cells
3. Family apartments
4. Nursery
5. School
6. Monorail
7. Commercial area
8. Helicopter pad

3

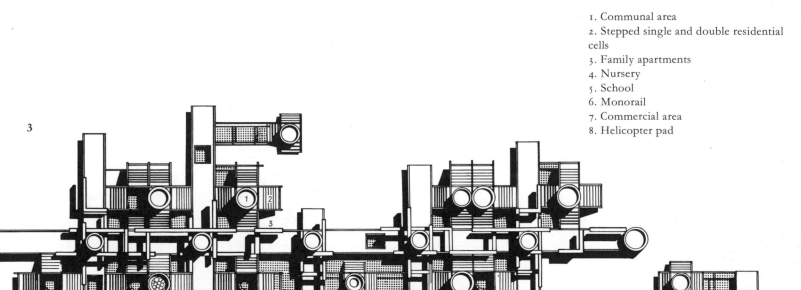

Bridge Structures

Yoichiro Hosaka

Proposed framework for urban living, 1965

Hosaka considers that most men lead a double life since they belong on the one hand to a small family group and on the other hand to a professional or occupational collective. They live a free life at home and an unfree life at work. In the post-industrial leisure society, of course, the collective work sphere will gradually recede into the background while family life and individual activities will become more and more important. Hosaka argues that town-planners have to create structures which reflect the duality between a man's working life, which is geared to efficiency, and his private life, which is devoted to individual pursuits and for which close contact with nature is an important requirement. In his view, this duality has to be visualized and expressed in architecture.

To this end Hosaka recommends the erection of megastructures for all collective activities, which would mean that the terrain itself could be used exclusively for the creative activities of individuals and small groups.

The design illustrated here features an interconnecting system of suspension bridges supported by cables attached to box girder towers (4–6). The bridges are set out in a quadratic pattern, which is pinpointed by the towers. The cable structure is arranged orthogonally and on its load-bearing axis supports traffic routes and a zone for communal activities (1–3). Access to this communications axis is provided by widely spaced multilane approach roads which spiral upwards into the megastructure. Multistoreyed platforms are suspended from the primary structure, where they provide support for the secondary structure which contains industrial installations.

By placing all communications, produc-

tion and distribution facilities in a spatial structure and reserving the actual terrain for the free, creative activities of private individuals, Hosaka is running counter to the general consensus of opinion, which favours the opposite system of constructing residential areas above communal installations. In marked contrast to his futuristic megastructure, Hosaka has designed a perfectly conventional residential sphere (4), containing detached family houses. Given his (dubious) premise that life should be polarized into a rational working sphere on the one hand and an idyllic leisure sphere on the other, this was perhaps only to be expected. But even if we were to accept Hosaka's premise, his proposal for a suspended megastructure would still be problematical because it would provide relatively little space—although this would still be too much for the proposed population density—in return for a very considerable technical outlay.

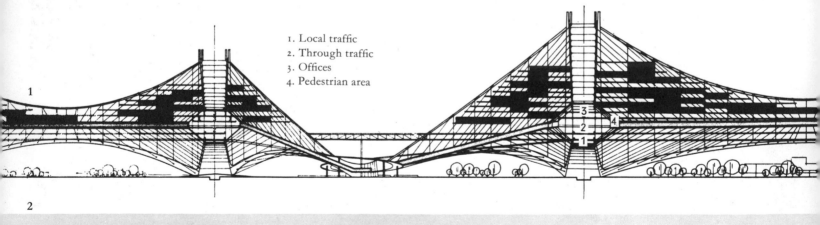

1. Local traffic
2. Through traffic
3. Offices
4. Pedestrian area

1

2

Bridge Structures

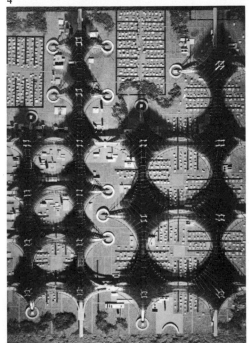

4

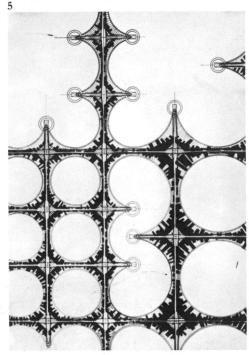

5

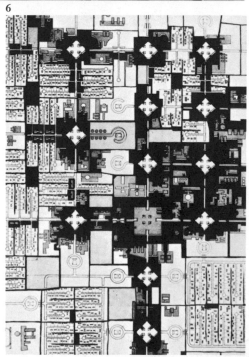

6

Bridge Structures

Kenzo Tange

City Centre for Skopje, 1965

When Skopje was destroyed by an earthquake in 1963, the Yugoslav authorities staged an international competition, in which four Yugoslav and four foreign groups of architects were invited to submit designs for a new city centre. The jury awarded sixty per cent of the first prize to Kenzo Tange and forty per cent to a group of Zagreb architects; it also recommended that Tange's entry should form the basis for a definitive design to be evolved by Tange in collaboration with the Zagreb group. The illustrations in this book are taken from Tange's original competition design.
In this design, the whole character of the city centre is shaped by the 'city gate' and the 'city wall' (**1**). The actual 'city gate' (**3–5**) is formed by an enormous road and rail junction which would break down the orthogonal network of fast and slow traffic routes by means of a simple multi-storeyed interchange system (**2**). The 'city gate' area would be situated on either side of the main axis that runs towards the river, and it would be built on the same impressive scale as the traffic junction.
This 'city gate', which is quite evidently intended to fulfil a symbolic function, would be flanked by two rows of enormous cylinders, one on either side of the main axis (**5**). These cylinders would be contiguous to a number of megastructures, to which they would provide vertical access, and would be linked by escalators to parallel rows of smaller cylinders providing access to the garages. The tall cylinders would also serve to support the megastructures, which would consist of space frames with suspended decks (**6**). The lower storeys would be used for shops and service installations, the upper storeys for offices. The 'city gate' area would also have cinemas, restaurants, a hotel, banks and other public buildings.
Tange's 'city wall' refers to an area lying

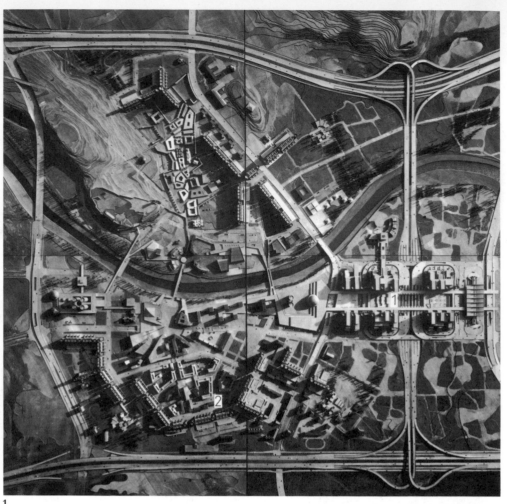

1

1. 'City Gate'
2. 'City Wall'

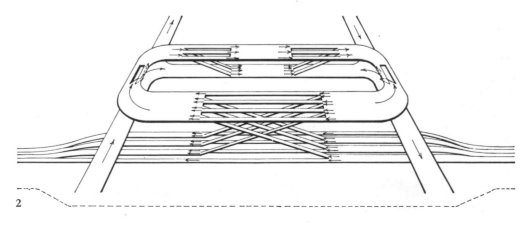

2

north and south of the river that would be developed as a residential district with rows of high-rise buildings (7).

It is quite evident from his use of historic concepts such as 'city gate' and 'city wall' that Tange has tried to create a design that would curb the excessive expansion found in virtually all modern towns. But whether his design will succeed in this remains to be seen. The introduction into the very heart of the city of a major traffic junction also seems a questionable procedure for, if the city centre is to be totally disrupted in this way, it is difficult to see how a viable public sphere can be created.

3

4

5

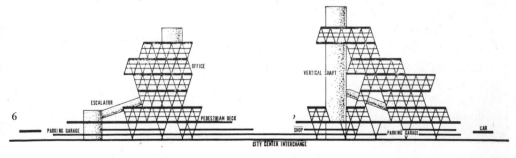

6

Bridge Structures

Engelbert Zobl, Helmut C. Schulitz and Dale Dashiell

Mojave Desert (Caravan park in a spatial grid), 1967

The sprawling expanse of single storey dwellings in Los Angeles, which cover the whole of the urban area like a vast homogeneous carpet, inspired these three architects to produce a design for an urban area that would be in complete contrast. They seek to create a new, effective urban environment in keeping with the life style of the post-industrial leisure society. In the controlled micro-climate of their Mojave Desert, they wish people to experience a desert landscape all the year round; by inte-grating the natural environment with their own artificial environment, they hope to create a fascinating new synthesis.

Mojave Desert is not so much a building, as a caravan park which is equipped with a wide variety of service installations, amusement and recreation centres and is extended into the natural environment by means of a spatial grid (**1**). Great importance is attached to mobility and provision has been made for mobile theatres, multi-storey cinemas and sports arenas, walk through aquaria, circuses, casinos and various multi-purpose areas, whose precise functions have not been spelt out. The proposed communications systems are of the usual kind: moving pavements, lifts, pedestrian ramps and arcades. In order to allow for expansion and contraction, provision has also been made for mobile platforms and for secondary construction systems, which could be erected rather quickly and easily.

The architects themselves speak in terms of a self-regulating structure, of an unspecified agglomeration of urban components, which would not only be capable of satisfying the needs of present-day users but could also be adapted to meet the requirements of future generations.

Certainly, this kind of spatial grid structure is likely to produce the sort of festive atmosphere and the lively aleatory character that are so desirable for the public areas of our towns.

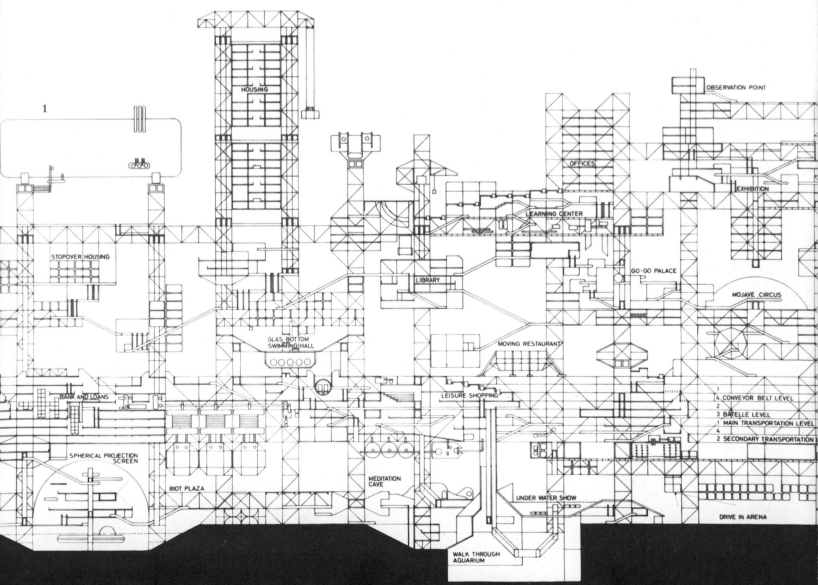

1

Günther Domenig and Eilfried Huth

Project for Ragnitz-Graz, 1966–9

Domenig and Huth's declared objective is to create urban settlements that would preserve the residential quality of the individual family house but not its traditional structure.

In order to achieve this objective, they propose to incorporate 'building sites' for both apartments and communal installations into a load-bearing frame (**1, 3**). Multi-storeyed parking areas would be provided in the basement (**2**). The load-bearing structure is composed of lattice beams, which intersect to form a wide-meshed orthogonal network, and cone-shaped stanchions. These then combine with the 'fixed points' (**4**)—the central cores, which house the lifts, staircases and service ducts—and the 'corridors' to create a spatial structural system that can be extended as desired. The 'functional volumes' which would be incorporated into the primary structure have been conceived as spatial cells with a controlled microclimate. The bathrooms and toilets would be concentrated in 'Hygiobiles' (sanitation cells) and audiovisual information facilities would be provided in 'Konzenträumen' (**5, 6**).

1

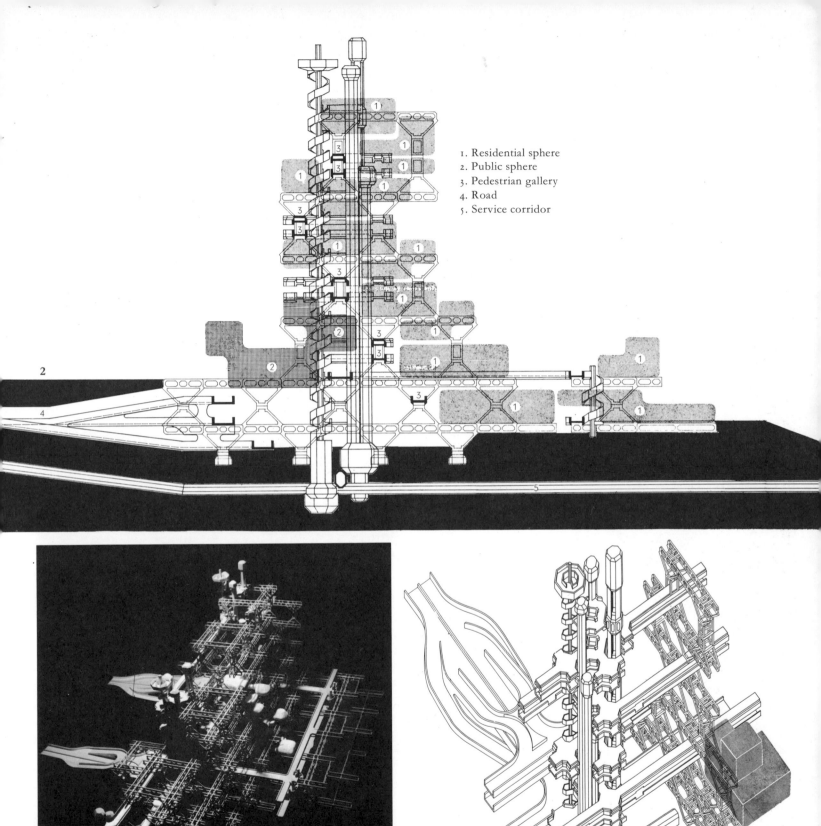

1. Residential sphere
2. Public sphere
3. Pedestrian gallery
4. Road
5. Service corridor

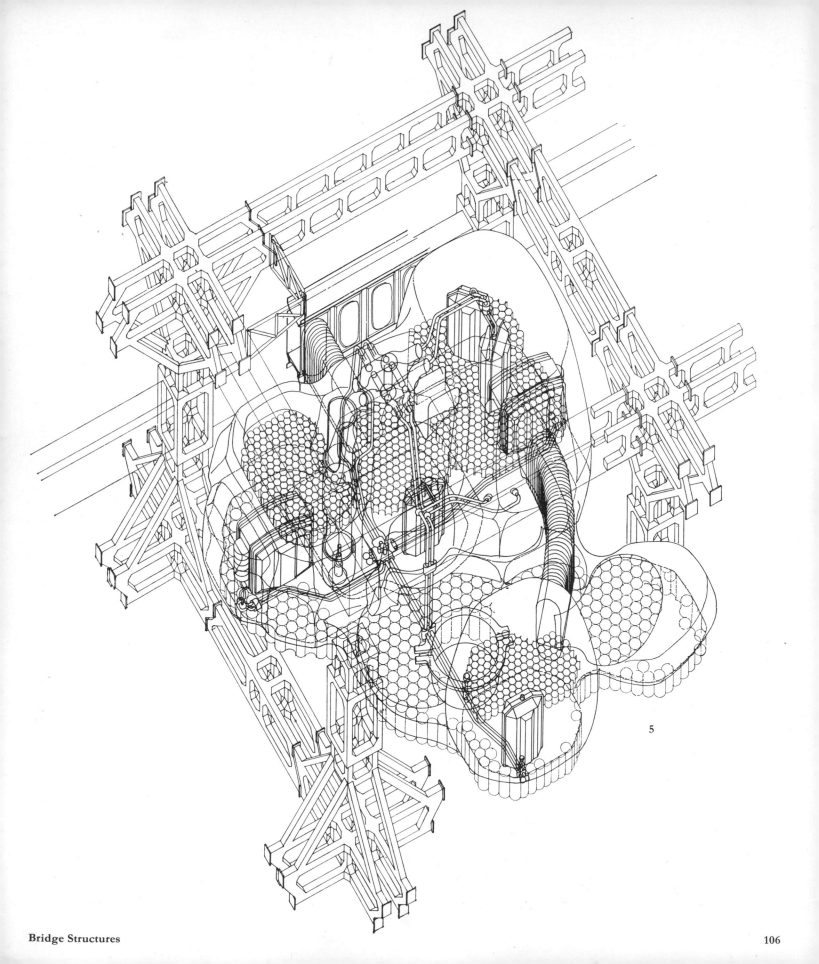

5

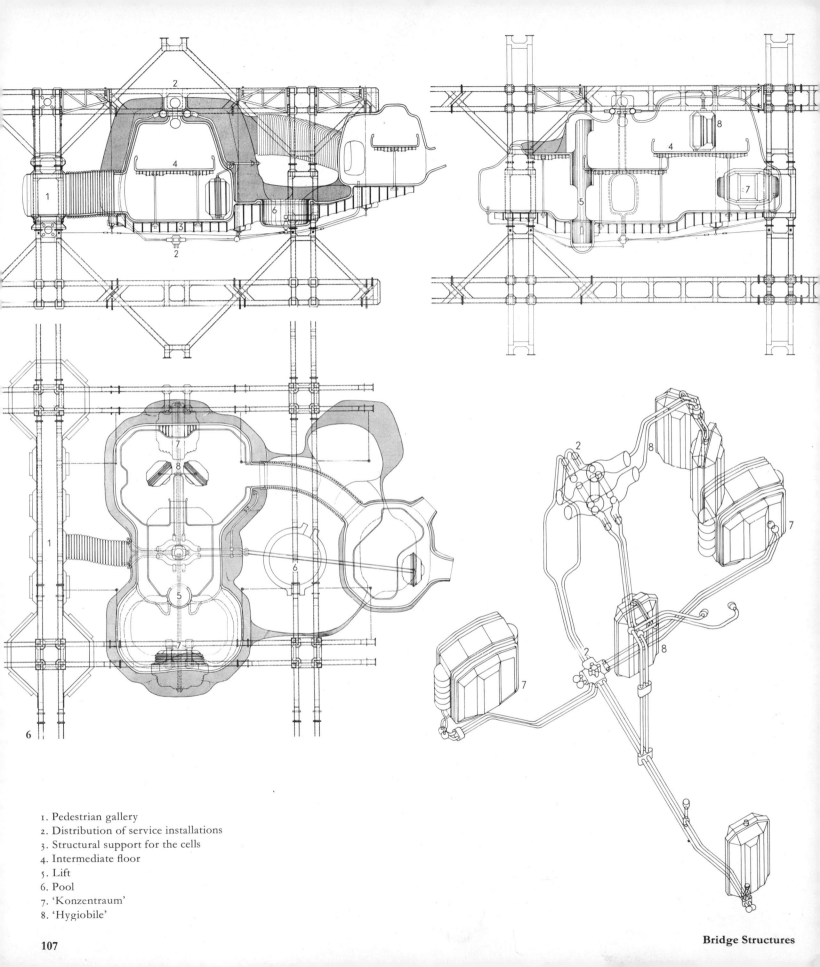

1. Pedestrian gallery
2. Distribution of service installations
3. Structural support for the cells
4. Intermediate floor
5. Lift
6. Pool
7. 'Konzentraum'
8. 'Hygiobile'

Bridge Structures

Jean-Paul Jungmann

Dyodon (Pneumatic residential cells), 1967

Of recent years we have learnt a great deal about pneumatic constructions, which have been used in many different ways: for children's toys, furniture, radar domes, exhibition buildings and even complete field hospitals.

In his Dyodon project Jungmann creates bulbous clusters of pneumatic cells from individual membranes (1–6).

But although the component membranes are quite stable in themselves, the clusters are not, and so they have to be stiffened. They differ in this respect from clusters composed of pressurized cells, in which the living areas are formed by the pressurized areas, for these are able to resist both internal and external forces. But, like pressurized cells, Jungmann's clusters can be stiffened by the simple expedient of pressurizing the inner area formed by the membranes.

The principal advantage of Jungmann's system is its flexibility, which enables the architect to create a wide variety of designs in almost any topography (7); its principal disadvantage is the high cost of its technical infrastructure.

1

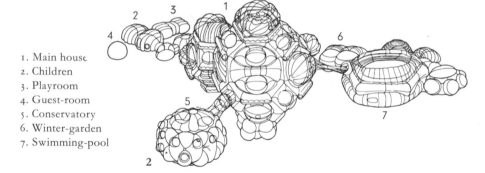

1. Main house
2. Children
3. Playroom
4. Guest-room
5. Conservatory
6. Winter-garden
7. Swimming-pool

3

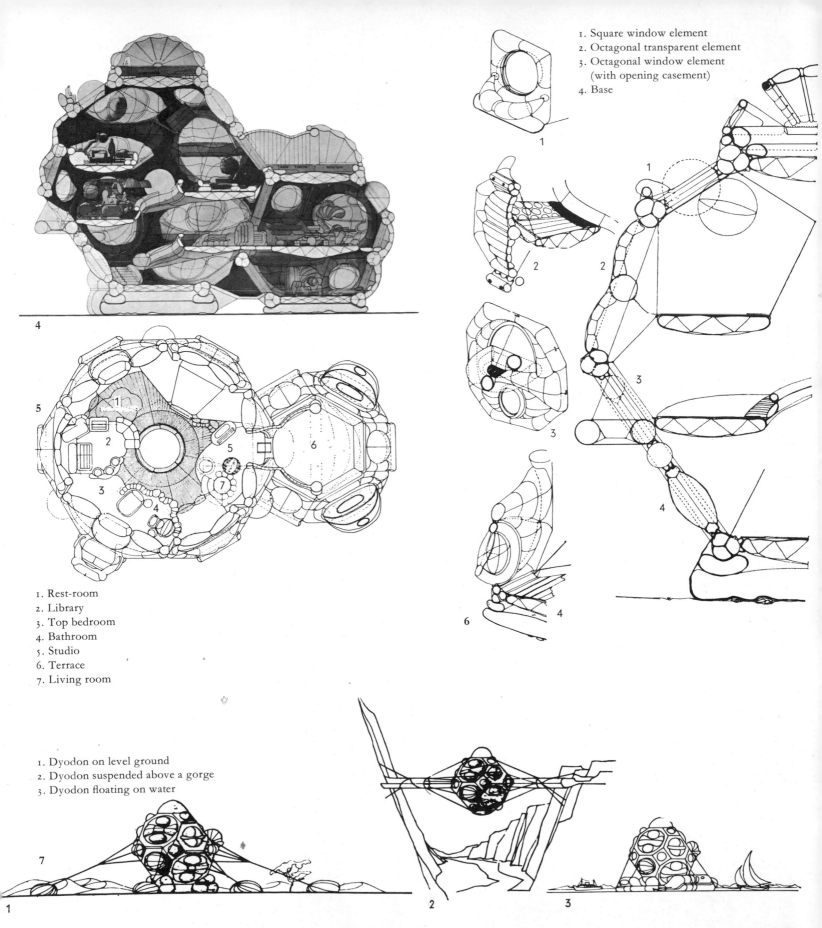

1. Square window element
2. Octagonal transparent element
3. Octagonal window element
   (with opening casement)
4. Base

1. Rest-room
2. Library
3. Top bedroom
4. Bathroom
5. Studio
6. Terrace
7. Living room

1. Dyodon on level ground
2. Dyodon suspended above a gorge
3. Dyodon floating on water

Containers

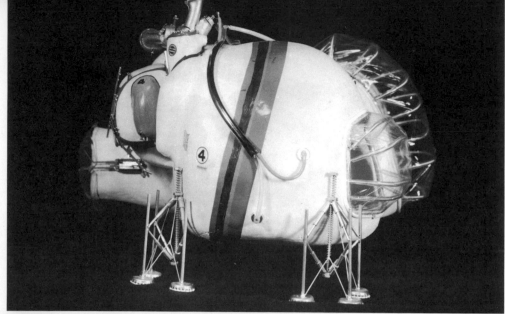

David Greene

Living Pod (Cell made of synthetic material with integrated power producing and waste disposal systems), 1966

Le Corbusier's conception of a 'machine to live in' has become one of the central themes of modern architecture, for over the years virtually every aspect of living has been influenced by the demand for technical apparatus of one kind or another. The most recent trend has been the development of residential units with integrated energy producing and waste disposal systems. This will have undoubtedly been inspired in the first instance by the advent of space travel, in which autonomous systems of this kind are essential.

In his project David Greene has carried the lessons learnt from the realm of space flight to their logical conclusion. His Living Pod is made up of two basic components: a cell made of synthetic material, and machinery. This structure, which is not unlike a moon vehicle (1, 2), stands on telescopic feet, which would compensate for any irregularities in the terrain on which it was sited. This unusual feature provides the outward sign of the complete independence vested in the Living Pod by its automatic climate, washing, bathing, cooking, waste disposal and learning machines.

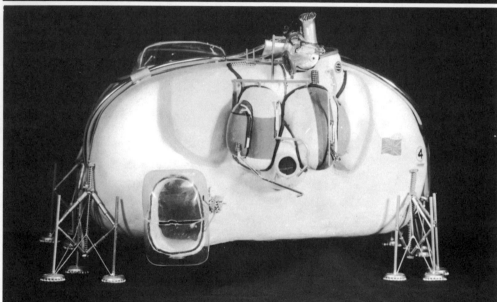

1

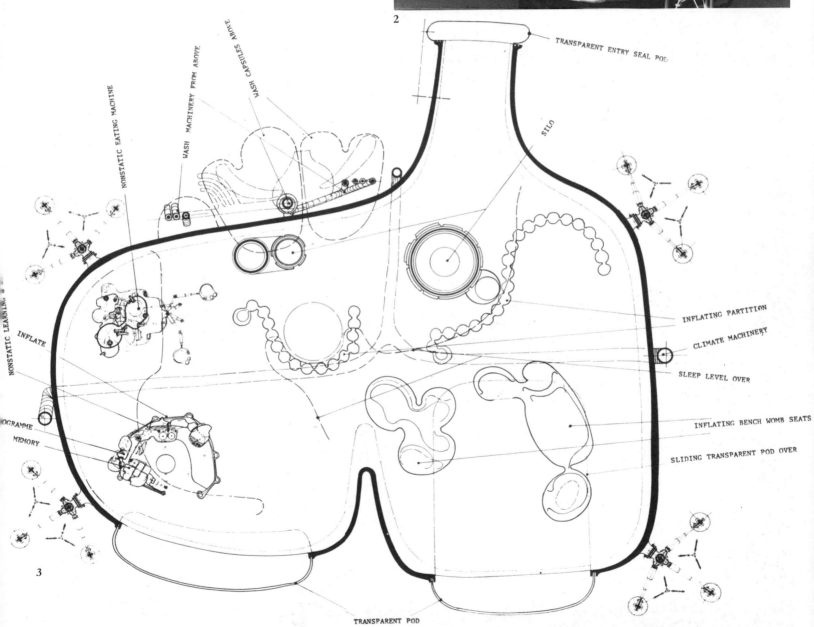

2

TRANSPARENT ENTRY SEAL POD

SILO

NONSTATIC EATING MACHINE

WASH MACHINERY FROM ABOVE

WASH CAPSULES ABOVE

NONSTATIC LEARNING

INFLATE

INFLATING PARTITION

CLIMATE MACHINERY

SLEEP LEVEL OVER

OGRAMME

MEMORY

INFLATING BENCH WOMB SEATS

SLIDING TRANSPARENT POD OVER

3

TRANSPARENT POD

Containers

Archigram Group (Peter Cook, Dennis Crompton, Ron Herron, Warren Chalk, Michael Webb, David Greene)

Living 1990, 1967

The intention of the exhibit 'Living 1990' was to demonstrate how computer technology might influence the form of future homes.

Warren Chalk wrote:

'The living space (1, 2, 5) is intended to be in a space frame or suspended within a tensegrity structure. Enclosure is created by skins which close together or separate electronically. The floor and ceiling can be transformed from hard to soft as acoustic/space/light regulators or inflated in certain areas as required for reclining and sleeping. The adjustable screens of the robot towers (robots Fred and James) (4) define smaller areas within the main volume where one can be totally enclosed—enveloped in an event generated by the projection of films, light, sound and smellies. The push of a button or a spoken command, a bat of an eyelid will set these transformations in motion—providing what you want where and when you need it (3, 5). Each member of a family will choose what they want—the shape and layout of their spaces, their activities or what have you. The hover chairs will provide an instant link-up with local amenities or access to the nearest transit interchange. A fully integrated systems approach to domestic bliss.

The importance we attach to the new technology is quite clear. To say that electronics is important to the future of architecture is a truism—something to talk about and discuss, yet feel unable to produce constructive and significant propositions about. This vision of the dwelling of the future takes an elementary and popularized form, but it is not a compromise. It makes clear, without any falsification of our beliefs, ideas that are otherwise difficult to grasp. Participation in an event such as this helps to redefine the problems we recognize to be important; clarifies our position before another step is taken. It might enable all of us to endure better the crisis we live in. Architecture remains well outside the orbit of technological forecasting—the ability to look ahead further than you can see—but inevitably and eventually it will be pressurized into a more receptive position![21]

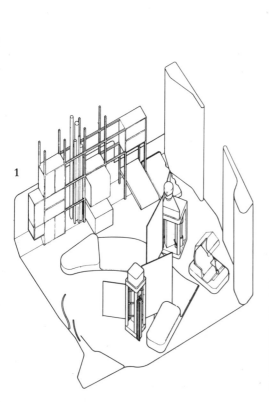

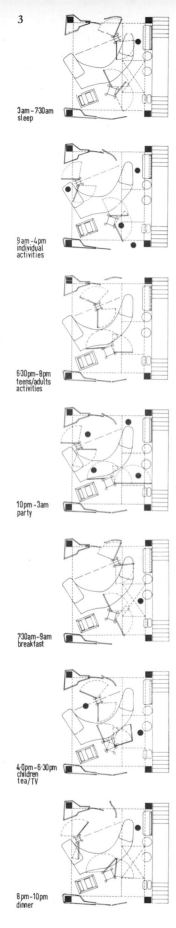

3am–7:30am
sleep

9am–4pm
individual
activities

6:30pm–8pm
teens/adults
activities

10pm–3am
party

7:30am–9am
breakfast

4:0pm–6:30pm
children
tea/TV

8pm–10pm
dinner

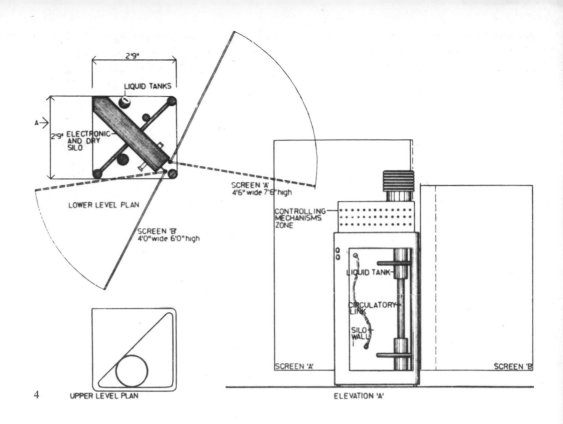

2'9"

LIQUID TANKS

2'9" ELECTRONIC
AND DRY
SILO

A

LOWER LEVEL PLAN

SCREEN 'A'
4'6" wide 7'8" high

SCREEN 'B'
4'0" wide 6'0" high

CONTROLLING
MECHANISMS
ZONE

LIQUID TANK

CIRCULATORY
LINK

SILO
WALL

SCREEN 'A'

SCREEN 'B'

4   UPPER LEVEL PLAN   ELEVATION 'A'

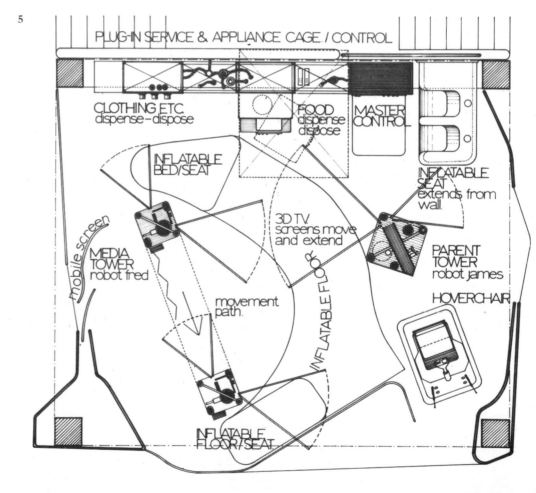

5

PLUG-IN SERVICE & APPLIANCE CAGE / CONTROL

CLOTHING ETC.
dispense–dispose

FOOD
dispense
dispose

MASTER
CONTROL

INFLATABLE
BED/SEAT

INFLATABLE
SEAT
extends from
wall.

3D T.V.
screens move
and extend

mobile screen

MEDIA
TOWER
robot fred

PARENT
TOWER
robot james

HOVERCHAIR

movement
path.

INFLATABLE FLOOR

INFLATABLE
FLOOR/SEAT

Ron Herron

Walking Cities, 1964

In his Walking Cities project, Herron has tried to incorporate a whole city into a few mobile super-containers (**1, 2**): these containers, which are supported by telescopic legs mounted on wheels, contain a complete urban structure; they are also fitted with sliding roofs to let in fresh air and sunlight (**3**). The different urban areas and residential districts are linked by corridors, which can be dismantled to allow the containers to be moved.

We are, of course, bound to ask ourselves whether this utopian conception of a completely mobile town, which at first sight appears to have more in common with science fiction than serious architecture, could ever be put into practice. But the basic ideas which prompted this project are perfectly serious and open up completely new vistas. Mobility, flexibility and optimum freedom of choice for the individual are the characteristic attributes of our times. Herron has simply expressed in architectural terms the extreme volatility of twentieth-century society and the explosion of science and technology.

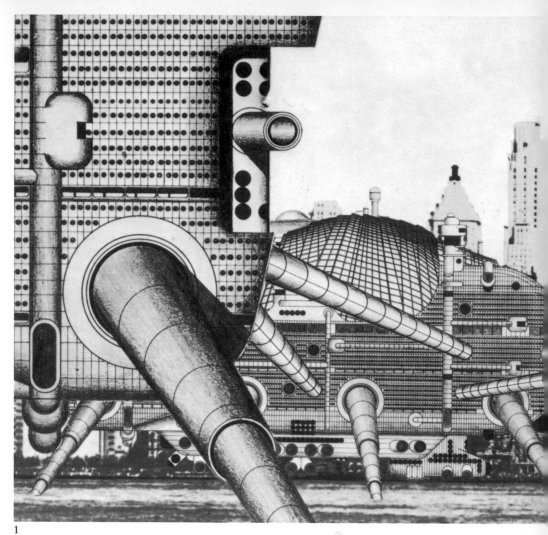

1

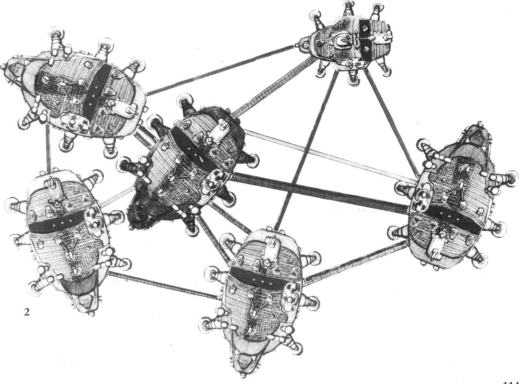

2

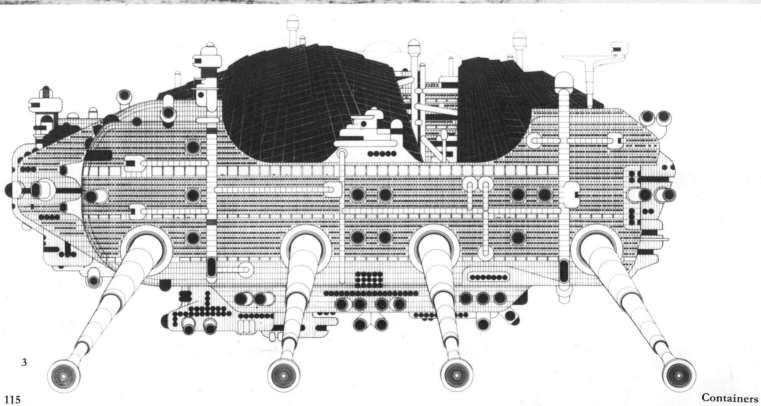

Frei Otto and Rolf Gutbrod with Hermann Kendel, Hermann Kiess and Larry Medlin

The German Pavilion at Expo '67, Montreal

The German Pavilion at Expo '67, Montreal, is the first really large light-weight structure that Frei Otto was asked to build. It consisted of a curved net made from galvanized wire and supported by eight sloping tubular masts of different heights (2, 3). The forces acting on the structure were discharged by the cables linking the tops of the tubular masts and by the lateral cables connected to anchorage points on the ground. The 'secondary structure', i.e. the actual canopy, was made of polyester fibre lined with PVC and was attached to the inside of the primary structure by turnbuckles (1). The canopy, net and masts were made in Germany and shipped to Canada for assembly.
In the interior of the pavilion an open prefabricated landscape was created which was made up of a number of parallel overlapping interactive planes (4).

1

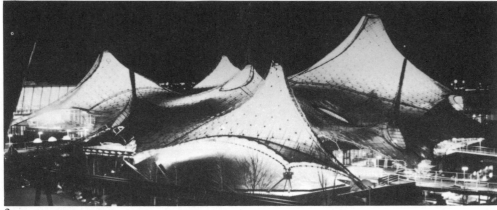

2

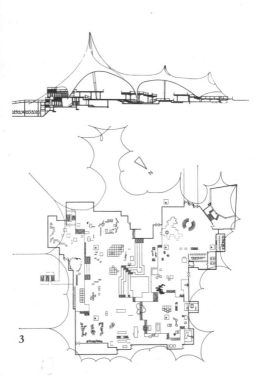

3

4

Atelier Warmbronn—Frei Otto and Ewald Bubner (design); Kenzo Tange and URTEC (town-planning); Arup Associates (structural design)

Arctic Town, 1971

In this project an inflated, transparent membrane to be manufactured by the Farbwerke Hoechst is designed to cover an area of three square kilometres without the use of supports. This would make it possible to create a Central European climate in arctic regions.

The structure, which would appear like a flattened dome, would have a maximum span of 2,000 metres and a maximum height of 240 metres (**3–5**). The membrane, which would be made of two layers of synthetic material, would be held in place by a rigid net constructed from polyester fibre and shackled to a circular foundation. The dome would be stormproof and any snow that fell on it would slide off its sloping surfaces.

Once the circular foundation had been laid, the pre-assembled membrane would be stretched out on the ground and inflated with air (**1**). The town could then be built under normal working conditions and in a normal climate.

The air used in the town would be drawn off from a height of 300 metres and brought to the requisite temperature by hot water from the cooling system of an atomic power station. Stale air would be released into the atmosphere. During the dark arctic winters, lighting would be provided by a mobile electric sun lamp positioned beneath the roof of the dome (**6**), while in the arctic summer mobile sails would be used to counter the effects of the long arctic days.

The cost of such a structure has been estimated at between 100 and 150 dollars per square metre. This figure would cover both the construction work and the supply of energy and is, therefore, relatively low.

This arctic town would accommodate fifteen to thirty thousand people. The buildings outside the dome would be linked by two subterranean storeys, which would house the air ducts. Transportation would be provided by conveyor belts, which would operate smoothly and silently. All walks would be carpeted. The roofs and any open areas not intended for pedestrian use would be planted with grass or shrubs. Two other attractive features would be a lake and a botanical garden.

The town could be expanded at any time by the addition of further domes (**7**).

1

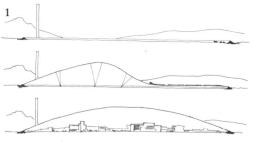

2

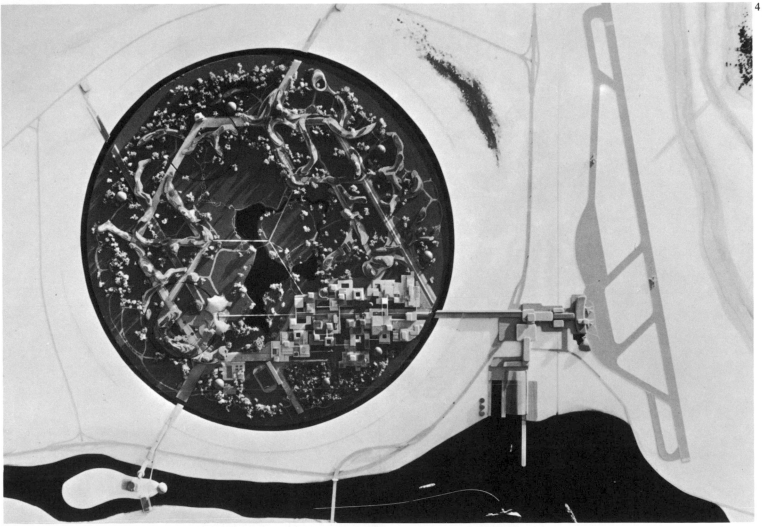

118

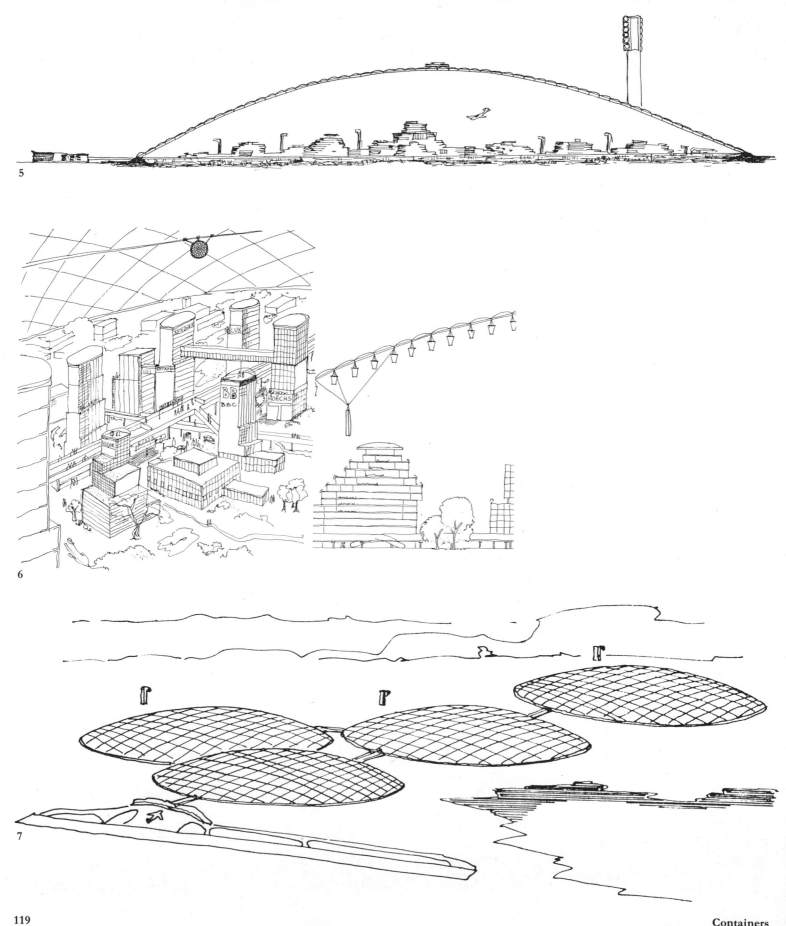

5

6

7

Containers

1

Richard Buckminster Fuller

American Pavilion at Expo '67,
Montreal
Geodesic Dome for Manhattan, 1962

The dome built by Fuller for the
American Pavilion at the Montreal
Expo (**1–3**) had a diameter of just over
seventy-two metres. The space frame
consisted of intersecting aluminium
tubes so arranged as to produce a triangular pattern on the inside of the frame
(**3**). The hexagonal panels were fitted
with concave plexiglass elements. This
structure was incredibly strong: it could
have withstood winds of up to 350 kilometres per hour and very high tensions
resulting from extreme changes of
temperature.

Speaking of his own transparent pneumatic constructions, Frei Otto once
observed that when they reached a
certain size people were no longer able
to relate to them (**2**). The same is true of
Fuller's pavilion. All that the observer is
aware of is a delicate network high above
his head; he has no real sense of a
physical demarcation between the interior
and the exterior. One of the most fascinating features of this dome was the way
in which its appearance changed with
changes in the weather. When it was
bright outside, the dome was transparent;

2

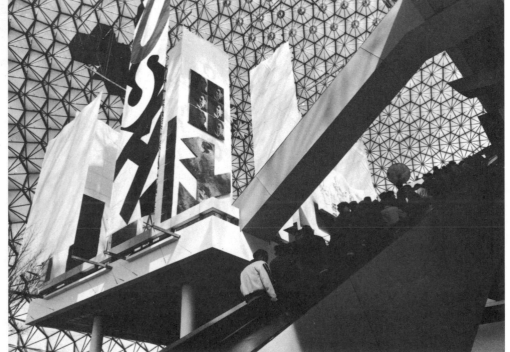

3

when it was overcast, the dome turned opaque.

A disadvantage of this type of structure is the fact that the diameter of the circular floor area is relatively small in comparison to the height of the dome, which means that accommodation is restricted. A further problem is the difficulty encountered in cleaning the translucent outer skin.

At an earlier stage, Fuller pointed out that it was technically feasible to cover a much larger area, such as a major city, with a geodesic dome and then to produce a controlled climate within the dome. His scheme for covering part of Manhattan is one of the pioneering projects in this sphere of architecture. But like Frei Otto's plans for pneumatic containers, Fuller's scheme for a geodesic dome over Manhattan would have to resolve a number of difficult problems, which call for practical experiment and consequently could only be tackled at a later stage (haze, condensation, rising and descending air currents, tension and so on). We do not yet know whether, in the present state of our technological knowledge, these problems could be economically resolved or not.

Containers

Kiyonori Kikutake

Unabara (Floating industrial city), 1960

The site envisaged by Kikutake for his project is in the Sagami-nada bay opposite Tokyo. There Unabara could be developed to become the centre of the Japanese industrial belt, which extends along the Pacific coast (1).
This floating urban macrostructure, which would accommodate five hundred thousand people, is made up of two concentric rings, an outer ring for industrial production and an inner ring for residential purposes (2). At one point the two rings converge and it is there that the communal administration and planning centre would be situated. A harbour for high speed submarine vessels consisting of a hollow cylinder submerged beneath the water and reaching to a considerable depth would be sited alongside the communal centre. The lagoon between the two rings would be used for the cultivation of marine products, and the expanse of water surrounding the outer ring for the production of energy generated by the sun and the waves. For the residential districts, Kikutake developed his 'Mova-blocks' (3). These consist of a central mast resting on a concrete base and fitted with three 'sails' which support prefabricated clip-on residential units. One Mova-block with a one hundred metre high mast would accommodate ten thousand people. Six Mova-blocks would form a residential unit (4) and six residential units grouped around a green area would form an urban unit (5).

1

2

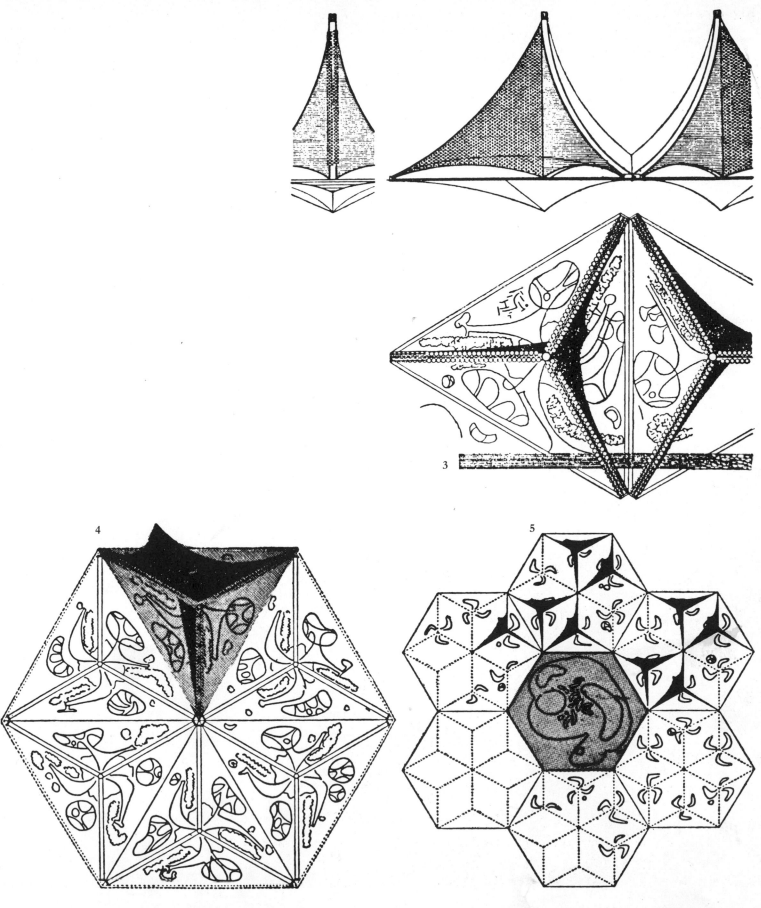

3

4

5

Marine Structures

Kenzo Tange with Arata Isozaki, Koji Kamiya, Heiki Koh, Noriaki Kurokawa and Sadao Watanabe

Plan for Tokyo, 1960

Of the many projects evolved by town planners to control the rapid growth of the population of Tokyo, this one has received the greatest amount of publicity.

Basically, it proposes the abolition of the existing concentric urban structure and its replacement by a process of linear development.

This would involve the construction of a wide urban axis extending across Tokyo Bay (**1**). The central strip on this axis would consist of a multi-storeyed orbital road network (**2**, **3**), which should prove considerably more efficient than the existing expressways since it would have no clover leaf or trumpet-shaped intersections.

One of the central features on this new urban axis would be the main line railway station, which would be flanked by two airports built on artificial islands just off the Tokyo waterfront. One of these would be for internal, the other for external services. The railway station and the airports would be linked by an underwater tube service.

Tange claims that the bridge structures (**4**, **5**) on the urban axis would establish an entirely new relationship between roads and buildings. Almost the whole of the base level would be used for a parking zone, which would be surmounted by elevated buildings. Service and access towers set out about two hundred metres apart in a square formation would link the different levels. Lattice frames could be erected between the towers to provide support for additional structures. The blocks of terraced houses designed for the residential areas (**6**, **7**) are to be organized as self-contained neighbourhoods with their own local amenities after the style of Le Corbusier's Unité d'Habitation. As far as the actual building of these houses is concerned, however, Tange and his associates propose that the occupants should be allowed to participate to a very considerable extent. Only the layout of the concrete load-bearing structure would be determined by the architects; the design of the apartments would be left to the occupants.

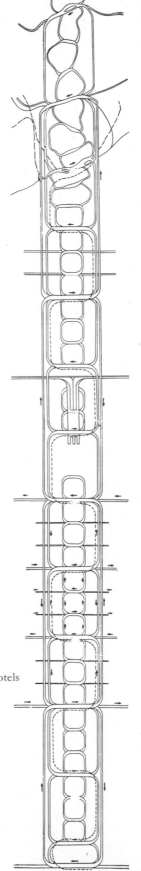

3

Tokyo railway station with underground connection

Office buildings

First Sphere: Office buildings

Second Sphere: New railway station

Third Sphere: Harbour

Fourth Sphere: Government buildings

Fifth Sphere: Office buildings

Sixth Sphere: Shopping centre and hotels

Seventh Sphere: Office buildings

Eighth Sphere: Recreational centre

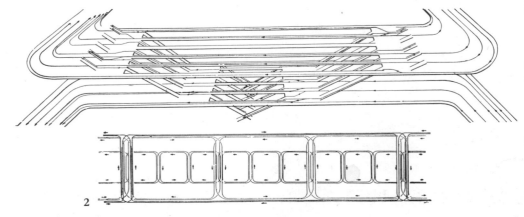

2

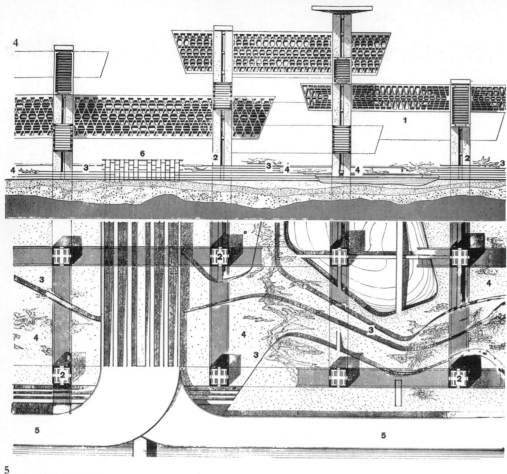

1. Office buildings
2. Vertical access
3. Parking areas
4. Plaza
5. Expressway
6. Traffic junction

1. Apartments
2. Public installations
3. Nursery
4. School
5. Shopping centre
6. Parking areas
7. Monorail station
8. Road

6

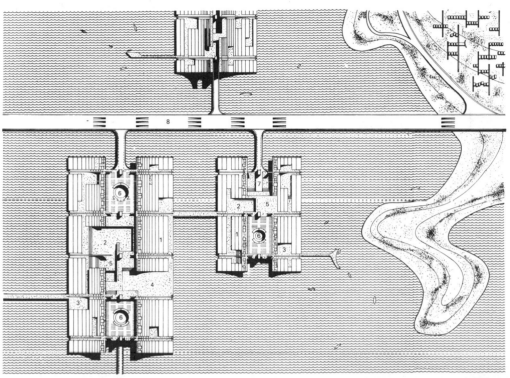

7

Marine Structures

Paul Maymont

Earthquake-resistant floating towns

Paul Maymont began to concern himself with the problem of safeguarding large buildings against seismic disturbances after visiting Japan. He studied the method developed by Japanese engineers, which involves laying blocks of reinforced concrete five or six storeys deep to provide a monolithic foundation whose mass renders the superstructure proof against shock waves. It then occurred to him that this process could be adapted for use in floating structures.

Like earlier Japanese architects, he chose Tokyo bay for his town-planning experiment, evolving a design in which the bay is covered by intersecting chains of floating settlements, each capable of accommodating between ten thousand and twenty-five thousand people (1). The foundations consist of multi-storeyed buoyant containers, which are anchored to the seabed and whose decks lie just below the surface. These containers are strengthened by bulkheads with the result that they are comparable in terms of stiffness to the concrete blocks used on land. Their interiors provide space for garages, shops, warehouses, factories and so on. The superstructures, i.e. those parts of the buildings above sea level, consist of a load-bearing frame and separate infilling that can be incorporated unit by unit. The load-bearing structure could be based on various figures of rotation and Maymont has made a number of sketches featuring different figures (2). The one he has worked out in greatest detail is the flattened cone (3, 4).

2

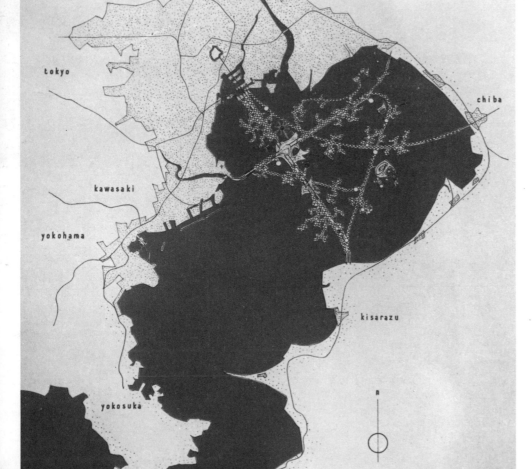

1

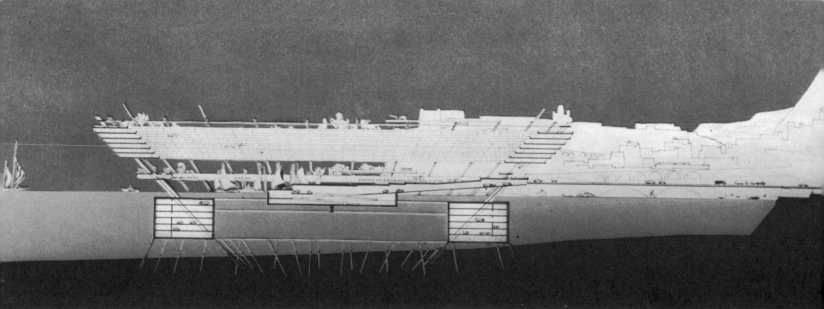

Marine Structures

Noriaki Kurokawa

Town on Lake Kasumigaura, 1961

This project for an overspill town for Tokyo (1)—Lake Kasumigaura lies about eighty miles north of the Japanese capital—is linked with the proposed reorganization of the Ginza district (p. 74).
In this design, however, the roads, which form an extension to the Tokyo motorway, run along the top of the helicoidal towers (2), which rise up within a hexagonal frame. This allows the residential terraces to run right down to the water's edge (3).

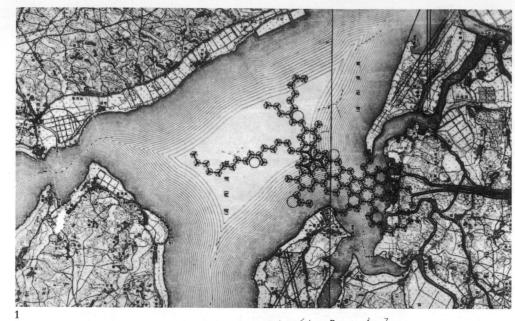

1

2

3

Richard Buckminster Fuller and Shoji Sadao

Triton City, 1968

This project (2), which was carried out under the auspices of the 'Triton Foundation' (President Richard Buckminster Fuller), was inspired in the first instance by the fact that eighty per cent of American towns with upwards of one million inhabitants are situated in the immediate vicinity of waterways deep enough to take large floating structures.

The basic components of Triton City are individual neighbourhoods of between 3,500 and 6,500 people. Some of these are made up of groups of four or six floating decks, each capable of accommodating approximately 1,000 people, while others consist of large self-contained triangular decks, which would accommodate approximately 6,500 people (1). When coupled together, between three and six of these neighbourhoods, plus an additional floating deck for inter-neighbourhood communal activities, would form an urban unit of between 15,000 and 30,000 inhabitants, while a group of between three and seven urban units, plus a large city centre, would constitute a 'full-scale city'.

The individual floating decks or islands consist of terraced megastructures, into which cellular units can be incorporated as required. In order to keep down costs, these units would be manufactured on a serial basis. Provision has been made for large garages on the islands and for link roads connecting them to the bank. But motor cars would only be used to provide easy access to and from the mainland. In view of the high population density of 300 occupants per acre, Fuller and Sadao have decided that all internal travel would be by public transport systems.

1

2

Stanley Tigerman

Urban Matrix (Floating town with tetrahedral residential units)

In this project, as in his better known 'Instant City' (p. 158), Tigerman shows how coastal towns can be expanded by the addition of marine structures.

Inverted tetrahedra are linked together in a composite structure (**1**, **2**) and are supported by multi-storeyed pontoons, which are anchored to the seabed by high strength cables. The tetrahedra can be stacked one upon the other up to a maximum of three storeys and, in order to reduce their weight, high strength aluminium is used throughout. The static backbone of the tetrahedra is formed by the outer trusses (**5**). These are octagonal in shape and have a diameter of 5.50 metres, which would allow both goods and people to be transported in electronically controlled capsules in any one of the eight compartments in each truss.

Any number of residential units, each containing 163 tetrahedra, can be incorporated into the Urban Matrix. Of the 163 tetrahedra, 130 are to be set aside purely for communal and commercial purposes. The remaining 33, which would be designated for mixed residential and public use, would each contain about 500 apartments (**3**) distributed over the first 24 floors. These apartments would be installed along the external faces of the tetrahedra, which would also serve communal, commercial and mechanical functions on their upper floors. The fact that relatively little space is allocated for residential purposes is due to Tigerman's overriding concern with the need to disencumber the city centre. On the other hand, he points out that the functional zoning within his Urban Matrix is highly flexible, which would mean that a reallocation of the available space in favour of residential use would be entirely feasible.

The buoyant but largely submerged multi-storeyed substructures would provide a large floor area for light

1

industrial purposes. Their decks, which would be above the water line, would be laid out as recreational parks (**4**).

No motor cars would be allowed in the Urban Matrix. Parking facilities would be provided in a large garage on the mainland.

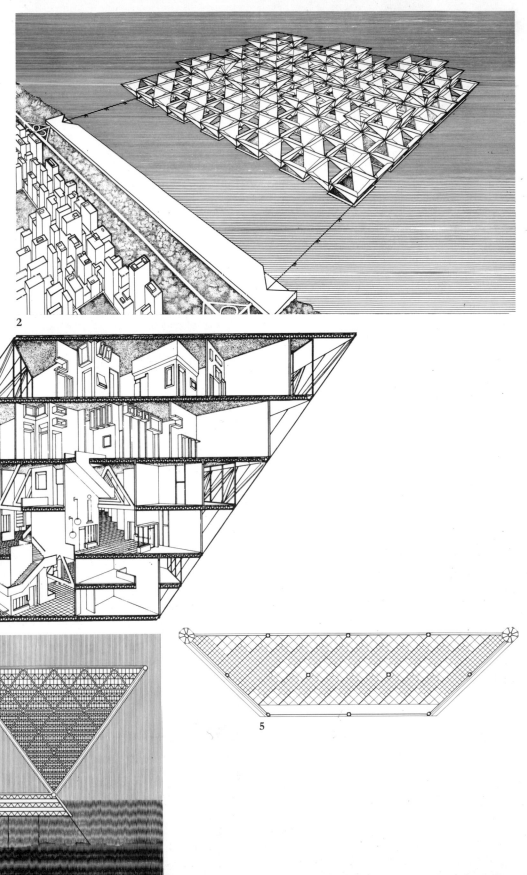

2

3

4

5

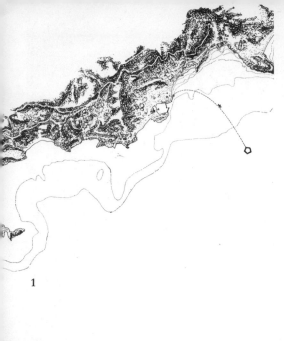

1

Edouard Albert and Jacques Cousteau

Artificial island in the Bay of Monaco, 1966

This artificial island, which it is hoped to construct three miles off the coast of Monaco (1), has been designed as a leisure town. The underwater section of the substructure would house research laboratories and night clubs; bathing beaches and swimming pools would be provided at sea level, while the superstructure would contain shops, restaurants, club rooms, cinemas, gymnasia and apartments.

The diameter of this pentagonal structure (3, 4) would be 220 metres at its widest point, and its height would be 50 metres, of which roughly half would be under water (2, 5). The principle underlying both the macro- and microstructures is derived from crystalline processes observable in nature (5, 6). Stability is maintained by a system of tubes shaped like a wreath; the buoyancy produced by the immersion of this primary structure keeps the whole of the structure in a state of balance. Buoyant foundations of this kind have already been successfully used for floating platforms. Five enormous concrete blocks, which lie on the seabed at points corresponding to the five corners of the pentagon, serve as anchors. But the anchor cables are slack, and so allow a certain amount of movement while at the same time preventing the leisure town from drifting too far (2). The tubular elements of the substructure are coated with a layer of synthetic material to prevent corrosion. It has been calculated that this island could withstand windspeeds of up to 185 kilometres per hour, and waves 9 metres high with amplitudes of 110 metres. In order to prevent the lower peripheral structures from being inundated, an extremely simple but effective safety precaution has been devised. In the event of a severe storm, the forty privately-owned swimming pools, which have a combined capacity of 13,000 cubic metres, would be drained, thus raising the whole island by up to ten metres.

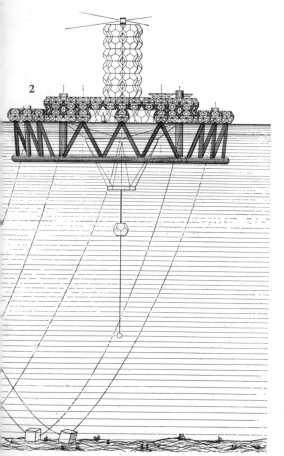

2

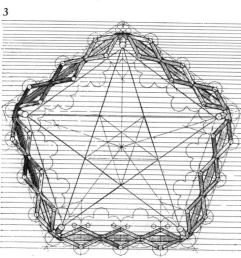

3

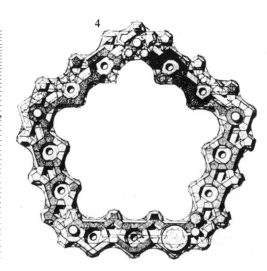

4

5

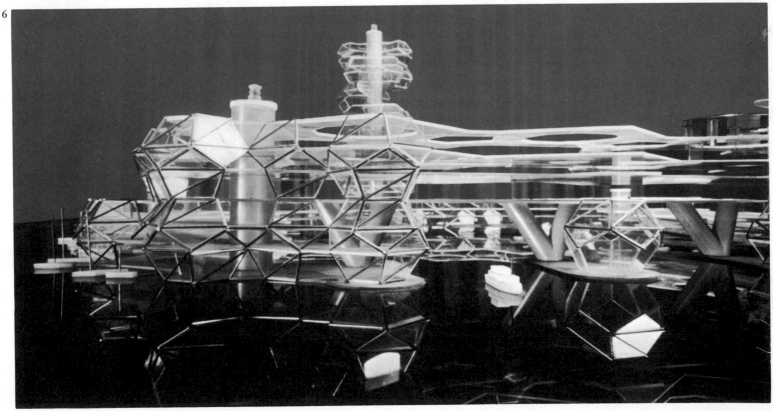

6

135

Hal Moggridge (Architect), John Martin (Structural Engineer), Ken Anthony (Climatologist and Oceanographer)

Sea City, 1968

It is hoped to build Sea City at a spot fifteen miles off the coast of Norfolk, England, where the average depth of water is 9 metres and the tide rises and falls between 1.80 and 2.40 metres (1). The population envisaged for this floating town is thirty thousand.

The principal structure in this complex is a sixteen-storey wall designed like an amphitheatre and built around a lagoon (2, 3). The edge of the wall would be shaped like an S (4, 5), an experimental form developed in order to protect the lagoon from high winds. Protection from sea swell would be provided by a belt of floating breakwaters made of synthetic material and filled with water to ninety per cent of their capacity, which would be placed in front of the wall. It is also planned to protect the entrance to the harbour from high seas, perhaps by creating a barrier of compressed air, which could be released from an underwater pipe line.

The terraced city wall would provide sufficient building space for apartments for twenty-one thousand people. The other nine thousand would be housed on pontoons in the lagoon. These triangular structures would have 18.30 metre sides and could be coupled together to form small or large units. Variations in the load carried by these pontoons would be compensated for by self-regulating buoyancy tanks.

Sea City would have its own power station for natural gas. According to calculations made by the engineers working on this project, the hot water from the cooling system of the power station would raise the temperature of the water in the lagoon by between three and four degrees centigrade.

This scheme undoubtedly has a very special architectural appeal, due primarily to the novel and highly stimulating form of the terraced wall.

The project was initiated by the Pilkington Glass Age Development Committee, which was set up by the firm of Pilkington Brothers Ltd. to promote new architectural ideas.

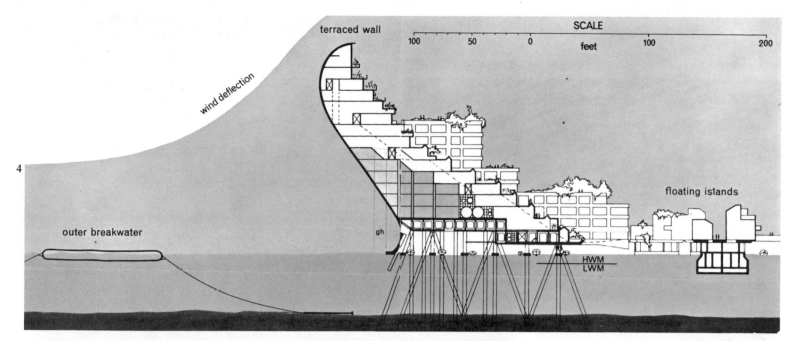

terraced wall

wind deflection

SCALE
100   50   0   feet   100   200

4

floating islands

outer breakwater

gh

HWM
LWM

5

Marine Structures

Cesar Pelli and A. J. Lumsden

Urban Nucleus (High density terraced town), Sunset Mountain Park, 1965

Pelli and Lumsden were asked to design a small town for a 14.4 square kilometre site in the Santa Monica mountains in California (**1, 2**). This mountainous region is subject to the Los Angeles building regulations for rural areas (Open Space Ordinance), which prescribe a density of two residential units per acre (4,047 square metres). But these two architects wanted to create a genuine urban centre, which would not have been possible if the living units had been spaced out over a wide area. Consequently, they circumvented the ordinance and designed a high density, cosmoform, stepped structure, in which the living units are laid out like rice fields (**3, 5, 6**).
The project provides for a total of 1500 living units, which are arranged diagonally, thus making it possible to create a highly concentrated urban nucleus while ensuring that each individual apartment has direct contact with the natural surroundings (**4, 8**). With their terraced gardens and panoramic views, the occupants would enjoy all the advantages of the traditional country house. Thus, the project offers a high density solution which none the less respects the human scale, a virtue that is often lacking in designs for terraced structures.
Some of the living units have been designed down to the last detail, while others have been left in a partly finished state so that the tenants can arrange the disposition of the interiors to suit their own tastes.
The urban centre on the top of the hill has been designed as a main square surrounded by low buildings. It is intended to serve, above all, as a meeting place. The public installations—such as the post office, bank, school, clinic, theatre, hotel, shopping centres, administration blocks, restaurants, clubs and the heliport—are grouped around the urban centre, which

1

2

3

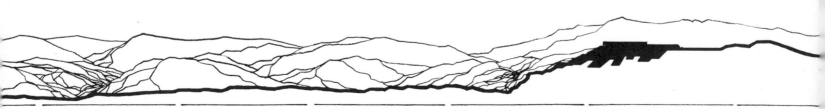

The Diagonal in Space

can be reached by both private and public transport (**7**). The access routes are all situated at the back of the urban nucleus so as to keep the noise levels in the residential areas to a minimum. Multistoreyed parking is provided beneath the main square (**8**).

Considerable thought has been given to the service and waste disposal systems. The available facilities would include closed circuit TV shopping, goods deliveries by pneumatic supply tubes, a meals delivery service from a central kitchen and electronically operated information centres, which would be connected to a large town library. Access to the apartments would be provided by inclined lifts (**4,8**), which would run alongside the supply tubes.

The load-bearing structure would be made of reinforced concrete. Inclined anchor walls fastened to the main structure at the parking level would counteract any accumulated thrust, which means that the secondary foundations beneath the terraced apartments could be greatly reduced.

4

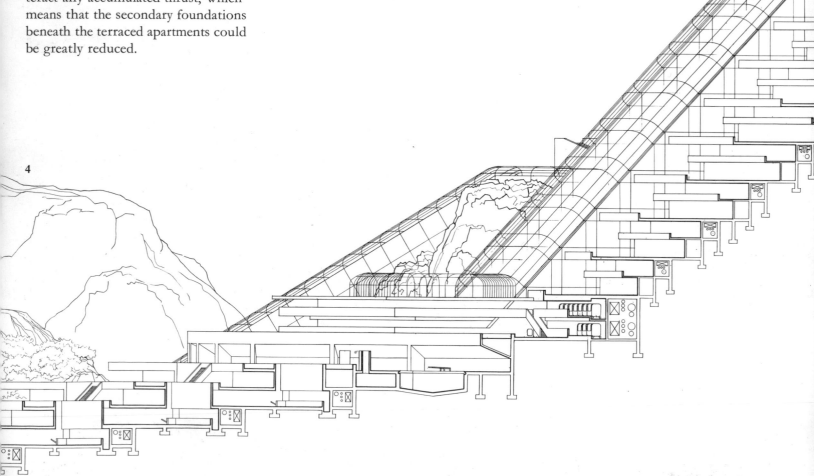

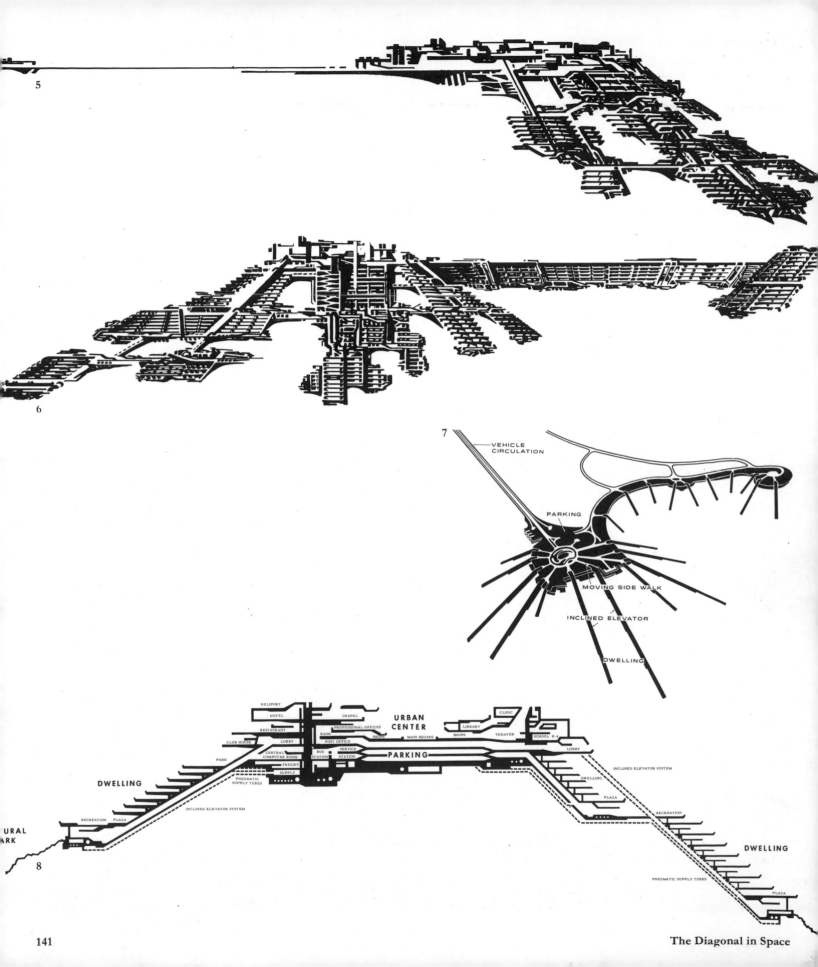

5

6

7

VEHICLE
CIRCULATION

PARKING

MOVING SIDE WALK

INCLINED ELEVATOR

DWELLING

HELIPORT
HOTEL   CHAPEL   URBAN   CLINIC
                                               CENTER
            RESTAURANT   PROFESSIONAL OFFICES   LIBRARY
                            BANK   SCHOOL K-4
CLUB HOUSE   LOBBY   POST OFFICE   SHOPS   MAIN SQUARE   SHOPS   THEATER
                    CENTRAL   BUS   SERVICE   LOBBY
            PARK   COMPUTER ROOM   STATION STATION   PARKING
                                FREIGHT   DWELLING
                                SUPPLY   INCLINED ELEVATOR SYSTEM
DWELLING   PNEUMATIC   PLAZA
                          SUPPLY TUBES
                                            INCLINED ELEVATOR SYSTEM   RECREATION
        RECREATION   PLAZA   DWELLING
URAL
RK
8   PNEUMATIC SUPPLY TUBES
                                                                                                      PLAZA

The Diagonal in Space

**Jan Lubicz-Nicz with Carlo Pellicia
(Architects)
Donald P. Reay (Adviser)
William Zuk (Structural Engineer)**

Project for Tel Aviv, 1963

This project was inspired by the new traffic plan for Tel Aviv, for which it proposes a number of extensions. A branch of the projected main traffic route leading to the coast would terminate in a parking zone for twelve thousand motor cars situated beneath the central linear complex running from east to west. The north-south communications axis would pass through the parking zone.

The cosmoform, multi-functional megastructures (1), which are shaped like saddles, would have twenty to fifty-five storeys. The area immediately above the parking zone (5) would be used for commercial undertakings and the loading and unloading of goods. Apartments and communal installations would be provided in the upper terraced storeys of the megastructures, while the towers which rise up above the terraces would contain offices and administrative centres. The area enclosed by the megastructures—the central area in the project—would be reserved for cultural buildings (theatre, cinema, museum, exhibition hall, library and synagogue) and for restaurants, bars and shops. This complex would be the focal point of the community, and consequently would form part of the first stage of the construction programme. The megastructures could be built in successive stages (2–4) on either side of the centre.

From this centre a pedestrian walk would lead to an artificially created island laid out parallel to the coast, which would also be linked to the north-south axis by two roads leading to the roundabouts situated outside the city centre. On the island, where pedestrian and vehicular traffic would be strictly segregated, approximately three thousand apartments and fifteen hundred parking places would be provided. The height of the buildings there would be restricted to four or five storeys. The pedestrian walk would terminate in an area given over to amusement centres and a hotel complex with some two thousand rooms. In this area, which motor cars would not be allowed to enter, moving pavements would be provided for the visitors. In the second construction phase, two further artificial islands equipped with bathing beaches would be erected between the residential area and the hotel and amusement area. These would provide an effective breakwater for the occupants of the residential area, who would then be able to pursue aquatic sports.

These artificial islands would not induce a sense of isolation, for they would not be very far removed from the mainland.

1

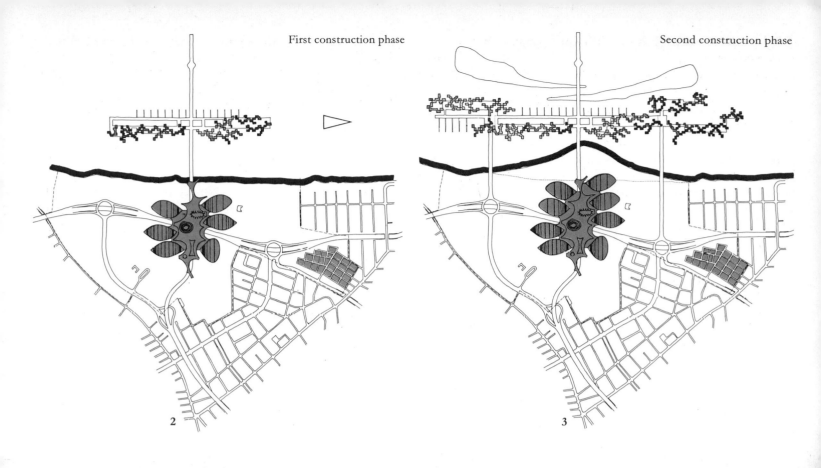

First construction phase

Second construction phase

2

3

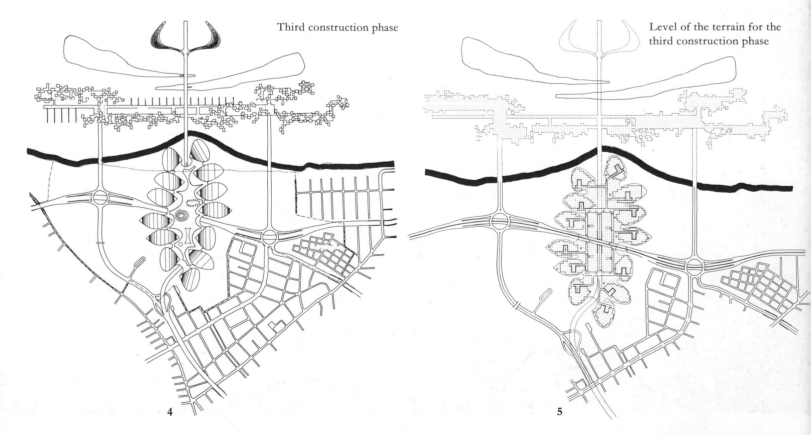

Third construction phase

Level of the terrain for the third construction phase

4

5

The Diagonal in Space

Lionel Mirabaud and Claude Parent

High Density Residential Units, 1960

Mirabaud and Parent set out to design groups of residential units (1) and not complete urban clusters. Consequently, their project makes no provision for communal facilities.

Each unit consists of three separate structures with a common foundation (5). These structures, which are shaped like segments of a cone, are of different heights and rise up at different angles, an arrangement which ensures that each apartment enjoys an unimpeded view of the surrounding countryside (2). Each unit would contain 1900 apartments. In a normal modern settlement with the customary density of sixty dwellings per acre, 1900 apartments would cover an area of 127,000 square metres. In this project, however, only 2700 square metres would be needed for the site (although the structures would project over a total area of 30,000 square metres).

All apartments would have their own terraces (4), which would greatly enhance their residential value *vis-à-vis* conventional high-rise apartments. The three structures in each unit would be linked by bridges. In the centre of each unit there would be a trumpet-shaped structure, which would house a high speed lift (5).

Vehicles would enter the units via tunnels (3). Garages and other service areas would be provided in the basement. The units would be sited in the open country so that their occupants would not be unduly disturbed by traffic.

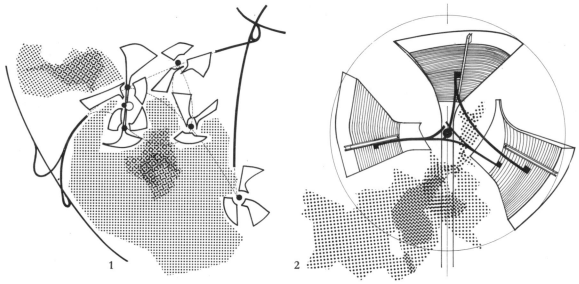

1

2

3

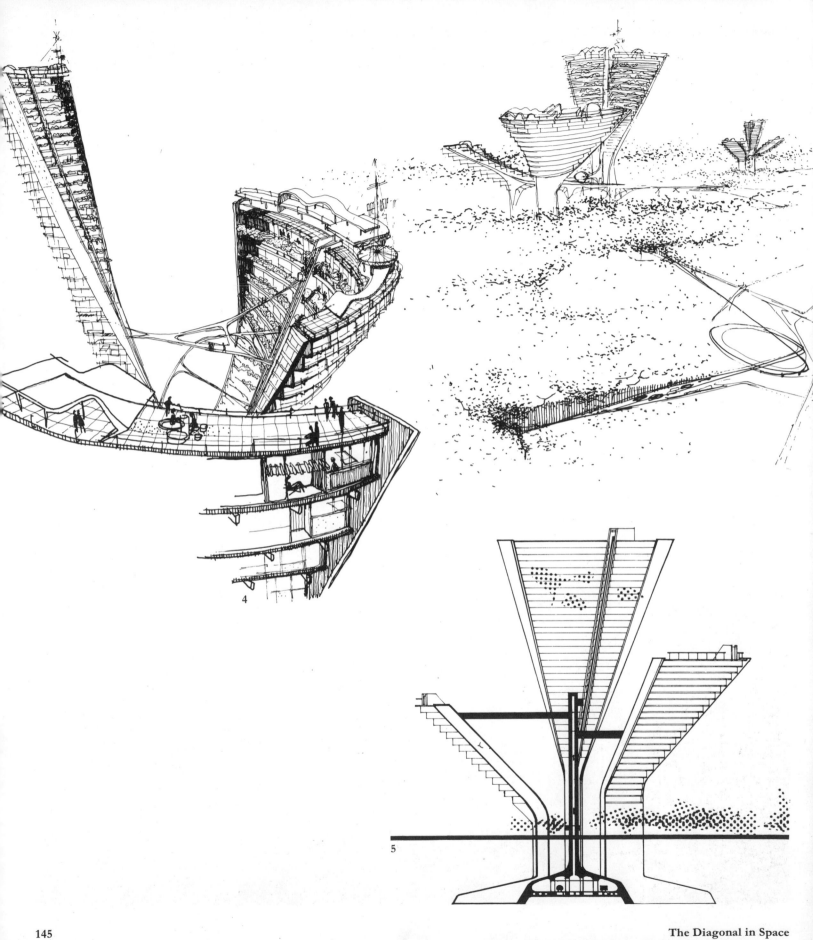

4

5

The Diagonal in Space

Manfredi Nicoletti

Overspill town for Monte Carlo, 1966

The tiny principality of Monaco is faced with a growing demand for residential accommodation, holiday apartments and amusement centres, and in view of its geographical situation the idea of building out over the sea in order to supplement the present limited supply of building land seems entirely appropriate. Nicoletti proposes to create an artificial peninsula (1). This would have two harbours, one opening into Monaco territorial waters, the other into French territorial waters. The settlement planned for the peninsula is designed to accommodate twenty thousand permanent residents and tourists and, although it would maintain close links with the mainland, it would none the less be a completely autonomous community. Despite the fact that Monaco is one of the

best known resorts in the whole of Europe, Nicoletti has succeeded in evolving an architectonic design entirely free of the phoney romanticism that is the bane of so many tourist centres. Working in collaboration with Gianfranco Gilardini, he made his first studies for this overspill town in 1961.
The back-to-back terraced buildings consist of reinforced concrete frames standing in containers which transmit the loads on to the seabed (4). The buildings are multi-storeyed. The concave shape of the structures creates an impression of great vitality and plasticity while preserving the human scale of the complex, which is so often distorted in projects of this kind. Nicoletti's structural design also makes for considerable flexibility in the distribution of internal space.
The general architectonic composition is most convincing (2, 3). The individual

segments have been arranged with great skill so that the apartments afford an unimpeded view and create a private sphere that is subject to only minimal disturbances. One particularly striking feature is the smooth transition from the base zone at the water's edge, which is laid out rather like a park, to the terraces, which rise up, very gradually at first, and then more and more steeply (3).
In addition to apartments, the Monte Carlo overspill town will contain facilities for light industry and for commerce and trade. The industrial centre is to be sited in the north, between the two larger groups of terraced structures, and the commercial centre in the south, between the two smaller groups. A cultural centre is to be built in the east, while offices will be provided at the rear of the lower floors in the terraced buildings.
The artificial peninsula is linked to the mainland by a major road. This

2

3

The Diagonal in Space

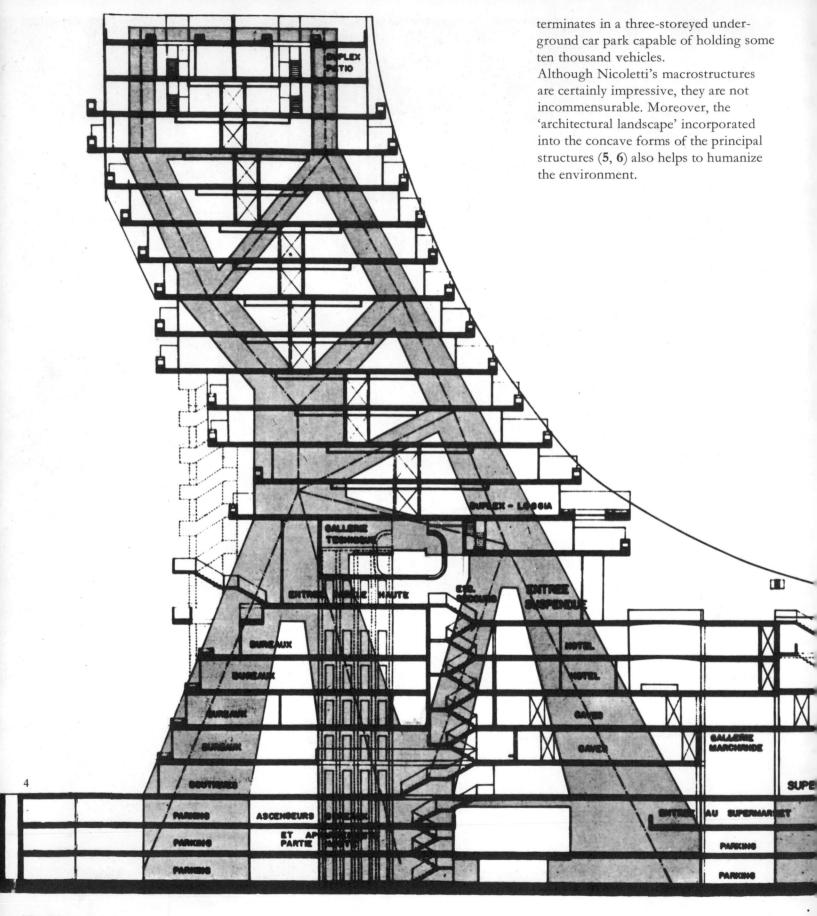

terminates in a three-storeyed underground car park capable of holding some ten thousand vehicles.

Although Nicoletti's macrostructures are certainly impressive, they are not incommensurable. Moreover, the 'architectural landscape' incorporated into the concave forms of the principal structures (5, 6) also helps to humanize the environment.

4

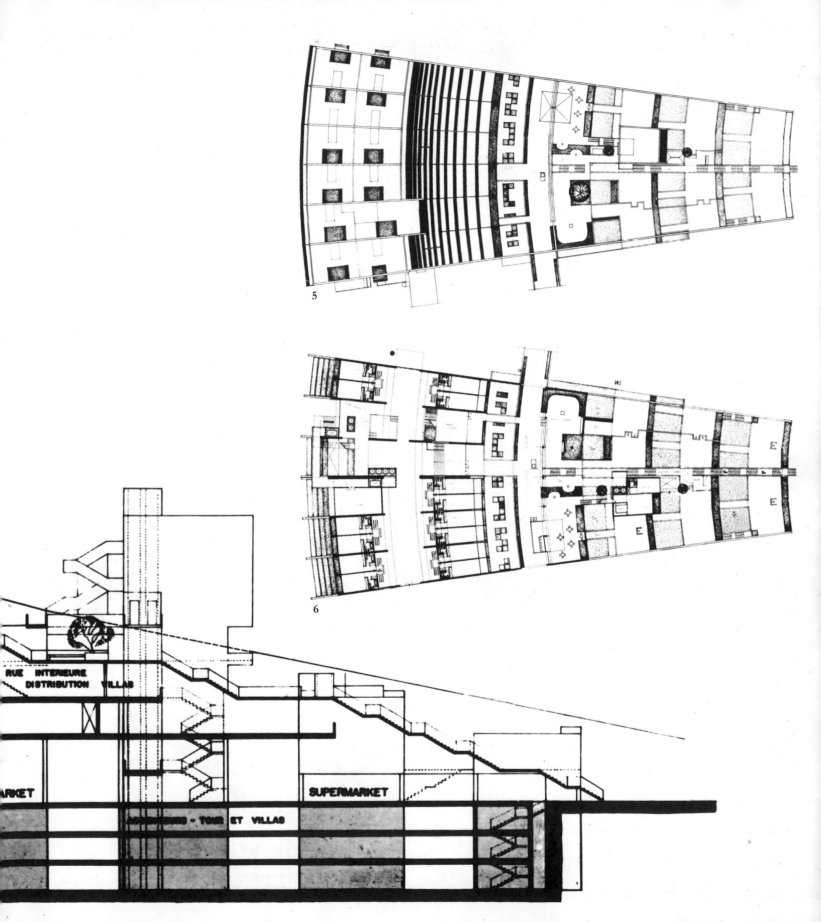

5

6

RUE INTERIEURE
DISTRIBUTION VILLAS

MARKET   SUPERMARKET

TOUR ET VILLAS

The Diagonal in Space

Walter Jonas

Intrapolis (Funnel town), 1960

Jonas has compared the labyrinthine structure of our major cities with the Brasilian jungle, and he has evolved his own impressive scheme for residential funnels (**4**) as an alternative. The idea for this scheme first came to him in Paris: 'Even in those early days (1932), I wanted the towering walls and apartments in the impoverished suburban districts to be integrated with the distant horizon and the sky; even in those days I wanted to have bridges running from roof to roof so that I could wander through the town in the airy heights beneath the open sky, far removed from the dangerous and distracting traffic.' In his funnel structure, Jonas has tried to create a patio-like residential area, whose inward-looking design would help to develop a strong community sense. Commenting on this project, he himself said: 'The term "Intrapolis" is intended to indicate that in this design an attempt has been made to correct the characteristic imbalance of present-day town planning by creating a counterpoise to the excessive extraversion that is progressively banishing the introversion which is so necessary for our psychological well-being.'

The funnel-shaped superstructures which between them make up Intrapolis would be built in varying sizes and set out in geometrical arrangements (**1, 5, 6, 7**) to form urban clusters. The tops of the funnels would be linked by footbridges, while vehicular traffic would be kept at ground level. Garages, underground stations and any other technical installations could be housed in the inverted subterranean cones (**3**).

Jonas considers that if his Intrapolis clusters are to function satisfactorily, the maximum population of the largest funnels should not be allowed to exceed six thousand people. Such funnels would be one hundred metres high and would have a top diameter of two hundred

1

2

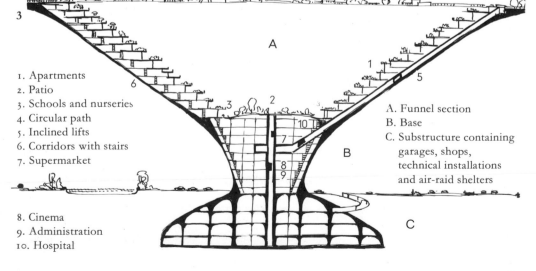

3

1. Apartments
2. Patio
3. Schools and nurseries
4. Circular path
5. Inclined lifts
6. Corridors with stairs
7. Supermarket

8. Cinema
9. Administration
10. Hospital

A. Funnel section
B. Base
C. Substructure containing garages, shops, technical installations and air-raid shelters

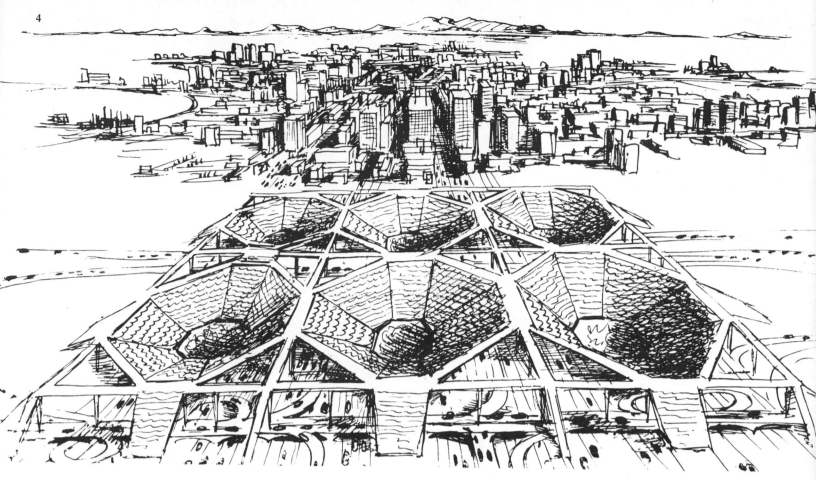

metres. The cellular residential units, which would be slotted into place, would be variable in so far as 'each occupant would be able to decide the interior design of his maisonnette'. Each apartment would have a terraced area laid out as a garden.

The first third of the inverted cone structure which links the funnel to the underground foundations would be fitted out with supplementary units, most of which would have to have artificial lighting and air-conditioning. The flat roof of this structure would be laid out as a communal patio and surrounded by public buildings. The top ring of the funnel structure would be used for communal purposes: pedestrian walks, restaurants, a helicopter pad and playgrounds. Access to the apartments would be provided by high-speed inclined lifts. Escalators and moving pavements would also be installed.

The funnel structures would be executed in pre-stressed concrete. They would be spatial frames (**2**) composed of horizontal and concentric tension rings, attached to a system of ribs extending from top to bottom and arranged like the ribs of a fan. The spaces between the ribs would be filled in to form solid walls, which would house the service and waste disposal systems and the communications network. The fixing point at ground level would be subjected to simultaneous pressure, tension and bending movements. It is at this point that the structure would be exposed to the most concentrated forces.

5

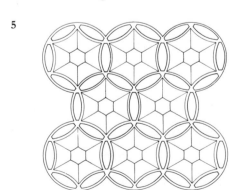

6

7

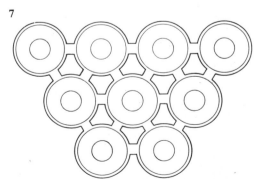

The Diagonal in Space

Chanéac

Crater City, 1968

Chanéac has been developing his project for a crater city ever since 1963. His attitude to town-planning problems is essentially visual; he attaches great importance to man's contact with his artificial environment and to the need for ecological harmony. The segregation of the production and consumer spheres, on which the structure of modern society is based, also features in Chanéac's town-planning projects.

It is Chanéac's declared intention to revitalize the mental attitudes of urban dwellers by formal measures in the sphere of architecture and town planning. In his view, a possible solution to this difficult task could be provided by the creation of an 'artificial' landscape (1, 4) based on—and in many respects forming an extension to—the existing natural landscape.

The framework for Chanéac's urban topography (3) would be provided by an

1

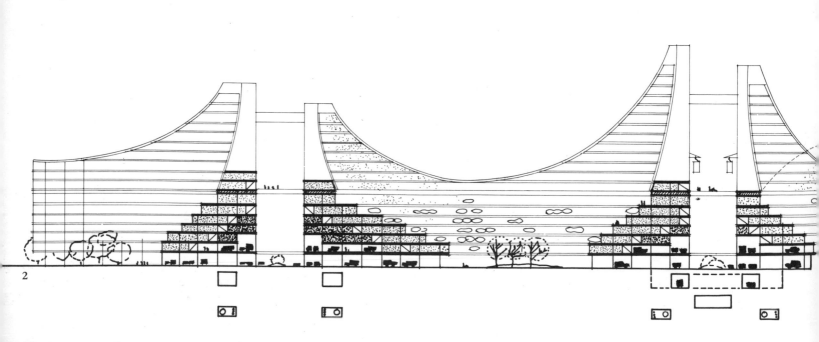

2

3

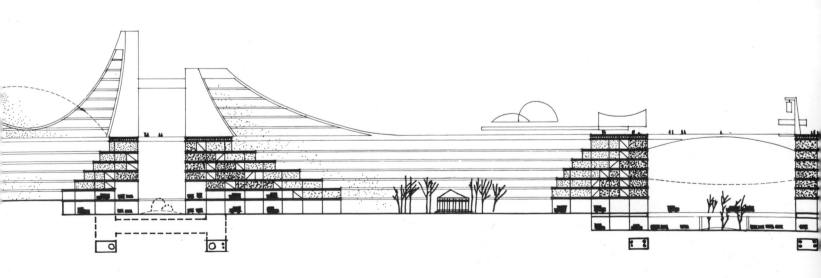

The Diagonal in Space

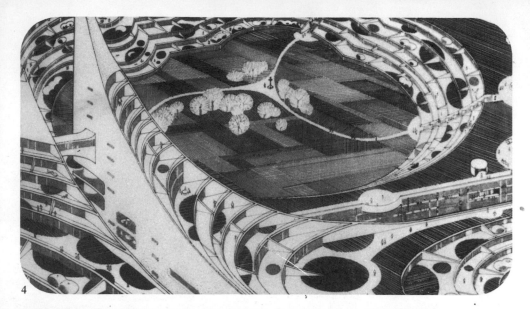

4

5

6

orthogonal traffic network. The rectangular areas formed by this grid would then be excavated to form craters, whose inner slopes would provide sites for terraced buildings and whose vertical rear façades would create cuttings which could be used for traffic routes (**2**, **6**). The lower storeys of the buildings would house parking, store and service areas, while the remaining storeys up to the main level would be laid out on a duplex principle with offices facing the traffic cuttings and apartments facing the craters (**7**). The terraces in front of the apartments would be very deep so that 'parasite cells' could be sited on them to provide temporary extensions to the dwellings. These cells would be assembled from prefabricated sections by the occupants themselves, who would also decide their function.

The main level (**8**), which would extend over the entire complex, would provide a monorail service for public transport within the city. Where necessary, bridges would be built spanning the traffic cuttings at this level (**6**), which would serve as the communal centre of the city and would be equipped with shopping arcades, parks, restaurants, walks and other communal facilities.

Sociologically speaking, Chanéac's residential craters create closed neighbourhoods (**5**), for—with the exception of the communal area—there would be no visual links between one neighbourhood and another. A comparison that springs to mind is that of the tenement blocks in our major cities, where the houses overlook the traffic routes. In Chanéac's project the traffic cuttings also serve to reinforce the sense of isolation. When people cross over one of these cuttings, they may well have the feeling that they are entering a foreign territory.

But, despite these disadvantages, the crater city opens up interesting prospects for the future.

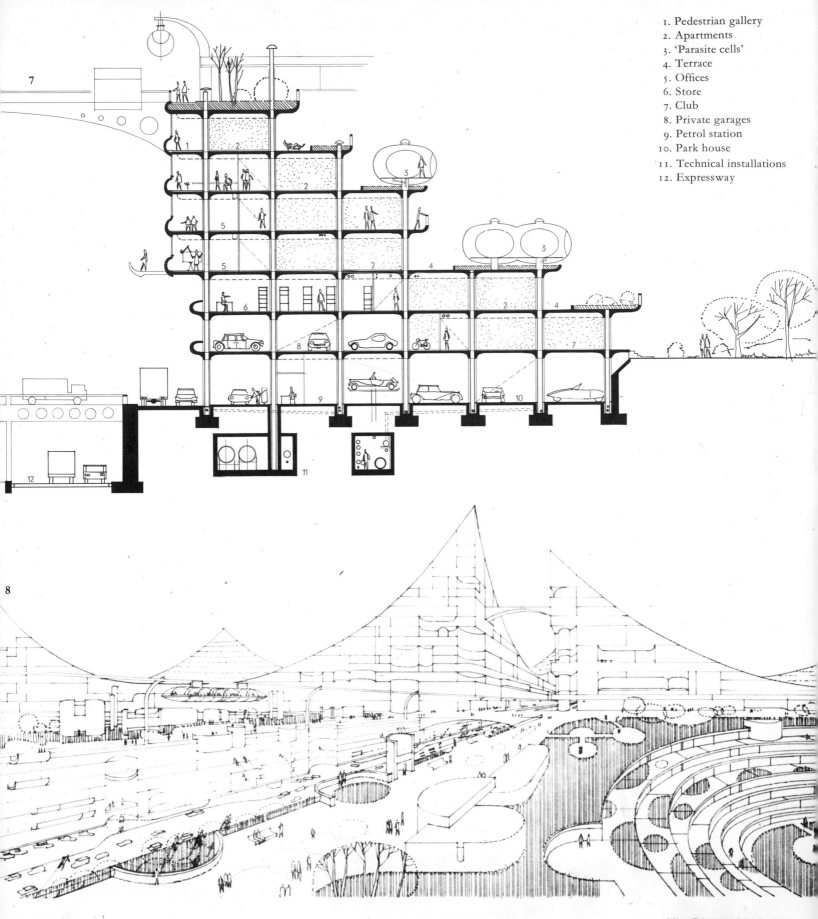

1. Pedestrian gallery
2. Apartments
3. 'Parasite cells'
4. Terrace
5. Offices
6. Store
7. Club
8. Private garages
9. Petrol station
10. Park house
11. Technical installations
12. Expressway

The Diagonal in Space

**Y. Akui and T. Nozawa, with
K. Yamamoto and T. Akaiwa**

Town-planning project for Tokyo, 1964

Like Tange and Kurokawa, Akui and Nozawa have built up their project around an orbital traffic network. This consists of a twin axis with interconnecting loop roads running immediately above the turbinate network of a secondary road system (2). The twin axis follows the coastline on either side of the city centre, where it branches off and runs away from the coast. It forms the infrastructure for a triple-branched linear town with a main-line railway station, a harbour and an airport in its central area (1).

New vertical residential megastructures would be built on the circular sites created by the secondary road network (4). These megastructures—or 'Neomastabas'—consist of four plane triangles arranged in the form of a pyramid (3). They would be erected in stages, working outwards from the centre, and when completed would each accommodate between twenty-five and thirty thousand people. The angle on the hypotenuse of each triangle would be forty-five degrees and the whole of the megastructure would be supported on pillars, leaving open spaces beneath the triangles. The structural design is simple and logical: the four plane triangles are load-bearing skeletons and, as such, provide support for residential units which are 'slotted' into place (5).

The central core of each megastructure contains eight shafts which house the lifts and the service and waste disposal systems. At the point where the inclined hollow sections join the base of the triangles, it is proposed to build a pedestrian walk. Access to the cellular residential units from the lift shafts is furnished by corridors designed like arcades. The base of the megastructure would be provided with a shopping centre, parking places and various other communal facilities.

Although these megastructures are certainly on a colossal scale, the architects have obviously done their best to make them acceptable to human beings. It is, of course, inevitable that those apartments with an eastern, southern or western aspect should receive more sunshine than those with a northern aspect. But, wherever possible, Akui and Nozawa have studied the interests of the individual occupants, with the result that the apartments are highly desirable from a residential point of view. The one major shortcoming in their design is the lack of a real community centre. The whole project is designed around the motor car; and although the landscaped areas between the mastabas would no doubt be attractive, they could never replace the public sphere of a real city.

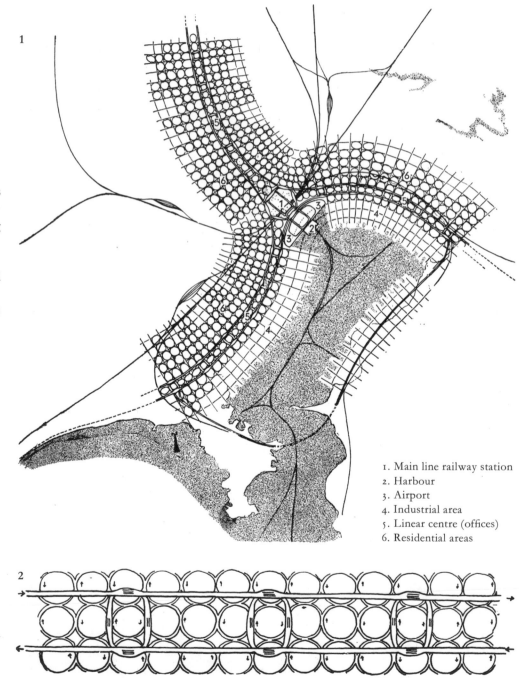

1. Main line railway station
2. Harbour
3. Airport
4. Industrial area
5. Linear centre (offices)
6. Residential areas

The Diagonal in Space

3

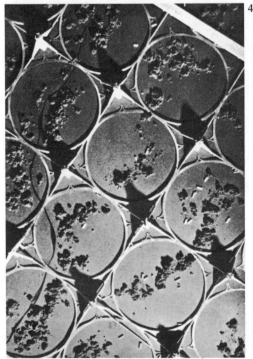

4

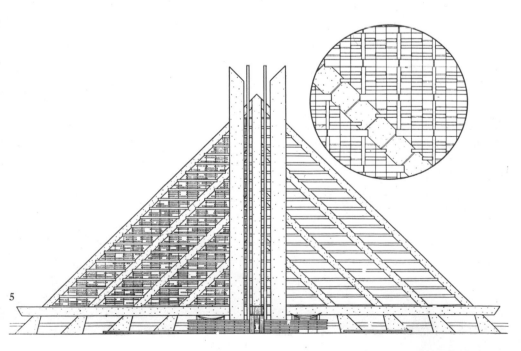

5

The Diagonal in Space

Stanley Tigerman

Instant City (Linear pyramidal city)

Tetrahedral megastructures would be erected above existing expressways, thus replacing the scattered settlements between our major cities which of recent years have been merging with one another to form continuous urban developments. Closely aligned triangular space frames with identical sides (200 metres long and 16.5 metres in depth) are erected in pairs above the expressway, sloping inwards from their bases to meet at their apexes (1). The main structure of each tetrahedron (2) is made up of thirty-six individual sections. These are also equilateral triangles: their sides measure 33 metres and they have the same depth as the main structure, namely 16.5 metres. Their component members are 65 centimetre diameter, fireproofed, clad steel tubes. The secondary structure, which is designed to shore up the primary structure and provide fixtures for the floors, also consists of steel tubes but of smaller diameter (3).

The loads of the entire megastructure are transferred through the points of intersection to a series of concrete buttresses supported by caissons. The horizontal forces are absorbed by tension cables running beneath the expressways and attached to the concrete buttresses (4).

The bottom section of each space frame, which lies between the buttress and the entry level (entrance is at ground level while the expressway is below ground), contains four storeys, which are used for service and parking installations. The next section contains three high storeys, which provide space for educational, institutional, light industrial and commercial activities. Above this there is a five storey section given over to offices, followed by three further sections, each with seven storeys, which are devoted to residential use. Finally, in the top section, there is a lower storey providing restaurant and recreational facilities and upper storeys which house mechanical services such as lifts.

1

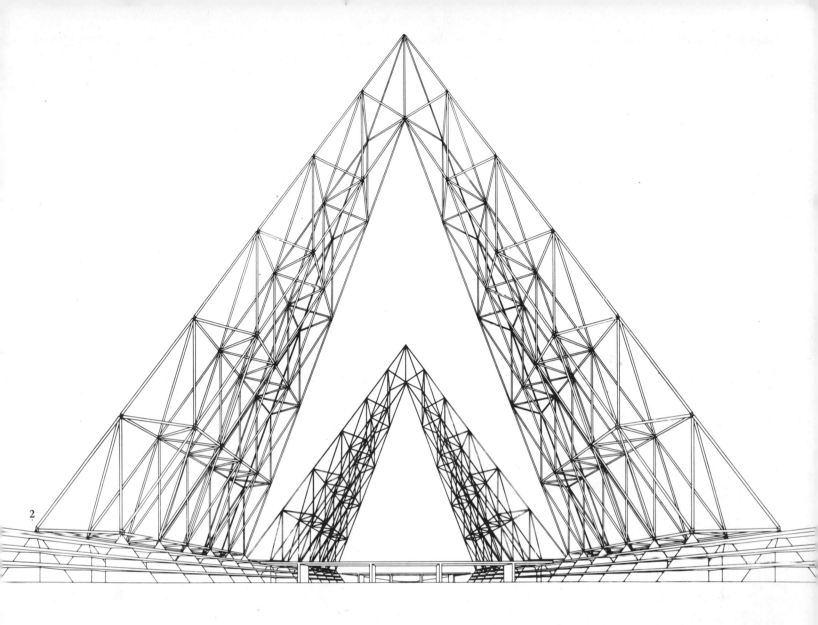

2

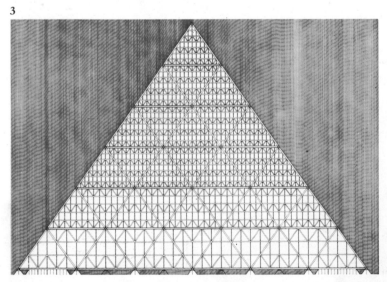

3

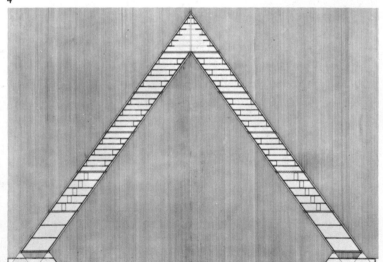

4

The Diagonal in Space

A. Schipkov and E. Schipkova (Architects) and A. Gravillin and A. Popov (Engineers)

Pyramidal residential structure for two thousand people in Siberia

The exploitation of the vast mineral deposits discovered in Siberia has always been greatly hampered by the extreme climatic conditions obtaining in that territory. This project (1) constitutes an entirely realistic attempt to improve those conditions for a large group of people by creating an artificial environment which would remove the terrors of the Siberian winter.

Three sides of the pyramidal structure would receive optimum sunshine; the fourth side would not be built on but fitted out to allow maximum light to enter the inner part of the structure (4, 5). This inner area would be laid out as a winter garden with a recreational park and sports facilities; it would have its own microclimate which could, however, be replaced by natural ventilation if desired. The winter garden would provide the occupants of the megastructure with an area for communal activities that would be in marked contrast to the winter landscape outside.

Between them the three built-up sections of the pyramid would contain 579 residential units of varying types (2), all of which would be provided with a small terrace. Since these apartments would have a controlled microclimate, they would tend to insulate the inner area, thus reducing the cost of heating this public sphere (3).

The sociological implications of this kind of building are very interesting. For example, it seems likely that the families living in the terraced apartments would come into frequent contact with one another, due to the provision of a communal area, and would join together to form groups and societies. This socializing tendency would be reinforced by the isolation from the outside world imposed by the harsh Siberian climate.

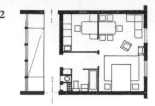

2

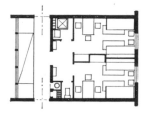

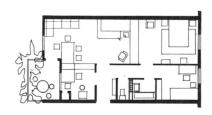

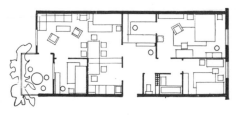

1

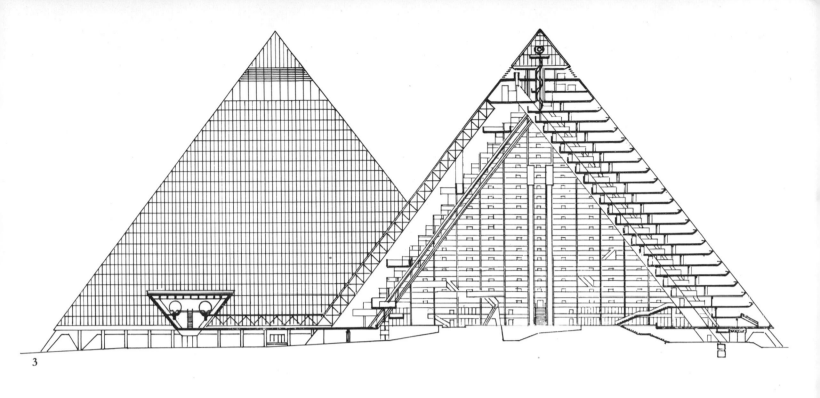

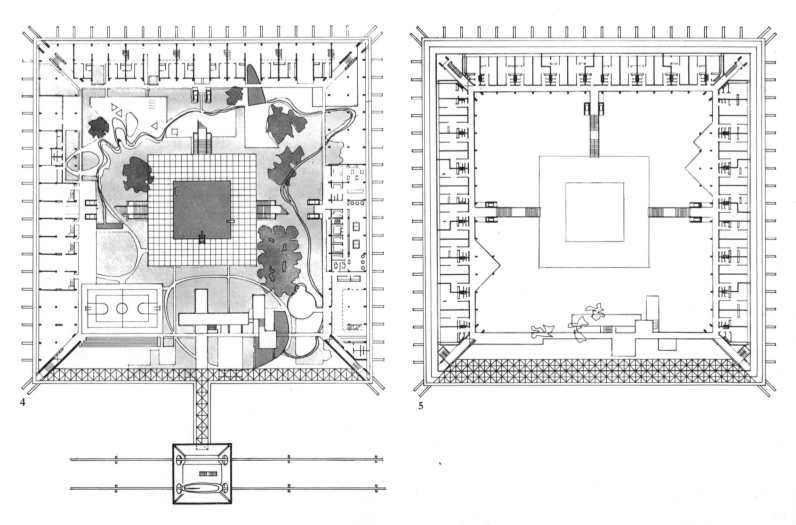

The Diagonal in Space

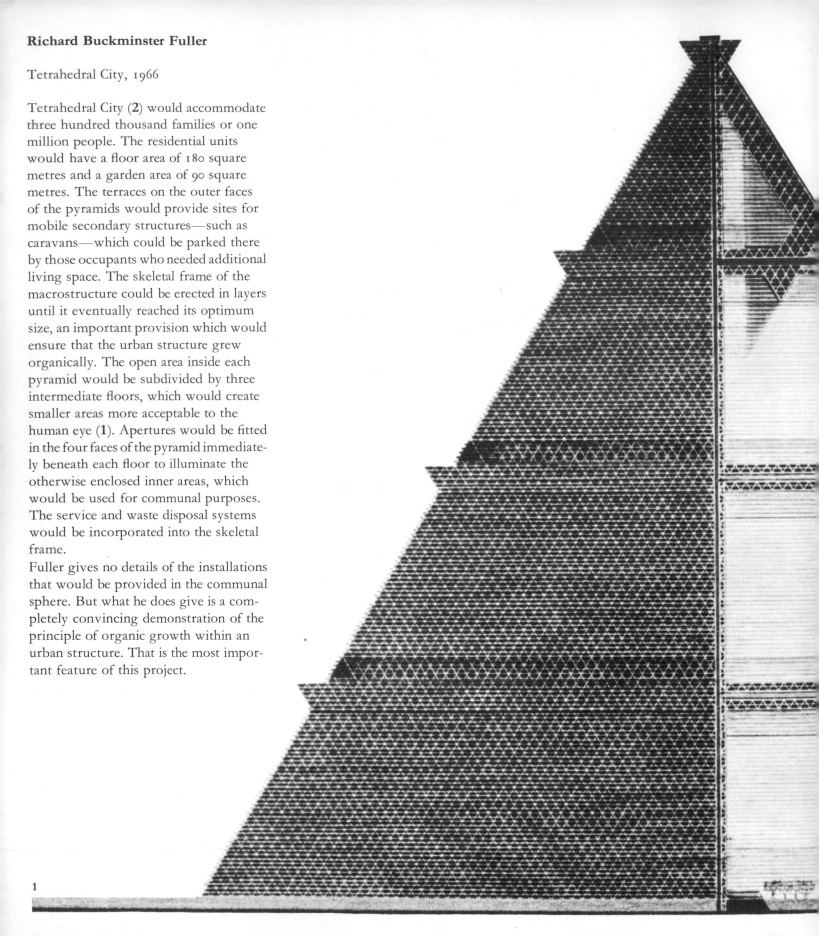

Richard Buckminster Fuller

Tetrahedral City, 1966

Tetrahedral City (**2**) would accommodate three hundred thousand families or one million people. The residential units would have a floor area of 180 square metres and a garden area of 90 square metres. The terraces on the outer faces of the pyramids would provide sites for mobile secondary structures—such as caravans—which could be parked there by those occupants who needed additional living space. The skeletal frame of the macrostructure could be erected in layers until it eventually reached its optimum size, an important provision which would ensure that the urban structure grew organically. The open area inside each pyramid would be subdivided by three intermediate floors, which would create smaller areas more acceptable to the human eye (**1**). Apertures would be fitted in the four faces of the pyramid immediately beneath each floor to illuminate the otherwise enclosed inner areas, which would be used for communal purposes. The service and waste disposal systems would be incorporated into the skeletal frame.

Fuller gives no details of the installations that would be provided in the communal sphere. But what he does give is a completely convincing demonstration of the principle of organic growth within an urban structure. That is the most important feature of this project.

1

2

The Diagonal in Space

Richard Buckminster Fuller and Shoji Sadao

Slum-clearance scheme for Harlem, New York City, 1965

The cosmoform suspension buildings designed by Fuller to replace the slums of Harlem are relatively low cost structures which would pose no intractable technical problems. There is no real reason, therefore, why this scheme should not be put into effect immediately.

The design provides for the erection of gigantic tubular 'moulds' which form the axes of figures of rotation (1). Sets of cables would be suspended from the top of each megastructure and anchored to the ground to form a circular base. The empty space between the inner and outer cables would be filled with decks, which would then provide the necessary support for the microstructure. No decks would be incorporated between the cables at the bottom of the megastructure since this would interfere with the existing urban cluster.

The principal rooms in the residential cells, which would be slotted into the circular storeys, would be outward-looking; the only parts of these cells that would look inwards would be the purely functional living areas (such as bathrooms, kitchens and corridors). Access to the residential cells would be provided by rear arcades.

Vehicular traffic would be carried by spiral ramps built in the innermost section of each megastructure and consisting of a three-lane street for ascending and descending vehicles and a parking zone. These would join up, via a clover leaf intersection, with a six-lane external highway, which would link all the megastructures in the district (2). Once the new megastructures had been built and the people now living in 'Old Harlem' had moved into them, the existing buildings would be demolished and replaced by a park with various centres for communal activities.

Since this project was conceived primarily in terms of slum clearance, it cannot really be expected to deal with all aspects of urban design. But, although it fails to provide adequate communal facilities, it succeeds in its principal aim of providing individual apartments fit for human habitation.

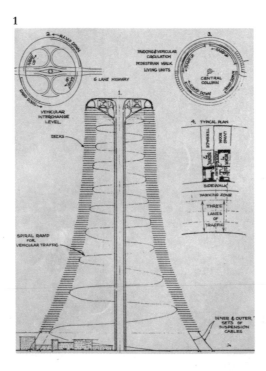

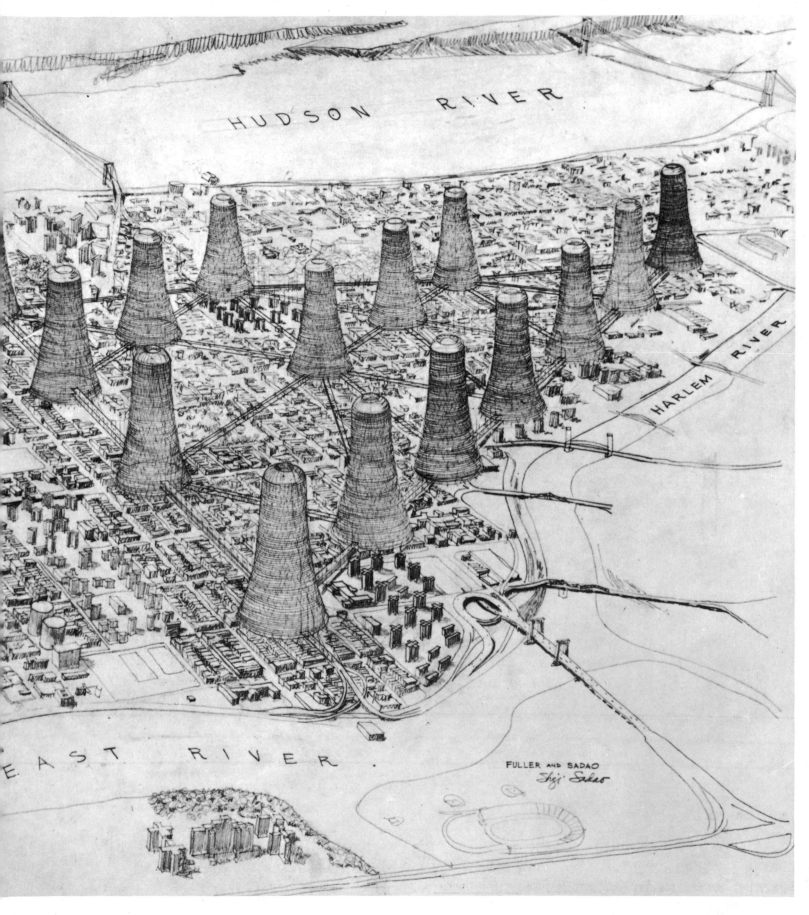

HUDSON RIVER

HARLEM RIVER

EAST RIVER

FULLER AND SADAO

The Diagonal in Space

Justus Dahinden

Radio City, 1968–70
Leisure City, Kiryat Ono, 1969–71

Radio City is an integrated urban system. Closely integrated urban units have been introduced with the object of organizing the urban structures in such a way as to bring out the polarity between the private and the public social spheres, which is an observable feature of present-day life. Although the interconnecting urban areas are arranged one above the other, there are no inhuman vertical structures and potential sources of disturbance have been eliminated (**1**). On the outside of the dome, whose spatial geometry corresponds to a rotatory paraboloid, a terraced garden city has been evolved (**2, 6**). The different areas which make up the city and which overlook the open countryside are mostly residential. The inside of the hill structure constitutes the public sphere and contains all the communal installations (**7**). The outer and inner areas form an organic and interconnecting whole, thus ensuring urban continuity.

The dome of Radio City is constructed in such a way that the individual units in the public area can grow inwards and those in the private area upwards (**4**). This organic process can be continued until such time as the units reach their maximum size, which has been predetermined. Subsequent changes to the structure are then restricted to metabolic regeneration. However, it is also possible to extend the whole of the urban organism by adding further hill structures which can be aligned in any given direction. The whole organism can, however, be expanded or retracted as desired with the addition or subtraction of hill structures. Three different types of internal communication have been provided. The residential districts are linked by high level roads, which circumnavigate the dome and are supported by its structural members. Elevators connect these roads to the public area, including the industrial and transportation installations in the basement of the city. Finally, pedestrian walks, moving pavements and electronically controlled 'personal-communal' transport (which is provided at the base of the dome) reduce the distances between the interconnecting communal areas (**3**) and enable the inhabitants to 'wander' effortlessly from one part of this big city complex to the next. External communications to and from Radio City

1

2

3

The Diagonal in Space

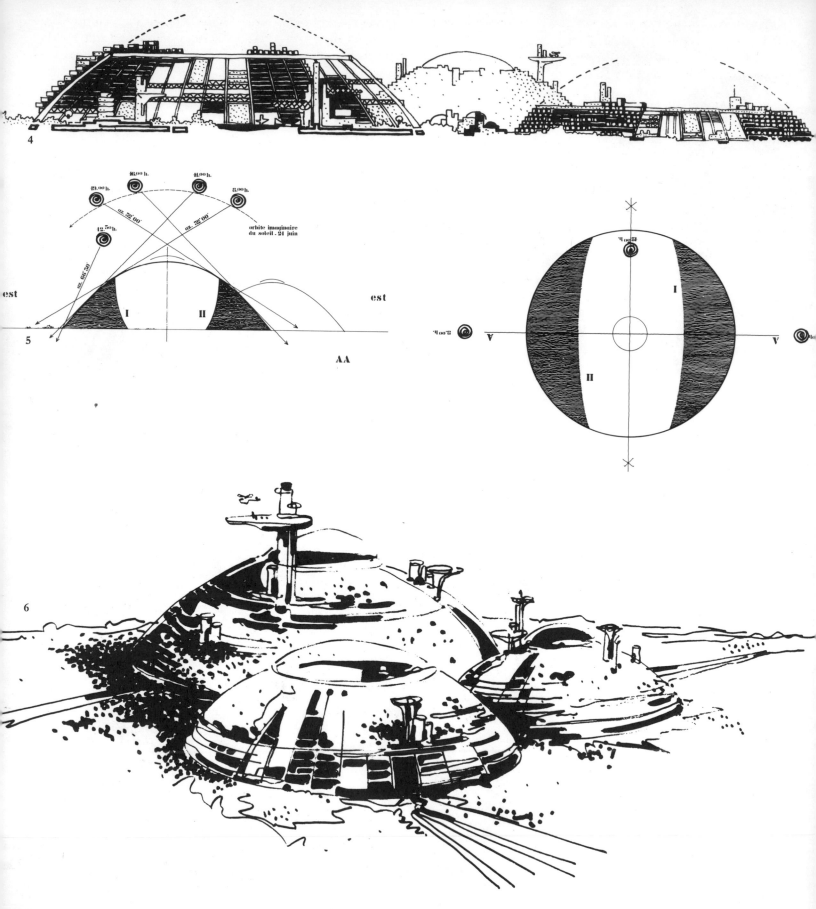

4

5

I   II

est

est

AA

I

II

orbite imaginaire
du soleil . 24 juin

6

The Diagonal in Space

are provided by subways for motor cars and express trains and by a helicopter service. A special pad is provided for the helicopters above the highest point of the dome on the tallest of the mega-structures (6).

A medium-sized hill structure would house about fifteen thousand inhabitants and cover an area of seventy acres; the megastructure has a radius of three hundred metres and the maximum height of the paraboloid primary structure is two hundred metres. The whole city has a total capacity of twenty-eight million cubic metres. No apartment would be more than five minutes walking distance from the nearest traffic route to the public area.

The dome of a hill structure is composed of a primary structural system of curved pre-stressed ribs, which carry the service and waste disposal systems, and a secondary system of horizontal stress and tension rings, which serve as access routes. The infilling is flexible: prefabri-cated spatial cells are incorporated into the load-bearing dome as required (4). A membrane of synthetic material is stretched across the inside of the dome to protect the whole of the urban area from climatic effects; this membrane also provides a screen for the projection of spatial lighting effects. At the very top—above the uppermost stress ring—the dome is rounded off with a translucent air cushion, which is like a gleaming canopy of light (6, 7). The installation costs and the cost of conditioning this urban con-tainer can only be assessed in the light of the overall economy of Radio City. Quite apart from the fact that such a system would be extremely efficient, the cost of building and maintenance would be low. It would also be relatively easy to provide a uniform microclimate for the public area since the residential structure on the outside of the dome would form a static temperature belt.

In other systems of this kind the primary structures are far more complex. In the case of Radio City such structures have been reduced to a minimum and, essentially, all that is required are a series of permanent installations with which to erect the secondary structures; these would be incorporated sector by sector in accordance with an established method of procedure.

Since the residential districts would face outwards, they would receive a maximum of sun and light (5) and would also over-look the open countryside. Consequently, their residential value would be high. The inward-looking public area would be equipped with audio-visual devices which could be used to intensify the urban experiences provided by this big city section of the complex. The richness of these experiences would depend largely on the kind of effects devised by the Gestalt psychologists, which would be programmed into the electronically con-trolled media and the robot mechanisms used for transforming the internal urban space.

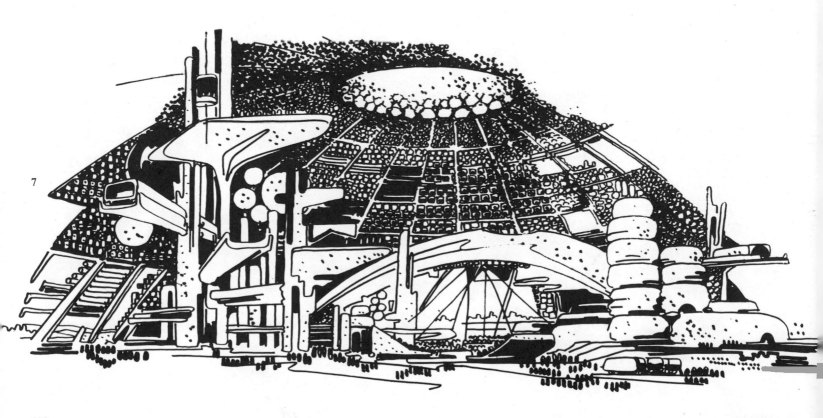

7

Kiryat Ono is a more sophisticated version of Radio City. It is an experimental urban system designed to test new living patterns for leisure.

Kiryat Ono will be situated in the densely populated part of Tel-Aviv (**9**), where it will serve as a centre not only for the inhabitants of the surrounding residential district, but also for people from much farther afield. The 'green hill' (**8, 10**) will have accommodation for three thousand people and facilities for every kind of communal activity (**14–17**).

These facilities will be provided in the main container, which will be in use all the year round and will have a controlled microclimate and air conditioning. With its sliding walls, hydraulic stages, mobile supply vehicles and other technical features (**11–13**), this container will be completely flexible and ideally suited for assemblies, exhibitions, theatrical performances, shows, concerts and ecclesiastical and indoor sports meetings. The only fixed installations will be the swimming-bath and the ice rink, al-

though they too will be adjustable in respect of size, for their spectator terraces can be removed if desired. A variable audio-visual environment will be produced by electronically controlled optical and acoustic effects, which will make a major contribution to the quality of the urban experience in the business area. Centres from which to direct and co-ordinate these effects will be installed on individual platforms attached to the vertical masts leading to the residential structure.

The complementary residential area of the private sphere (**18, 20, 21**) has been developed 'diagonally'. The macrostructure, which is shaped like the base of a cone, carries the spatial, outward-looking cells. Each level has its own communications link with the public area, which can be reached quickly and easily. The cells are produced by a sandwich construction method and consist of shells covered with synthetic foam; they are prefabricated and interchangeable, and can also be coupled together and consequently used to form a wide range

of spatial designs. The cells are lifted into position by a mobile crane, which runs around the macrostructure, and they are used for motels, studios, students' rooms, assembly rooms, youth hostels, old people's homes and offices. Each individual cell can be broken down into smaller modular units for ease of transportation. Its equipment functions autonomously within the microclimate. The substructure of the leisure town will be made of reinforced concrete and will house the energy control-station, the parking floor and the fixed installations (air duct controls) for the microclimate in the main container. By contrast, the superstructure (**19**) will be built up from modular units in the form of a space frame. The inner surface of this polygonal structure will be covered by a membrane which will maintain the microclimate and also serve as a screen for the projection of visual images. The inward-looking communal sphere is closed at the top by an air cushion that is divided into two sections by a metal strip which reflects the light.

8

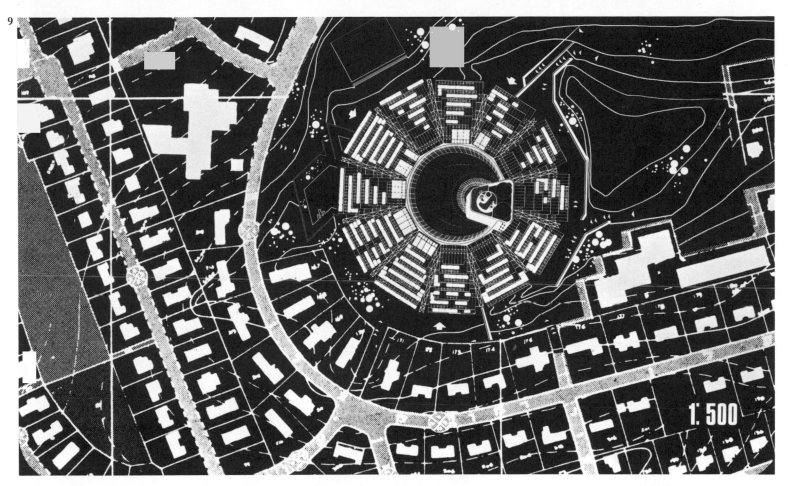

The Diagonal in Space

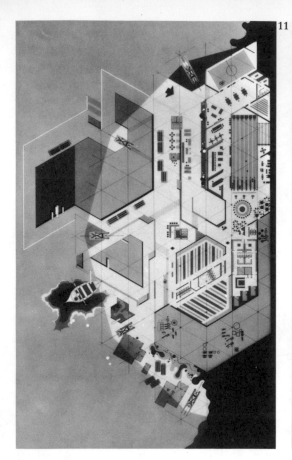

11

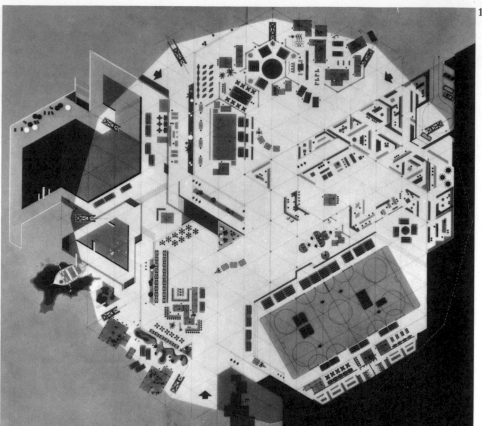

12

13

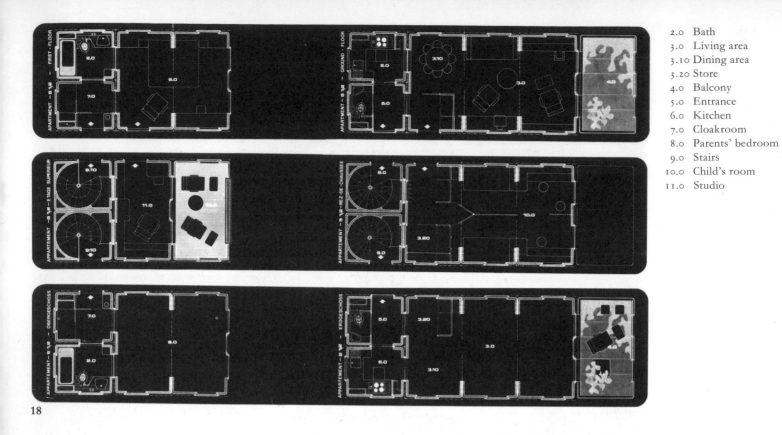

18

- 2.0 Bath
- 3.0 Living area
- 3.10 Dining area
- 3.20 Store
- 4.0 Balcony
- 5.0 Entrance
- 6.0 Kitchen
- 7.0 Cloakroom
- 8.0 Parents' bedroom
- 9.0 Stairs
- 10.0 Child's room
- 11.0 Studio

19

The Diagonal in Space

1.0   Entrance
1.10 Store
1.20 Hotel lobby
1.30 Lobby with cloakroom
2.0   Bath
3.0   Lounge and bedroom
3.10 Bar, T.V.
4.0   Balcony
5.0   Kitchen for preparing
tea
6.0   Kitchen
7.0   Secretariat
8.0   Bedroom
8.10 Dining-room
9.0   Stair

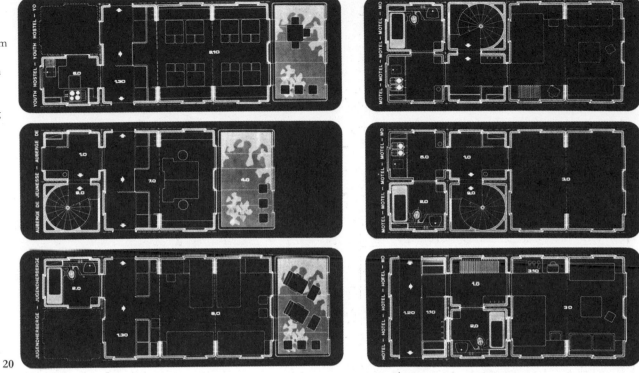

20

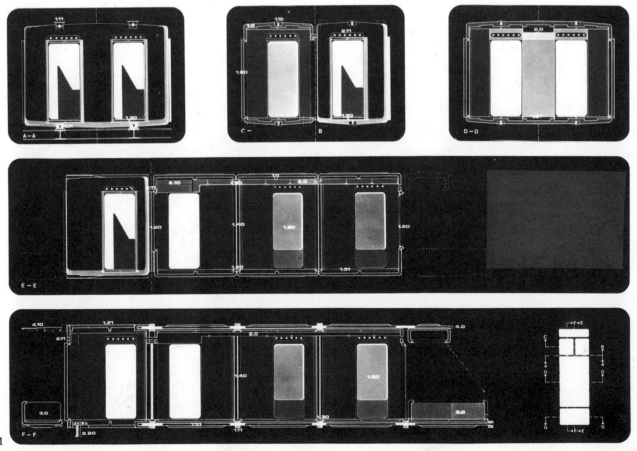

21

The Diagonal in Space

Equipe MIASTO
Michel Lefebvre, Jan Karczewski and Witold Zandfos

Manifestation plastique (Sculptured urban landscape)

The most striking aspect of this project is undoubtedly the pneumatic communications system which provides vertical as well as horizontal access. The central feature of this system is a large ring designed to encircle the small town of Vetheuil, which lies on a bend in the river Seine (**1**). Deceleration lines branch off from this ring to join extensive loop systems, whose arched lines supported on powerful pillars pass through the residential landscapes (**2–4**). A central junction connects the local traffic with the long distance road, rail and air traffic systems. This junction lies between the main ring and the branch line leading to the motorway, which passes to the south-east of Vetheuil where it is flanked by the commercial and administrative centre of the town. The imaginative residential landscapes (**5, 6**) reach heights of up to 150 metres. No details of their construction have been published.

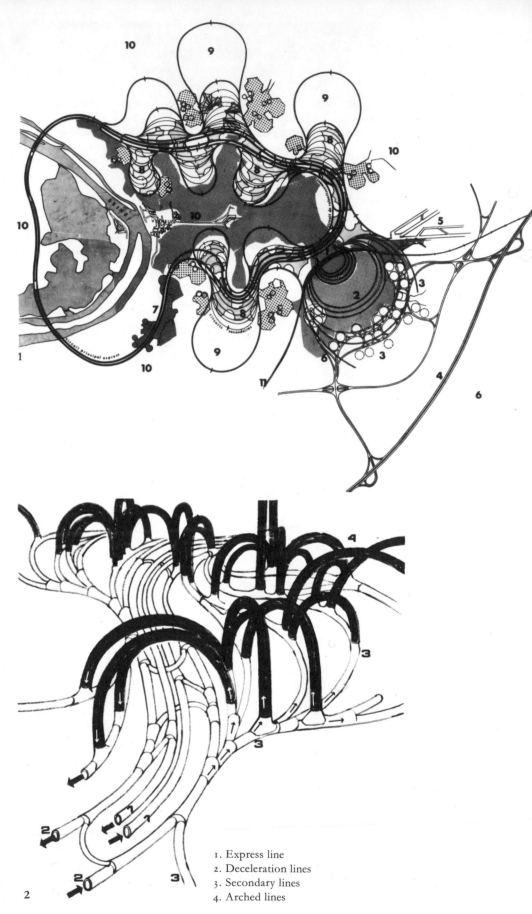

1. Express line
2. Deceleration lines
3. Secondary lines
4. Arched lines

1. Central junction
2. Commercial and administrative centre
3. Garages
4. Motorway
5. Airport
6. Service area
7. University
8. Residential area
9. Possible extension
10. Leisure park
11. Railway line

3

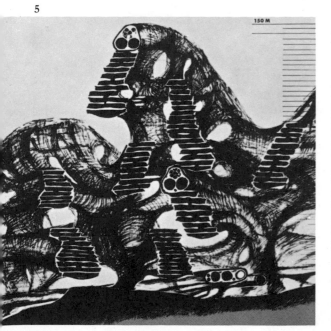

4

5

6

Biostructures

Paolo Soleri

Arcology

Paolo Soleri has produced designs for thirty super-cities, all extremely compact and all based on his own theories of town planning[22]. He evolved his arcological conception of the compact city, which he compares with the self-contained and highly functional design of the great ocean liners, as a counterpoise to the modern big city, which seems bent on constant expansion (2).

Soleri developed a number of his projects as alternatives to existing cities. His Hexahedron, for example, is conceived as an antithesis to New York City (1). Four of his projects are illustrated in this book: Veladiga (4), Hexahedron (5), Asteromo (6) and Arcosanti (7). Although Soleri does not actually advocate the incorporation of arcologies into existing cities, it would be quite feasible to renew an urban area in this way; only three or four per cent of the population would have to vacate their homes during the construction period.

Soleri distinguishes eleven successive phases in the development of an arcology (3). In the first phase, the architect would choose the site with due regard to all economic and social factors. In the second phase, the site would be excavated and work would begin on the production of the necessary building materials. Then, in the third phase, any special installations needed for the production of building components would be set up, and in the fourth phase those components would be produced and put into store. In the fifth phase, the macrostructure would be erected, ready to receive the infillings in the sixth phase. In the seventh phase, the industrial plant used during the first six phases for the production of building materials and components would be switched to the production of consumer articles, a process involving greater diversification. In the eighth phase, the city would begin to emerge in all its complexity: living, culture, industry and leisure would be integrated to form a balanced whole. In phase nine, the city would pass through a metamorphosis by adapting to new needs. In phase ten,

this process of adaptation would be completed and the urban structure would achieve its final and necessary form. This would pave the way for a new cycle, which would set in in the eleventh phase, starting from the point reached at the end of the third phase.

Soleri's thirtieth Arcology—Arcosanti— is now being built under the auspices of

1

New York City:
33 occupants per acre

Hexahedron:
200 occupants per acre

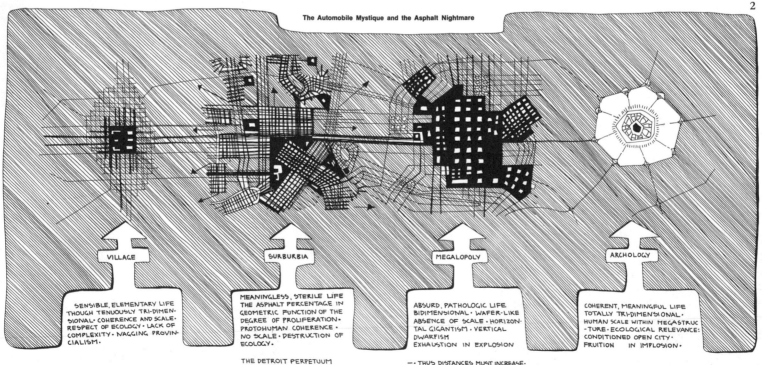

2

The Automobile Mystique and the Asphalt Nightmare

VILLAGE

SENSIBLE, ELEMENTARY LIFE THOUGH TENUOUSLY TRI-DIMEN-SIONAL · COHERENCE AND SCALE · RESPECT OF ECOLOGY · LACK OF COMPLEXITY · NAGGING PROVIN-CIALISM.

SURBURBIA

MEANINGLESS, STERILE LIFE THE ASPHALT PERCENTAGE IN GEOMETRIC FUNCTION OF THE DEGREE OF PROLIFERATION · PROTOHUMAN COHERENCE · NO SCALE · DESTRUCTION OF ECOLOGY.

THE DETROIT PERPETUUM [AUTO] · MOBILE: WHENEVER DISTANCE INCREASES MORE CARS ARE NEEDED · MORE CARS DEMAND MORE SPACE · —

MEGALOPOLY

ABSURD, PATHOLOGIC LIFE BIDIMENSIONAL · WAFER-LIKE ABSENCE OF SCALE · HORIZON-TAL GIGANTISM · VERTICAL DWARFISM EXHAUSTION IN EXPLOSION

— · THUS DISTANCES MUST INCREASE · WHENEVER DISTANCES INCREASE MORE CARS ARE NEEDED · MORE CARS DEMAND MORE SPACE · THUS DISTANCES MUST INCREASE · WHEN · · ·

ARCHOLOGY

COHERENT, MEANINGFUL LIFE TOTALLY TRI-DIMENSIONAL · HUMAN SCALE WITHIN MEGASTRUC-TURE · ECOLOGICAL RELEVANCE: CONDITIONED OPEN CITY · FRUITION IN IMPLOSION.

the Cosanti-Foundation, a non profit-making body which anybody may join, that was established for the express purpose of testing Soleri's ideas by launching an experimental project. The design for Arcosanti provides for a population of three thousand people. In 1969 the Foundation acquired land in Arizona; in 1970 work was started.

3
_____

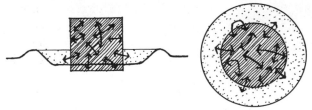
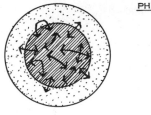

PHASE 6

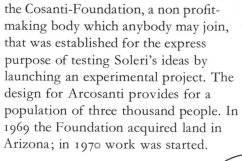

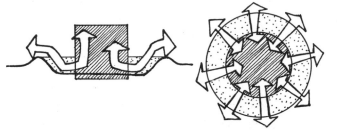

PHASE 1

PHASE 7

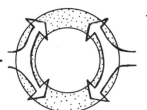

PHASE 2

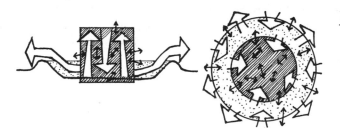

PHASE 8

PHASE 3

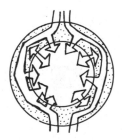

PHASE 4

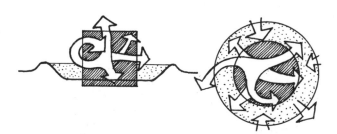

PHASE 9

PHASE 10

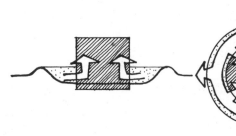

PHASE 5

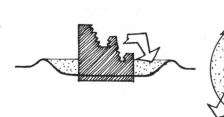
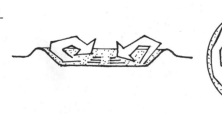

PHASE 11

Biostructures

Veladiga
Dam site

Population: 15,000
Density: 125 occupants per acre
Height: 250 metres
Surface covered: 120 acres

1. Veladiga, section
2. Veladiga, plan
3. Veladiga, top view
4. Veladiga, detail

Comparative Arcologies:
5. Babel Canyon, view
6. Arcoforte, view
7. Arcvillage II, top view
8. Arcollective, plan
9. Arckibuz, elevation
10. Empire State Building

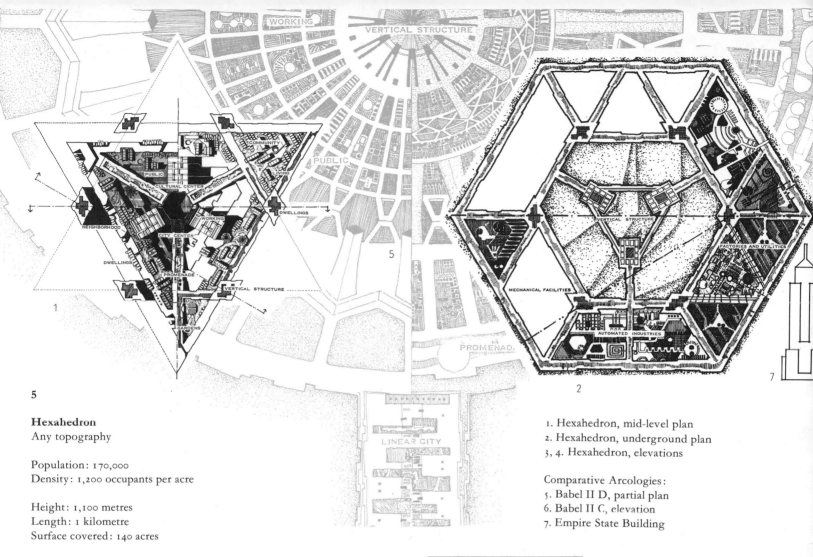

5

Hexahedron
Any topography

Population: 170,000
Density: 1,200 occupants per acre

Height: 1,100 metres
Length: 1 kilometre
Surface covered: 140 acres

1. Hexahedron, mid-level plan
2. Hexahedron, underground plan
3, 4. Hexahedron, elevations

Comparative Arcologies:
5. Babel II D, partial plan
6. Babel II C, elevation
7. Empire State Building

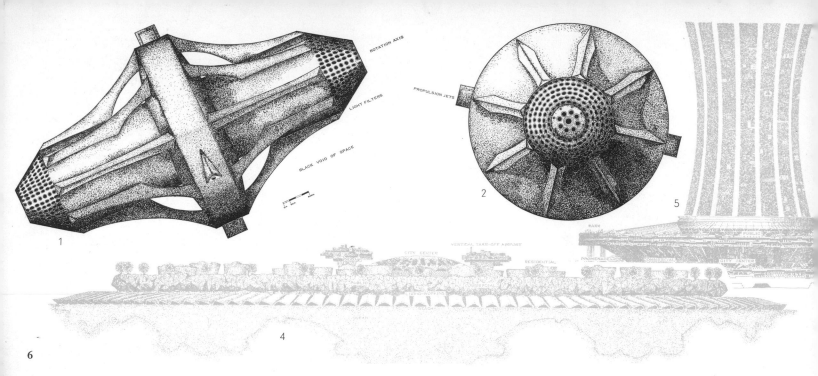

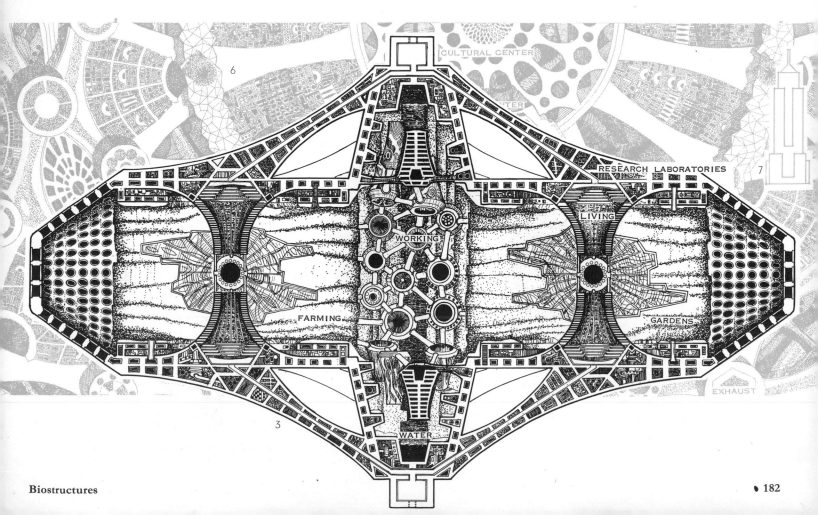

Asteromo
Space

Population: 70,000
Density: 162 occupants per acre
Major Diameter: 1,400 metres
Length of longitudinal axis: 2,600 metres
Surface of interior: 466 acres

1. Asteromo, side view
2. Asteromo, front view
3. Asteromo, longitudinal section

Comparative Arcologies
4. Novanoah I, elevation
5. Babel II D, view
6. Novanoah I, partial plan
7. Empire State Building

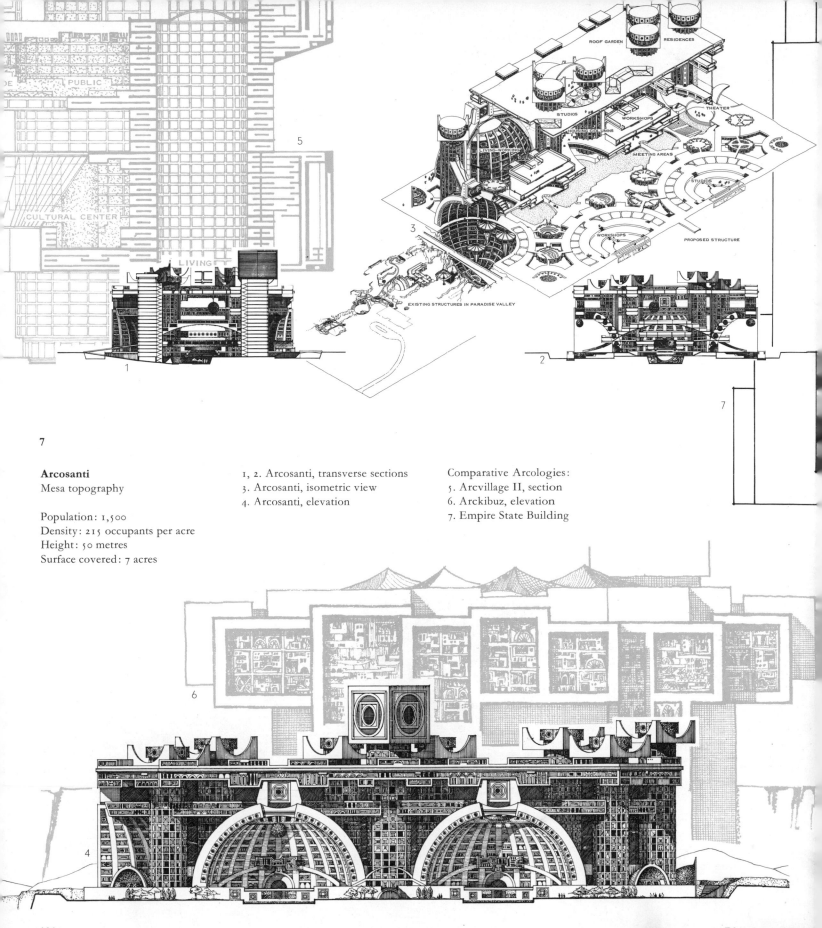

ROOF GARDEN   RESIDENCES

STUDIOS   WORKSHOPS

THEATER

HOUSING COLUMNS

LIVING-WORKING

MEETING AREAS

STUDIOS

WORKSHOPS

PROPOSED STRUCTURE

EXISTING STRUCTURES IN PARADISE VALLEY

5

3

1

2

7

CULTURAL CENTER

PUBLIC

LIVING

Arcosanti
Mesa topography

Population: 1,500
Density: 215 occupants per acre
Height: 50 metres
Surface covered: 7 acres

1, 2. Arcosanti, transverse sections
3. Arcosanti, isometric view
4. Arcosanti, elevation

Comparative Arcologies:
5. Arcvillage II, section
6. Arckibuz, elevation
7. Empire State Building

6

4

Merete Mattern

Stadtlandschaft Berlin (Berlin Town-
scape), 1955–9
Design for the 1967 Ratingen Com-
petition (with Herta Hammerbacher,
Yoshitaka Akui, Uwe Damm, Ernst
Dettmann, Nils Krieger, Mike Mott and
Hans Stegemann)
Design for the 1968 Bratislava Town-
planning Competition (with Hermann
Mattern, Yoshitaka Akui and Manfred
Walz)
Laboratory City, Fort Lincoln,
Washington D.C., 1969 (with Mario Sama)

Merete Mattern regards human beings
and human society as 'partially
autonomous' links in a biological
environment that is controlled
at both a microcosmic and a macro-
cosmic level and she considers that every
cultural system constitutes an encroachment on a natural system. Consequently,
she believes that the task facing the
architect and town-planner—and allied
workers—consists in the constant integration of cultural and natural values at a
higher level. In practical terms this
objective is to be achieved by using a
combination of closed integral structures
and variable individual components in
all architectural and town-planning
designs, the same sort of combination
that is found in natural processes and
one that would strike a continuing or, to
be more precise, self-regulating balance
between natural and cultural factors.
The Stadtlandschaft Berlin (1) is one of
Merete Mattern's first works. It shows,
albeit in a somewhat abstract form, that
even at this early stage in her career she
is concerned with the integration of architecture and nature into a comprehensive
ecological system.
For the Ratingen competition—which
was for a new urban development
scheme capable of housing 25,000
people—she has produced several
designs at the same time. The one finally
submitted (2–5) is based on a series of
frame structures which rise up at

1

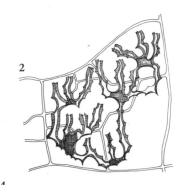

2

3

4

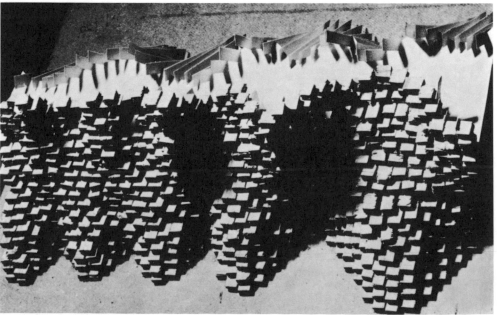

5

6

Biostructures

8

9

7

different angles, thus forming a plastic complex of ridges and hollows (4, 5). Between, above and beneath the frames, infillings can be incorporated as desired. Those areas left unfilled—and also the structural members of the frames which would be big enough for footpaths—would be used for communal activities, leading to a close integration of the private and the public spheres.

In her design for the Bratislava competition (6), which called for the extension of the existing town to accommodate another 160,000 people, Merete Mattern further developed the kind of ideas that she had first used in her Ratingen project. By introducing special structural forms (high sloping structures to break the wind) and special kinds of vegetation, she tried to extend the internal microclimate by effecting some measure of control over the external climate. The town has five main focal points: the university, the school complex, the social, health and sports complex, the exhibition centre and the administrative centre.

The massive appearance of the new structures found in the Laboratory City at Fort Lincoln (7–9)—which are intended to provide a centre in which to test new environments before they are introduced on a wide scale—is due to the fact that the buildings in this town have been sited on top of existing hills. In this project a more ambitious attempt has been made to control the external climate. In addition to the angled buildings and the vegetation used in the Bratislava design, in Fort Lincoln Merete Mattern has also introduced a series of towers capable of spraying water and transmitting trapped solar energy. The intellectual and cultural centre of the town is a musical and information centre (9), which would enable the inhabitants to express themselves in new artistic media. The urban area of Fort Lincoln would be limited in size, but environmental experiments could also be carried out in the surrounding district by means of mobile aerial or marine communities (8).

Constant

New Babylon[23]

Individualist culture is at an end; its institutions are exhausted. The present task of the artist can only be to prepare the way for a future mass culture. For if there is still to be any talk of culture it will have to carry a mass society, and then the means can be sought only within mechanization. The shaping of the material environment and the liberation and organization of everyday life are the points of departure for new cultural forms. My New Babylon project arose as an illustrative sketch and elaboration of these ideas. It is the experimental thought and play model for the establishment of principles for a new and different culture.

New Babylon is not primarily a town-planning project. Equally, it is not intended as a work of art in the traditional sense nor as an example of architectonic structure.

New Babylon in its present form may be construed as a proposal, as an attempt to give material shape to the theory of unitary town-planning, to maintain a creative game with an imaginary environment that is set in place of the inadequate, unsatisfying environment of contemporary life.

The modern city is dead; it has fallen victim to utility. New Babylon is a project for a city in which it is possible to live. And to live means to be creative. New Babylon is the object of a mass creativity; it reckons with the activation of the enormous creative potential which, now unused, is present in the masses. It reckons with the disappearance of non-creative work as the result of automation; it reckons with the transformation of morality and thought; it reckons with a new social organization. But it also reckons with facts like the rapid spread of the world population, the perpetual growth of traffic, the cultivation of the whole planet, and total urbanization. Thus the project takes account of the purely functional problems of current town-planning, traffic and housing and strives for extreme solutions. But its main theme is a new regard for social space. It is the medium for a new creativity that is to manifest itself in daily life, by means of a continually varied arrangement of the environment, in harmony with a dynamic way of life. In a technical respect, it is a simple, thoroughly structured framework, a scaffolding set on pillars and raised up in toto from the ground. Thus the ground is left at the free disposal of traffic.

Division of the scaffolding into smaller units (sectors), each twelve to twenty-four acres large, gives rise to a complicated, netlike pattern interspersed by remnants of landscape and criss-crossed by a traffic grid, which can run independently of the built-up area.

On the raised platform, dwelling and social space form a vast coherent edifice which, in all its several storeys, is artificially air-conditioned and lit. The upper terrace, the 'roof', can include sports areas and airports.

Apart from dwelling quarters, the interior of these sectional buildings consists of a large public space serving the purposes of social life. It is divided up by means of movable walls and constructional parts into variable volumes that can be linked by a play of stairs, platforms and corridors. This gives rise to a multiplicity of different ambiences that can be altered at any given moment. Their character can be influenced and determined by an abundant manipulation of colour, sound, light, climate, by the use of the most varied kinds of technical apparatus, and by psychological procedures. The shaping of the interior at any given moment, the interplay of the various environments takes place in harmony with the experimental life-play of the inhabitants. The city brings about a dynamically active, creative unfolding of life.

One can wander for prolonged periods through the interconnected sectors, entering into the adventure afforded by

1–3. Constant, New Babylon, 1959.

188

this unlimited labyrinth. The express traffic on the ground and the helicopters over the terraces cover great distances, making possible a spontaneous change of location.

The function of dwelling is adapted to this adventurous and dynamic life. It can scarcely be planned any longer to cater for permanent dwelling. The dwelling spaces, as parts of the rest of the interior space above which they are scattered, are best regarded as a kind of residential hotel in a non-commercial sense, favouring frequent change of domicile.

Such a project is dependent upon sociological, psychological, scientific, technological, organizational, and artistic factors.

Already at this Utopian stage a collective collaboration of the most varied interests is an inescapable condition.

But New Babylon will first be realized by its inhabitants.

Peter Cook

Eight Alternative Futures[24]

I wish to discuss recent work by the Archigram Group in the context of eight abstract notions of the future, since these can serve to profile the real objectives of the Archigram experiment.

Proposition 1: the future will be geared-up

Each generation deserves the artefacts that are directly the product of its culture and its technological potential. This is its right. Sometimes these artefacts carry over much dross of previous cultures: this can be dangerous. Each generation will recognize its own iconography, and recognize it in its own terms: therefore to assess the power or aptness of environmental machinery for tomorrow in today's or yesterday's recognizable yardsticks is foolish, yet we all do it. We postulate a future in terms of a complete set of interdependent icons: the Plug-in-City (1964–6) contained a suspiciously consistent looking assembly, the future (in early Archigram work) could be seen as a total image, in the Utopian tradition perhaps. We would not necessarily serve-up a future aesthetic in the same way at this time.

The idea that the future will be geared-up implies that it will contain the 'gear' of the time, and as 'gear' it will shout about itself (and its world) out loud. We think of Robots in terms of giant machines doing directly the morphological jerks of humans (as early experiments in robotry had to be, simply because they are unsophisticated), we think of the future in terms of (really quite traditional) engineering structures: oil refineries, channel ports, heavy engineering, machines.

The question remains whether the future need be so obviously geared-up, or whether it will be as dramatically different from now, but in its colloquy rather than its iconography?

Proposition 2: the future will have an expendable environment

During the last six years, much Archigram work has been concerned with the demonstration of a throw-away architecture. Not only as architects should we avoid setting-up nice architecture as a monument to our own *coterie* discussions, but realize that people using and enjoying the environment want to get on with living. They could not care less whether we 'plan on the diagonal' (or whatever) or not.

Plug-in City, the Living Capsules (1964–7), the Living Pod (1966) and several other projects look at architecture from the point of view of a market researcher responding with a choice of alternative bits and pieces that are put together by the person living in them. Our attitude has progressively moved towards the point where we expect the designer to be more of an 'agent' or 'broker' than a dictator. The future will almost certainly be expendable (the signs of it have already been absorbed into daily life as now). We are prepared to accept shifts in the recognition of social balance (to the good), social mobility and environmental mobility (we all pay good money to achieve some minimal once-a-year environmental change, if not more), and we have (in fact) come to absorb considerable change in our cities, not as much of it as bad as we would pretend.

It is perhaps a fundamental issue of survival that we 'shed our skin', let us also work at the application of the next skin by the animal himself.

Proposition 3: the future must be comfortable

Comfort here means reassurance, lack of tension, peace of mind as well as peace of posture. The most frequent criticism of modern architecture (of all kinds) is its 'uncomfortableness' in the mind of laymen. One of the reasons for this is (again) the architect's preoccupation with architectural (formal, professional) satisfaction before anything else. In several Archigram projects of the middle period (1966–8) the basis of the project has been a series of 'comfort-responses' to selected social units. The 'Control and Choice Housing' (prepared for the Paris Biennale, 1967) was a dialogue between an invented family, each member of which had particular characteristics. This was shown in the cartoon, with 'Frank and Doris' . . . the mum and dad, son Bob' who is a sports fanatic, 'Uncle Wilf' whose predilection is for food, daughter 'Rita' who really wants to be left alone most of the time, and the young 'Mark' and 'Simon': these two are looked after by the robots, making the point that we see the new cybernetic technology in the direct service of the individual rather than as a science-monster.

Comfort is seen by the Group as a fundamental objective of our work. If an environment cannot be satisfying or satisfactory from the point of view of the user, it remains a designer's toy. The future must be comfortable, and can be the more comfortable by the juxtaposition and regard of all types of hardware and software. This question is a useful one for any piece of environment: 'Is it comfortable?'.

Proposition 4: the future will be personalized

From choice it is one step to the consideration of the personal environment. For example, the use of the car is an interesting case in this context (as well as that of the previous proposition). Often it is in his car that today's frustrated and conditioned man once more becomes an individual. It may not be ergonomically as comfortable as an easy chair in front of the fire but it gives him more relaxation; in his car he can live out some of his wish-dreams.

The advent of do-it-yourself is another manifestation of the will to involve; the actual do-it-yourself apparatus may really be prepackaged and the result

imperfect, but one has been creating one's own environment. Another aspect of personalization is the immediacy and variety it may involve. David Greene's suit-that-becomes-a-room is an example. Mike Webb has also been developing this idea with the 'Cushicle' and the idea of 'Rent a Wall', which is as it suggests, a system of rentable and interchangeable wall elements by which you are able to recreate your domestic surroundings week by week, to chat up a girlfriend or impress mother-in-law. Arabian Nights or clinical efficiency can be summoned-up in your living room. (A do-it-yourself instruction kit is coming in the next issue of *Archigram,* with a choice of changeable room or audio-visual helmet as personalized environments.)

Proposition 5: the future will be responsive

From 'Control and Choice' onwards, we have been involved in response-design. The future will probably respond to our needs in a smoother, less demonstrative way than most architecture. Architecture tends to inhibit anyway. In a truly responsive environment, time and circumstance are added to the critical factors along with space and organization. It has been technically difficult to show this on traditional drawings: time and movement and interference are part of the demonstration. The responsive mechanism will probably be increasingly based on a software assembly, dependent upon hardware only for some of the responses. Sensory mechanisms are at the moment only primitive (and probably over-rhetorical about their prowess) but the experiments have begun.

The 'Soft-Scene Monitor' which we built in Oslo in 1968 was the first run at what we now call an 'Environmental Jukebox'. A means by which the person sitting in a space can sift through a series of offerings and at the press of a button be enveloped by a place and sound and condition of his choice.

It is only a further step on from this to more subtly responsive apparatus. Once

more with the condition that the response is to a need.

Proposition 6: the future will offer 'features'

If you are buying a camera you may be interested in the potential of a superbly machined lens, but more likely you will be looking to see what 'Features' you can get for £X. The whole commercial basis of 'Look—these features' is one that concentrates on value for money, or things that do something for you. Another example; if you are buying a house in the London area, there is a limit of probably not more than three computes to what you can get for £6000. You will buy the place that has got the best features. These might not be equally equitable. Good location will have to be measured against good drainage.

This is not a bad way of going about things. The preference for or against square windows retreats into the background. The future will certainly offer features that we cannot even conject. The architecture of the present will be pretty 'featureless' by comparison, so we should not be surprised if nobody will want it. But then, we can reverse the architectural question from compatibility to open up the possibility of acquiring and discarding features. Once again the public will be disinterested in the finer points. It will ask: what are the features offered? What optional extras can be added? How much? and when?

Proposition 7: the future will be softer

The likely design relationship of 'hardware' and 'software' has been alluded to already. The potential of this cannot really be imagined. In some of the more recent Archigram work, the idea of 'Manzak', a kind of service-dog is proposed. An environment that need only be imagined as three-dimensional (by way of laser beams: holograms) is possible. Perhaps the taking of pills is more environmental than we have imagined? Certainly there is evidence of a way of structuring the environment by acute monitoring and responding by every means possible that will show little on the ground for the considerable energy and intelligence that is displaced. Already in the computer world (from whence the terms came), the importance of the software over the incidental hardware can easily be understood.

The future will very likely be gentler and more integrated between different environmental options.

Proposition 8: the future environment will be where you find it

In recent Archigram work, we have been interested in the mobility of current society; but more than this, we have been seeing how facilities can be mobilized so that previous limitations of location and institution can be overriden by regarding the whole of a territory as part of a responsive environment. Two projects characterize this work—the 'Ideas Circus' and 'Instant City'. Buckminster Fuller has shown us how the world can be regarded as a village. Coming closer to home, the Ideas Circus is an assembly of vehicles and equipment that can be travelled round from place to place taking a programme of Seminars that are reprogrammed by the input of comment and document from each place that they visit. In this way the circuit is part of the event.

Instant City is a more complex collection of parts; a series of trucks that carry teaching machines, enclosures, exhibits, electrical gear and so-on. The idea is that provincial culture could be made part of a network by catalyzing a series of towns. Each town visited by the 'city' assemblage would be linked by landline to the rest of the network. The 'Event' would be an important part of the process, the town would be a City for a week—a city in terms of Event, sophistry and offering. The assembly would contain some of the previously isolated elements such as the Soft-Scene Monitor,

Ideas Circus, inflatable tents, etc., as well as absorbing the output of local schools and groups, beamed from the city to other places visited. Eventually the IC would be phased out as a caravan, the whole network being a 'City' but there need be no conurbation necessary for enjoyment of the choice of the traditional city.

The future might well contain elements of the environment that are not hierarchically linked as of now: a place, a home or a city might be where you find it or YOU want it.

Justus Dahinden

Leisure Society and Leisure City

Social and Urban Utopia of the Affluent Society

The concept of a social and urban utopia in the form of a leisure city is based on the assumption that we still need urban concentrations and will continue to have them in the future. Future societies will be urban societies and, as such, will regard their towns as universal centres, which cater for every aspect of living. The social utopia of urban society is the leisure society, its urban utopia is the leisure city. But our present urban and social structures are not conducive to the kind of socio-economic behaviour patterns envisaged for the leisure city. Consequently, the structures which now determine the relationship between society, city and leisure will have to be changed.

We are all told by the ideologists that our work is a necessary service, on which the maintenance of the system depends. But it is, of course, this very system which prevents the individual from developing his personality within society.

The *Lebensraum* of urban man is circumscribed by economic and monopoly interests.

The urban environment is determined by the profit motive. The places in which we live and work are simply endured. Road cuttings and asphalt deserts bear witness to the passing of an aesthetically aware urban culture. Road traffic is killing the human environment.

In our consumer society, in which economic necessity is being superseded by economic affluence, those who were once free to buy as they pleased are subject to intense pressures. Group behaviour is determined by considerations of social status and class consciousness.

Individual creativity, spontaneity and intuition are suppressed by coercive conditions. Complex production processes make people completely dependent and leave no scope for personal expression.

Our urban biosphere is threatened. Our environment is being denaturalized by the pollution of air, land and water. Our towns are short of breath. Man has become an enemy of nature.

The educational and economic systems in force today have been designed to create a form of social organization which elicits compliance and consequently provides an effective control mechanism. Because of the automation of modern technological processes the freedom of action ascribed to man is illusory.
The greatly increased amount of leisure that man now has at his disposal appears to him as a solid mass in his space time continuum, which gives him the impression that his position in space and time is being determined by an alien will.

There is no longer any interaction between the private and the public spheres. No suitable space provision is made for leisure activities. The only place left for such activities is the urban backyard.

Social injustice is reflected in the contrast between rich and poor areas. The break-up of socially integrated districts has led to a growing sense of alienation between the generations.

Protests

Any attempt to change existing structures must inevitably lead to conflicts. At present these are finding expression in symbols, protests and romanticized attempts at reversal. Because it has acquired awareness of social and political problems, youth is anti-Establishment.

Leisure as Emancipation

The socio-economic behaviour patterns envisaged for the leisure society would allow for the spontaneous interaction of independent and non-profitmaking activities. Consequently, although it has yet to be put into practice by any of the industrialized nations, this scheme does in fact offer considerable practical advantages. For people learn from their leisure activities and, since these embrace an infinite variety of subjects, they form a natural complement to occupational work and must therefore improve the quality of the work force.

But, above all, leisure activities involve participation, a change from the working routine, and a recreational occupation free from group rivalry and egotism. It has a genuinely recuperative effect and is only possible within a re-humanized urban environment.

Leisure City

The leisure city is representative of our changed society, who views leisure as an opportunity for self-realization.

Rudolf Doernach

Biotecture[26]

Provolution into post-industrial society is 'resurrection' of enviro-fur lost millions of years ago, when a genetic mis-position (? god) drove man (the ape without fur?) out of paradise. (Religion: a symptom of disintegrated systems?)

If we try to define the relationship between the disciplines of biology and architecture, we find that the primitive distinction between animate and inanimate phenomena is not particularly helpful. We first had biological systems which then gave rise to architecture—as a complementary system. This is trite but important.

First we had the arch-a-itecture of biology, and this then gave rise to architecture.

Both of these disciplines—architecture and biology—are structural disciplines, for both investigate the structural patterns of matter:

1. Certain structural patterns—the so-called 'open systems'—are animate, for they exchange substances and information with the environment. This is the biological sphere. Biological systems act on the environment in such a way that it helps to promote their own growth.

2. Other structural patterns are inanimate. This is the physical sphere, which embraces architecture. The atoms and molecules in these systems maintain themselves, without any interchange with the environment, simply by means of the energetic interaction between their component elements. In these there is no renewal.

To define biology and architecture as complementary structural disciplines is meaningful only if we are able to explain why architecture was evolved. The problem is complicated by the fact that, although we naturally know that the evolution of architecture was preceded by the evolution of man, we do not know why man was evolved.

But just how did the interaction between a 'biosystem' and the environment lead to the development of architecture?

1. In the first place we find an environment that is subject to continuous change (heat and cold . . .)

2. Then, in this constantly changing environment, we find living creatures evolving from primeval slime, who stand in continuous need (of energy, living space, social amenities) and who are also subject to constant change (e.g. they become hungry and tired, and they grow old).

These living creatures have tried to ensure their own individual survival and the survival of their species by adapting to their environment, and by evolving more or less successful patterns of behaviour.

There were two possible ways in which this could be done:

1. The long drawn-out biological way, which called for adaptation, for biological automation (based on instinct).

2. The more rapid non-biological way, which led to the construction of nests, cave dwellings, machines, computers and towns.

And so architecture has emerged as a result of man's search for a quicker, more permanent and reversible means of survival (in other words, one that is not based on the instincts and is not automated). But, of course, non-biological buildings have led to biological adaptation. The whole process involves the interaction of highly complex forces at numerous individual and social levels. Soon these survival mechanisms were sublimated, differentiated and individuated, thus leading to the emergence of towns with numerous sub-systems: Houses acquired kitchens as an extension of the human mouth; living rooms acquired television sets (macroscopes) as an extension of the human eye; institutes acquired microscopes as an extension of the scientific eye; garages were built to house motor cars, the modern equivalent of the seven-league boot.

Because they are non-biological, these

new acquisitions constitute permanent extensions of human power. But, although permanent in one sense, they are ephemeral in another: today articles such as clothes, flats, houses, ships and motor cars can be exchanged very quickly.

In general we may say that—apart from the cerebral cortex which is still developing—man's biological evolution has been completed and has now been replaced by a wide variety of extrabiological activities. As a result man has become extremely powerful and regards himself as a super system in the 'system of systems'. He has quite forgotten that he is really only a complementary system of the vegetable world, its source of CO_2.

Hypotheses and Speculations

We know that man contains within him traces of all his ancestors and of their behaviour patterns, which each successive generation has to live out.

Now that our technocrats are engaging in bionics, it is time for our biocrats to assert themselves, although this does not necessarily mean that they must oppose this development. But greater stress must be placed on behavioural research into man's archaic forebears (arch-a-itecture) and also into social psychology (sociotecture), which should be treated as creative (and not just analytical) disciplines.

In the science of bionics, the functions fulfilled by biological systems are transferred to technological spheres which operate on a larger scale, such as aircraft construction and ship and house building.

Man reproduces his internal biological organisms in his external organisms, in other words in houses, towns and vehicles. This is one of the insights and one of the spheres of activity of bionics. In this sphere we have already made discoveries of considerable importance: In the microsphere we have succeeded in developing new materials such as 'regenerable' building materials.

In the macrosphere we are now able to

employ regenerative urban building systems, which operate in accordance with the biological hardware-software principle: a steel frame supports 'cellular' units capable of fulfilling different functions, which can be exchanged at will and allow constant regeneration within the total organism of the town.

It is also possible to use small marine organisms for the construction of floating towns.

The simple and basically systematic technocratic studies which have been carried out within the framework of bionics over the past few years have posed a question of immense importance. Namely, whether living systems are able to live in living systems; in other words whether man can live in self-generating buildings which are capable of growth. We have called this process biotecture; and, although it has not yet been possible to carry out practical experiments in this sphere, the idea is quite fascinating: Living systems live off living systems. But they are not only able to live off them, they can also live in them.

So far the advantages which have accrued from the limited research carried out in this field are purely strategic:

1. It strengthens the case for an interdisciplinary approach based on the marriage of such disciplines as physics, chemistry, biology and behaviour research: we do not know what the children of this marriage will be like, but we can be reasonably confident that there will be children.

1. Rudolf Doernach, Iceland, 1964. Artificial icebergs produced by a condensation process, in which living areas can be created in any desired form by melting sections of the ice.
2. Rudolf Doernach, Edible City, 1964. A city considered as a total ecological system, as a 'Gingerbread House'.
3. Rudolf Doernach, Hydropolis 'La Marseillaise', 1966–7. Pneumatic structure with an adaptable 'skin' on which the skeleton of the town is built up by micro-organisms.
4. Rudolf Doernach, Hydropolis II, 1969. A structure made of foam material overgrown with micro-organisms and fashioned by environmental forces.

2. It would oppose the established system of non-biological development and, by doing so, might conceivably place it in sharper relief.

3. It would ensure that people would once again be made aware of, and could help to determine, the closed ecological cycle of plants, animals and man. In other words, it would ensure integral biological development.

4. In the immediate future the world will be convulsed by revolutions on the part of the starving masses with the result that billions of people will have to be rehoused. It is conceivable that the development of self-generating houses capable of growth for use in developing countries might make an important contribution to peace research.

5. Finally, there is one long term advantage. The greatest social problem facing the industrialized world is the problem of leisure, which has been caused by automation. Eventually all technical processes will be automated; so too will the production and distribution of food; and this means that people will have a great deal of time for biological self-realization, so much in fact that they will probably only be able to utilize it without undue frustration in a reintegrated ecological cycle incorporating plants, animals and man.

But man is a highly automated being with only a minimal degree of self-awareness. Consequently, it might be felt that he is more likely to achieve self-realization on a comprehensive scale by living out his automated characteristics in a living environment rather than in dead buildings.

We see, therefore, that the question as to whether it is desirable to experiment with the development of a living environment has strong social implications.

It is possible to produce a living environment—but it is not possible to predict with any degree of accuracy the relationship between this living environment and the living beings who would use it. Both would be highly complex, open and dynamic systems, whose likely inter-action could only be assessed in very general terms.

It is hardly likely, therefore, that we will be able to develop precise, purpose directed systems.

None the less, it would seem to be both useful and extremely interesting to carry out practical experiments with self-generating building systems. This would presuppose the translation of the architecture of living beings into biological architecture.

Appendix: crucial problems of environmental research

1. Is structure slow function and function fast structure—in the final analysis, is everything geometrically determined (i.e. 'by arrangement')?

2. What are the common factors between structure and function, waves and particles, hypothesis and theory, cause and effect, space and time, differentiation and integration, quality and quantity?

3. Does the geometric-energetic structure of the 'chemical system of the elements' have a counterpart in the macrosphere, the social structure and the urban structure?

4. Does the genetic code have geometric-structural and functional-energetic counterparts in the macrosphere?

5. Is it possible to evolve a 'system of systems' that would structure the links between the microsphere and the macrosphere?

6. Are there common factors in architecture and sociotecture, psychotecture and genotecture?

7. Are architecture and biology complementary systems for short term extra-biological or long term biological adaptation?

8. How do primary, secondary and tertiary drives in biological systems like sex, hunger, aggression, territoriality interact as a system of 'communicating tubes'?

9. What biological and psychical dangers or, alternatively, advantages stem from extra-biological development and how is this development brought about (density, enemies, food . . .)?

10. Does man reproduce his own biological system and his ancestral system in the form of 'external organisms' (brain computer etc)?

11. Will man's non-biological (external) organisms be automated in the same way as his biological organisms (transportation of food)?

12. The full ecological cycle, which embraces the environment, plants, animals and man, is disrupted by specialization. What are the consequences, both for the population at large and for the individual, when such ecological (archaic) cycles which are perceptible to the senses, are disrupted in this way?

13. Biological systems (unlike physical systems) force their environment to develop in a way that promotes their own growth. Will man—who is the most successful of all biological systems—eventually also live in a completely biological environment? In other words, apart from living *off*, will he also live *in*, a living environment in the same way as he himself already provides a living environment for micro-organisms?

Yona Friedman

Dare to Live[27]

A somewhat simplistic view has been carefully cultivated for some considerable time now (although it has not always prevailed), according to which the act of 'creation' (artistic or architectural) is the prerogative of 'specialists' (artists or architects); these specialists, who are endowed with a superior culture and education, are able to 'create works of art', works which can be classified according to a scale of values that is universally applicable.

But public opinion has relinquished certain activities despised by the aesthetes to ordinary mortals, and has conceded that they too are capable of creating works of genius: two examples that spring to mind are the art of cooking and the art of making love.

In this article I want to discuss the question of 'democratization', in other words the ability vested in every individual to create his own environment, an activity that is at present restricted to architects, town-planners and artists. This means, of course, that I shall be trying to free the 'user' (or occupant) from the often more than dictatorial tutelage of these specialists.

In the final analysis, all creative acts (shaping the environment, art etc) are necessarily and rightly the concern of the user, for he is the one who is condemned to suffer their consequences—the constant influence (appearance, function etc) of the environment. But since he is to be 'condemned', he must also be the most competent to 'judge', and should therefore be allowed to decide which personal environment he is prepared to endure in his daily life.

If we now take the next logical step along this path we see that this person, who is capable of deciding about his own environment, is also capable of creating his own environment. Although I am not trying to plead the cause of the do-it-yourself merchant, I would certainly wish to argue that every individual is capable of producing or choosing or arranging the objects which make up his environment and that he will derive great satisfaction from his 'creation'. (This simple principle is openly conceded in respect of 'culinary art', so why should it not be conceded where the art of spatial organization is concerned?)

Thus, the emotional content of a particular environment need only please its 'user' (it goes without saying that the particular environment referred to here is the user's own personal environment or the environment of a homogeneous group such as the occupants of a particular apartment or the children in a particular schoolroom and so on), whereby this 'user' is the only person qualified to decide about, and to create his environment. As far as his assessment of the emotional content of his environment is concerned, this is necessarily superior to any assessment made by any specialist (artist, architect or town-planner).

Every individual has an inalienable right to form such an assessment. It is as much a part of his personality as his face (and the right to remodel his face), his choice of clothing and so on.

Although commonplace, I have none the less emphasized these points because, after centuries of indoctrination, our users are convinced that they are quite incapable of creating their own environment.

But . . . the environment does not consist of emotional factors alone. It also has a number of much more prosaic features. For example, if I consider a particular environment as an assemblage of different objects, then, in addition to emotional factors, this environment will contain certain material factors deriving, on the one hand, from the technical properties of the objects and, on the other hand, from the way in which these objects are assembled. And if I consider the components of a particular environment (an apartment, for example) as 'enclosed spaces' (rooms, for example), then of course the environment will consist of 'enclosures' (partitions, walls) pierced at certain points by 'passages' (doors). The emotional content of such an environment will depend primarily on the visible surfaces of these 'enclosures' (walls, ceilings), the technical properties will depend on the materials used in the construction of the enclosures, while the properties of the 'assemblages' will depend on the way in which the 'passages' (doors) linking the different enclosures have been arranged. Far from being exclusively determined by emotional conditions, these two last types of properties (the technical properties of the assemblages) are largely determined by strictly scientific conditions. Consequently, they can be accurately distinguished and are predictable, which means that we are able to choose between them and decide their use.

I will deal only very briefly with the technical question, not because technical properties are not important for the user (on the contrary, they are very important), but because there is no need for me to go to any great length in order to persuade the user (occupant) that he really is able to choose—from the articles shown in specialist brochures, exhibitions and so on—those industrial products that he would like to use in different parts of his apartment (particular environment). It is already perfectly obvious that he has this choice. We all of us choose and buy our own chairs, television sets, cooking pots or curtains without help from anyone.

The problem posed by the properties of the 'assemblages' is more important. The way in which rooms (enclosed spaces) are assembled or arranged influences the user's behaviour (the way in which he uses his apartment). For example, the mere fact that a nursery is placed next to the parents' room or that a kitchen opens on to the 'communal living-room' exerts a crucial influence on the daily life of a family. The style of living in a given environment is determined to a considerable extent by its assemblage.

The firmly established belief that the

properties of the 'assemblage' are known only to 'specialists' (architects) is false. These properties (which can be stated in mathematical terms) can be learnt and understood by anyone.

Once they had mastered their multiplication tables, primary schoolchildren could learn these properties, especially if they were learning the new mathematics, which are now being taught in numerous countries. It would be both desirable and easy to give these children a working knowledge of the properties of assemblages which—as we have seen—determine their style of living, the style of their future lives.

And so this part of the specialist's work could be done by the user (in the case of particular environments, such as apartments) and by a group of users (in the case of a public environment, such as a town or, alternatively, a district zoned for redevelopment). I cannot go into details in such a short article, but it should be clear by now that an undertaking of this kind would be entirely feasible.

To recapitulate: the democratization programme which I have outlined presupposes three kinds of decisions:
a. Decisions concerning the assemblage, which are of an essentially scientific nature and can be taken by anyone from primary school age onwards (provided he has learnt the basic facts),
b. Decisions concerning the technical properties of the components of a given environment, which can be taken on the basis of brochures, in which industrial (or other) products are listed for the convenience of users,
c. Decisions concerning the emotional content of the environment, which can be taken by anyone, provided he does not allow himself to be disheartened by the long and painful indoctrination to which all users have been subjected.

I have now dealt briefly with the fundamental questions raised by the choice of assemblages and the decisions concerning the emotional content. As for the decisions concerning the technical properties of the environment, I have already indicated that I do not propose to comment on these because it seems to me that such decisions are now taken more or less automatically by the vast majority of people.

The act of 'fashioning' something (transforming some 'thing' by the application of human will power) involves a process of information. A person (whom I shall call the artisan) 'informs' a piece of inanimate matter that it must assume such and such a form because the artisan prefers that particular form. We might say that the artisan 'imposes' his will on to the object because it is his will. Of course, before imposing his will (or his preference) the artisan has made a choice: he has taken a decision. But he will not know if his choice or his decision was just or correct until he has finished fashioning the object (in other words, until he has actually imposed his will). If, when he has fashioned the object, it come up to his expectations, he will consider that his choice was a just one.

We can now reformulate this method of procedure in the following terms: the user, who has chosen to fashion his environment in a particular way, will not know whether his choice was a just one until he has finished fashioning it; consequently, he bears the entire responsibility for his choice and runs all the risks.

This idyllic state of affairs was soon spoilt. At a very early stage, the user ceased to be his own artisan. The artisan then entered the 'information circuit' as a 'translator'; he became 'confidential interpreter' to the user.

This new situation was naturally less satisfactory than the first, but after a certain period of adjustment the translation reflected the user's decisions fairly faithfully (according to one celebrated architect of my acquaintance the 'adjustment' period is about six months).

The trouble started when the number of users increased. For example, to 'translate' the choices of ten thousand users (occupants) an artisan would have to allow an adjustment period of sixty thousand months (five thousand years), which would have a singularly retarding effect on the information process . . .

This is the problem facing the modern architect.

He has to make a choice for users (occupants) whom he does not know. Being naturally benevolent, he chooses for all these people the sort of thing that he himself would prefer. Unfortunately, he has no means of knowing whether the real people for whom he is acting share his preference. Thus, the real occupant becomes a potential (and, not infrequently, an actual) victim of the architect's benevolence.

This is the worst possible state of affairs, and it is not simply a case of the information circuit having developed a bottleneck. The fact of the matter is that it has been completely broken; the link between the real user (occupant) and the interpreter (architect) is completely illusory because it is maintained only by recourse to a fictitious entity known as 'the average man'.

Today occupants and architects the world over are deeply disturbed and are accusing one another in their search for the guilty party. But that the situation should have proved untenable was only to be expected.

In point of fact, there is no guilty party. The only guilt is that of ignorance. Whether one likes it or not, an 'information circuit' embracing the occupant and the architect is indispensable. If the circuit is badly designed, this is not the fault of those who are 'parties' to it (the occupant with his decision and the architect with his end-product). We should, however, know how to redesign the circuit.

Let us try to do so:
1. The occupant is entitled to choose his environment and to decide about his environment, because he is the one who takes all the risks. This applies both at an individual and at a collective level.

2. It is impossible to choose or decide unless a complete inventory of possible solutions has been drawn up. An inventory of this kind would necessarily be simplified (individual solutions would be subsumed under general headings) but it would still be complete (all real solutions would be reflected in one or other of the items listed on the inventory).

3. To choose or decide between different possible solutions is meaningless unless the occupant has been advised of the consequences of different choices. Such information would have to be provided for individual users.

4. To choose or decide between the possible solutions listed on an inventory and to be advised of the consequences of different choices is still not enough. The choice and the decision must be capable of being implemented and realized.

5. To choose and decide and to implement a choice and a decision is only possible —where there is a large number of individual users—if each user is advised of the consequences for his own plans of the choices and decisions made by all the other individual users. Such information would have to be provided on a collective basis.

I shall now try to illustrate this process with a practical example, one which is not directly concerned with the environment as such and which is so simple that one is not immediately aware of its systematic implications. What I have in mind is a typical telephone system such as the one operated in Paris.

In this system:

our inventory of possible solutions is represented by the total number of seven figure combinations, each of which constitutes a potential telephone number; our proposal that individual occupants should be provided with an advisory service is reflected in the provision of a telephone directory, which advises every individual subscriber wishing to make a call of the consequences of his action,

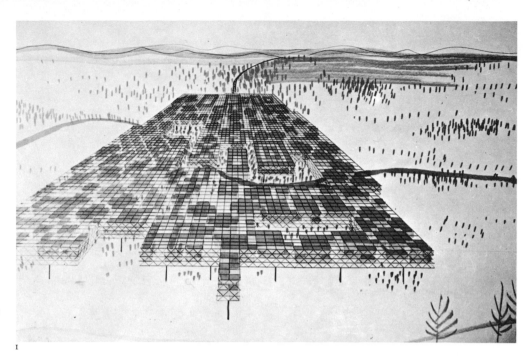

1

2

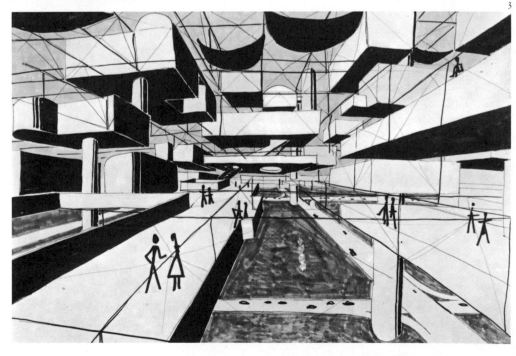

3

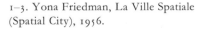

1–3. Yona Friedman, La Ville Spatiale (Spatial City), 1956.

namely the name of the person who will answer his call;

our further proposal that a collective advisory service should be provided is reflected in the provision of automatic signalling devices; if you are talking to another subscriber and a third party tries to ring either of you, he will hear a signal indicating that the number is engaged;

and, finally, the telephone system provides a technical (or electronic) network, which corresponds to the kind of infrastructure envisaged for our own system. This network is able to connect any number with any other number automatically (provided it has been properly constructed). Thus, the subscriber is not dependent on the benevolence of technicians; they do not tell him who he can talk to or what he must say. The infrastructure is impersonal.

Admittedly, this is only a rough and ready illustration but it does show quite clearly that real users are able to express extremely personal emotions by means of a system as highly technical and impersonal as our telephone system. It also shows that technicians are concerned, not with the emotional or intuitive aspects of utilization (the telephone technicians did not decide the content of the subscribers' conversations), but with the preparation of an inventory and the provision of an infrastructure and an advisory service.

That is why I find it so important that schoolchildren (between seven and ten years of age) should become accustomed to the idea that they are able to choose their environment (apartment, town etc) and that any choice they make is a 'good' choice.

Although I have avoided going into technical detail, it should be clear by now that the concrete basis of this new conception is provided by the 'infrastructure', which (in the case of our present industrialized countries) resembles a bare skeleton and (in the case of the developing countries) takes the form of separate enclosed areas. The bare

skeleton can be 'fitted out' by incorporating different building components such as walls, floors, ceilings, partitions and sanitary equipment. The arrangement of these 'infillings', which will of course be decided by the 'individual occupants', can be effected in an enormous number of different ways (the 'Flatwriter' solution, for example, envisages several million different designs for private dwellings and several hundred million for 'public' environments or public areas).

This method will enable us to incorporate architecture and town-planning into a direct democracy, in which all decisions will be taken by the occupants (either individually or collectively). In this system democracy is defined as a type of organization, in which the majority is always right without the minority being wrong.

We have seen that (in practical terms) the key to this new type of architecture is the complete segregation of the rigid and unchangeable infrastructure from the highly individualized 'infillings'. I have already referred to the strict rules laid down for the design of the infrastructure (rules which ensure that any user will be able to choose any combination he wishes, on the basis of the complete list of possible combinations, without inconveniencing other users who have made other choices) and, although I have not explained in this article how such a list should be drawn up (one which would enumerate every possible solution to the problems of interior and urban design but which would contain nothing superfluous and nothing contradictory), I have done so in earlier publications.

This is the 'mechanistic' aspect of democratized architecture and in the following pages I shall try to demonstrate the 'aesthetic' aspect to which this could lead.

To this day our architects are still trying to dress up the buildings and towns entrusted to their care in accordance with their own pet schemas and precepts, which vary from one architect to the

next; they regard these buildings as their works of art, 'their' creations; and the occupants are left to install themselves as best they may. We have already seen that this method of procedure has provoked a crisis situation and produced feelings of resentment which are shared by occupants and architects alike, who blame one another for this state of affairs.

The technique which I am trying to analyze is geared to a different solution, namely the aesthetic of fortuitous composition. In this system what counts is not the concept of 'beauty' favoured by a particular architect or even by a particular occupant (save in his own personal environment, i.e. his apartment), but the aleatory ensemble which results from the interaction of all the individual tastes of *all* the occupants. The fact of the matter is, of course, that once these ('mechanistic') general rules— such as the observance of the correct quantitative ratio between empty areas and infillings or of minimum distances between different infillings—are respected, fortuitous composition arising out of the unpredictable preferences displayed by individual users will follow as a matter of course. At this juncture it should perhaps be pointed out that this 'fortuitous' composition is very well organized (thanks to the rules mentioned above), and will look every bit as picturesque as any of the primitive forms of 'architect-less architecture' (to which our art critics are so attached). Moreover, it is likely to be every bit as colourful as a large crowd of people, whose composition is also 'fortuitous' due to the forming and reforming of different groups within the crowd and the capricious and highly distinctive way in which different people like to dress. Some of the individual members of a crowd may be unattractive, others may wear unattractive clothes, but the crowd itself is never unattractive.

Continuing with this image of the crowd, I would suggest that the kind of architecture in vogue today has a great deal in common with a military parade, in other words with an organized crowd formed on the concept of the leader, whereas the kind of architecture that I am advocating corresponds more to the spontaneous crowds encountered at festivals. The comparison is crude, but for that very reason it effectively demonstrates the difference between these two methods (which is not only aesthetic).

In point of fact, of course, the image of present-day towns is already far more 'spontaneous' than is generally supposed, for the impression created on the observer by shop windows, posters, motor cars and pedestrians is far more powerful than that produced by the aesthetic ideas of urban architects. An urban resident is more likely to notice that the window display in one of his neighbourhood shops has been changed than that four extra storeys are being added to one of the buildings on his way to work. We see, therefore, that it is the aesthetic and essentially fortuitous elements (such as shop windows) that have the strongest effect on the urban population.

I now propose to pursue this idea still further by suggesting a combination of events which, for the time being at least, must still be regarded as belonging to the sphere of science fiction.

But first let me set the scene.

If I am in a room or on a road, there are very few 'real' objects that I can actually touch with my hand. In a room I very rarely touch the ceiling, while on a road I never touch the areas of the walls and the decorations that are out of reach of my outstretched arms (220 cm). And yet I can see all of these objects (ceiling, decorations etc); it is simply that I cannot touch them. Consequently, as far as I am concerned (both as an observer and as a user), these objects are really no more than optical illusions.

Now it so happens that, today, we possess a technique which, although still under course of development, is already capable of producing three-dimensional 'optical illusions': holography. Holographic 'illusions' were demonstrated a

few years ago at an exhibition, where images were seen to 'emerge' from a screen. Until recently it was only possible to produce holograms with the aid of laser beams. Now, however, ordinary light is all that is needed. It is perfectly true that, at present, the size of holograms is still limited. But will that always be the case?

I have no desire to set myself up as a prophet and I must stress that this whole idea has been conceived purely as an illustration, as a 'mental experiment'. But let us suppose that holographic projections can be made on a really large scale—say, the size of a cinema screen. By using this technique we could project (and change at will) the external appearance of all the 'untouchable' parts of rooms, buildings, roads etc, thus creating an illusion of reality, one that was perfect in every way and could not be invalidated by our sense of touch. And so, if we postulate the existence of 'holographic diapositives', it would be entirely logical to assume that users (or groups of users) will one day possess collections of such diapositives, each one of which will be capable of creating a different and well defined (but illusory) view that will replace for the individual concerned the 'untouchable' parts of any construction (ceiling, upper areas of walls etc). As I have already mentioned, the users will be able to change this (illusory) view of rooms, roads and so on at will.

Once this stage had been reached, it would not be difficult to imagine that 'holographic decoration', which is able to convey the emotional quality of a given environment would become a popular art form (like amateur photography). I need hardly add that, to my mind, the individual user would very soon be 'creating' his own holograms (and, consequently, the aesthetic aspect of his environment) without allowing himself to be influenced in any way by specialists. After all, this is virtually what he is already doing in 'culinary art' and the 'art of making love'.

Thus, the power of individual expression

would lead to the emergence of a fortuitous composition, in which each user would be responsible only for his own projection and whose aesthetic quality would change from day to day, hour to hour and place to place. A road could look like a Brazilian jungle one day, a medieval fair the next day and an abstract sculpture the day after that. Why not? Artistic expression would not be lost, it would simply be transformed into a new folklore. And this folklore, which would represent 'the spontaneous and anonymous creation of forms and customs as practised by a large number of individuals', this 'creative activity', would present no difficulties, thanks to the techniques I have mentioned. It is to be hoped that, in this new capacity (as folklore), architecture and town-planning (which in actual fact have always been a kind of folklore) will enrich modern life.

Dare to live! The moral (if there is one) of this article is that the occupant, the user, is able to decide what he wants, that nobody else is able to decide for him and that he must, therefore, dare to decide for himself! In the final analysis this moral is intended to discourage all those who try to intimidate the user and persuade him that, since he himself is incapable, the best thing he can do is accept their services (because they know about such things), thus granting them power of attorney.

This moral is strict but it is not pessimistic: I am convinced that primary schools in all countries should be teaching architecture (as one of their basic disciplines); they should be teaching their pupils that they must dare to decide about their environment, for it is my firm belief that 'natural laws' (which are also the laws of a combinatory science) are perfectly simple and can be taught to very young children. The concept of scientific architecture and the freedom of expression vested in the individual are two different facets of the same subject.

Richard Buckminster Fuller

Domed Cities [28]

There are inexorably persuasive arguments in favour of cities under single umbrella shells. It is no aesthetic accident that nature encased our brains and regenerative organs in compoundly curvilinear structures. There are no cubical heads, eggs, nuts or planets. Whether the economic advantages can overcome the anti-change inertias of large social bodies, however, can be questioned. When whole new human settlements are to be installed on virgin sites as, for instance, on the Antarctic continent, the doming over may be promptly realized. The doming over of established cities in the moderate climates will probably not occur until domed-over cities in virgin lands have proved successful enough to persuade the established cities to employ comprehensive umbrellaing. The established cities will probably not adopt the domed umbrellaing until environmental and other emergencies make it imperative.

A number of advantages are provided by domed-over cities. First is the advantage accruing exclusively to energy quantum changes inherent in size changes and growth rates. When we double the diameter of a dome, its surface area increases four-fold and its volume increases eight-fold. This also means that the number of molecules and atoms of the gases of the atmosphere enclosed by the double size dome is multiplied eight-fold, while simultaneously the number of atoms of the shell is multiplied only four-fold. Variations in atmospheric temperature are caused by increased motion and resultant crowding of the atmospheric molecules. Therefore, each time we double the size of a dome, the amount of surface of the dome through which each molecule of interior atmospheric gas could dissipate its heat outwardly or gain heat from outside is halved; also, the number of molecules able to reach the surface in a given time.

We can say that the larger the dome the slower the rate of energy loss as heat—that is, when the heat is greater inside than outside—or conversely, when the exterior heat is greater—the larger the dome the lower the rate of energy gain or loss through the dome's surface by the gaseous molecules inside the dome. The energy conservation of a closed local system improves two-fold each time the system's linear dimensions are doubled. This principle is demonstrated in stars and in icebergs. Icebergs can melt only as fast as they can absorb heat from their surrounding environment of air and ocean through the surface of the iceberg. The larger the iceberg, the lower the ratio of surface area to its volume or mass. However, as icebergs melt, their mass gets smaller at a mathematical velocity of the third power while their surface area decreases only at a velocity of the second power. This is to say the volume decreases much more rapidly than does the surface area, for each unit of volume of its interior mass increases at a geometrically accelerating rate. Therefore, icebergs melt faster and faster and when the final piece of ice dwindles to pea size it can be seen, by the human eye, to accelerate extinction. The most magnificent demonstration of the increase of local energy conservation by progressively larger geometrical systems—in particular of spherical systems which of all geometrical forms contain the most volume with the least surface—is demonstrated by the gargantuan spherical fireballs which we call 'stars'. The sun's fiery volume is so vast and its surface so relatively meagre that it will take billions of 'eons' (whatever those incomprehensible time magnitudes may be) for it to completely dissipate its energy.

Due to the principle of energy conservation improvement with size, the larger the domed-over city the more stable its atmospheric conditions become, and at ever-decreasing cost per unit of volume. A second advantage also relates to relative surfaces. When we wish to design a good air-cooled gasoline engine, the greater the external surface the more effectively will the heat be conducted from the small interior to the large exterior surface. Though it would be impractical from a service viewpoint, the surface of the air-cooled engine could be further increased by modifying the same amount of metal, used in the fins, to take the form of spines or spindles like the quills of a porcupine.

If one looks at an aerial photograph of Manhattan Island, New York, there is seen just such a spined, or spindled, high-speed cooling system. The energy consumed by New York City to heat it in winter and cool it in summer is employed in a structural system that operates most effectively in the swift release of the energy to the surrounding atmosphere. There is no structural method of enclosing the circulation space of the city's dwellers that is more effective in wasting heating and cooling energy than the structural system employed by New York and other skyscraper cities of the world. Spheres enclose the most volume with the least surface and, as we have seen before, the larger the sphere the lower the ratio of surface atoms to enclosed atmospheric atoms.

A dome over mid-Manhattan, reaching from the Hudson to the East River at Forty-second Street on its east-west axis, and from Twenty-second to Sixty-fourth Street on its north-south axis, would consist of a hemisphere two miles in diameter and one mile high at its centre. The peak of the Empire State Building's television tower would reach only a third of the distance from the street to the domed surface above it. The total surface of the dome is just twice that of the base area of Manhattan that it would occupy.

A cube has six square faces. If we build a cubical building on a square of land, five of its six faces are exposed to the air. If we build a square-based building, two cubes high, the exposed, vertical and top surfaces of the building are exactly nine times the area of the land occupied by its base. If twenty stories high, it is eighty-one times the base area. Using such calculations and taking an inventory of the building heights in each of the city blocks of midtown Manhattan that would be covered by the dome, we find that the total surface of the dome is only one-fiftieth of the total exposed surface areas of the buildings which it would cover. The energy losses of midtown Manhattan, under such a dome, would be reduced approximately fifty-fold and the energy lost through the building walls, during both the heated winter and air-cooled summer conditions, would not be lost to the outer atmosphere but lost only to the controlled interior environment of the dome, and therefore could not be considered as lost. We have already learned of the extraordinary energy conservation of big domes, so that the very moderate temperature level of the dome would be effectively maintained, with energy savings to the city and its inhabitants of probably better than ninety per cent as against the undomed conditions.

The cost of snow removal in New York City would pay for the dome in ten years. Studies made at the Snow Institute of Japan and by Mitsubishi Company (the General Electric of Japan) indicate the cost of heating the surface of the domes with electric resistance wires bedded in the skin, to maintain a temperature sufficient to melt snow and ice—with the electric heat turned on only during the time of snow and ice formation, for cities in the snowfall magnitude of New York—would be far less than the cost of amortizing the expense of the additional structure necessary to support the cumulative snow loads throughout the winter months.

When rain falls on New York City and its counterparts around the world, it runs down the buildings into the streets, then into the gutters and on to the sewers to be polluted with all the other waters. Year after year New York and other cities have suffered water shortages, though they are deluged with summer thundershowers when enough water falls to take care of the city for days. With a domed-over city, both the melted snow water and the rain would run neatly to a guttering, clear of the pollution of the streets, down into a canal around the dome's lower rim from whence it would flow to great collecting reservoirs. There would be enough altitude in the dome to cause the water to flow gravitationally back to the storage reservoirs in Westchester. Because the energy losses would be so greatly reduced for the covered portion of the city, the heating and cooling could be handled most economically by electrical energy wired in from generators, far from the domed-over city. A new ultra-high-voltage electrical conducting system will soon bring New York electrical energy, by wire, all the way from the Pennsylvania Hills, where the coal is to be mined and burned in steamdriven electric generators at the mine mouths. This will eliminate all fumes from the atmosphere covered by the dome. The dome would also be able to umbrella away the fumes occurring outside the dome and originating inside the satellite industrial areas.

Those who have had the pleasure of walking through the great sky-lighted arcades, such as the one in Milan, Italy, are familiar with the delights of covered city streets in which it is practical to have outdoor restaurants and exhibits. They will be able to envision the arcaded effect of a domed-over city in which windows may be open the year round, gardens in bloom and general displays practical in the dust-free atmosphere. The daylight will be bright inside the domes without direct sun. All the parts of the dome through which the sun does not shine directly will be transparent. These domed-over cities in the northern hemisphere will have the southern part of the dome, which receives the approximately perpendicular rays of the sun, protected in summer by polarized glass so that the dome will not gain heat during the sunny hours. In the winter the sun will be allowed to penetrate to impound the sun's energy.

Structural calculations on the two-mile dome for mid-Manhattan indicate that the individual structural elements would have a girth less than that of the mast of the S.S. Queen Mary. If we imagine this diameter dome hypothetically imposed on an aerial view of Manhattan, the Queen Mary might be seen through the lower left part of the dome, lying at her dock at Fifty-eighth Street and the Hudson River. The smokestacks of the ship could be discerned but the masts, which are just a fraction of the diameter of the funnels, would be invisible from the height of the photographing airplane. For the same reason, the structural members of the dome also would be invisible: invisible as are the wires of a screened-in porch when viewed from a hundred foot distance. For this reason the appearance of the dome would be seen as a glistening translucent form. One would get the same effect if we photographed an ordinary kitchen wire strainer, turned upside down and placed one hundred feet away. Such a shielding dome would also, very effectively, exclude the sound of passing jet planes. The lower edge of the dome over the city would be at such a height above the city as to make it appear as a high umbrella, with plenty of blue sky visible under its rim. The dome would appear from below as a translucent film through which the sky, clouds and stars would be visible. It would not create a shut-in feeling any more than carrying a parasol above one's head on a summer day.

William Katavolos

Organics[29]

A new architecture is possible through the matrix of chemistry. Man must stop making and manipulating, and instead allow architecture to happen. There is a way beyond building just as the principles of waves, parabolas and plummet lines exist beyond the mediums in which they form. So must architecture free itself from traditional patterns and become organic.

New discoveries in chemistry have led to the production of powdered and liquid materials which when suitably treated with certain activating agents expand to great size and then catalize and become rigid. We are rapidly gaining the necessary knowledge of the molecular structure of these chemicals, together with the necessary techniques that will lead to the production of materials which will have a specific programme of behaviour built into them while still in the submicroscopic stage. Accordingly it will be possible to take minute quantities of powder and make them expand into predetermined shapes, such as spheres, tubes, and toruses.

Visualize the new city grow moulded on the sea, of great circles of oil substances producing patterns in which plastics pour to form a network of strips and discs that expand into toruses and spheres, and further perforate for many purposes. Double walls are windowed in new ways containing chemicals to heat, to cool, and to clean, ceiling patterns created like crystals, floors formed like corals, surfaces structurally ornamented with visible stress patterns that leap weightlessly above us. The fixed floors provide the paraphernalia for living, a vast variety of disposable pods plugged into more permanent cellular grids.

Let us discuss the principles of organics in how it might affect something as simple and as complicated as a chair. To be comfortable a chair must vibrate, must flex, must massage, must be high off the floor to allow for easy access or vacation. It should be also low to the floor, when sitting, to take pressure off those areas of the body which easily constrict. It must also be capable of educating its occupant, of having sounds come stereophonically to his ears, it must create correct ionic fields, it must have the ability to disappear when not in use, and above all it must be beautiful. A chair like this does not exist. My researches have led toward these needs again and again. We could create a mechanical contrivance which would do all of these things, but from my own experience with such machines in which to sit, they would not fully satisfy or delight the eye of the beholder. Now this becomes very possible using blow moulded methods of plastics with a double wall, which could be filled with chemicals of various densities, which could allow the outside surface to be structurally ribbed in a beautiful pattern, which would allow the inner shell to flex and to receive the body, a chair which could rise through pressure to receive the sitter, then softly decend for closer contact with the floor, a chair which could easily again bring coolness or heat through chemical action, vibration and flex, a chair which could incorporate electronic devices for sound, and also for creating correct ionic fields. A chair which would be an affirmation of all that has gone before and that which is now necessary. This we can do without mechanics, organically in much the same manner as similar actions, such as respiration, peristalsis, pulse rhythms, occur in many natural forms.

Carrying the principle further from furniture into the idea of containers for food, for liquids, we find that again the double wall structurally ribbed on the outside, smooth on the inside, could eliminate the need for refrigeration by chemically cooling the product within, or when activated or opened such a container might then chemically cook the soup, provide the disposable bowl itself from which to drink, and thereby

1

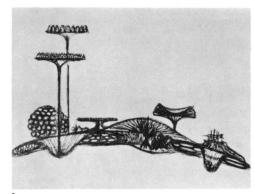
2

3

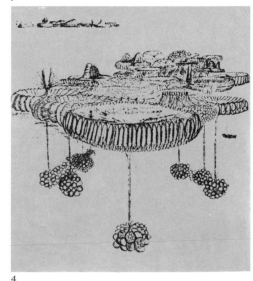
4

1–4. William Katavolos, Organics, 1960.

204

make the stove, the sinks for cleaning, and areas for storage unnecessary, as we know them.

Again the organic process creates an immense simplification and allows a great freedom for the positioning of areas within the environment. As in the case of the bath and showers we find the double-walled container, which would enclose the form to the neck and chemically steam the occupant, would clean the body and then dry it.

To carry the point further the individual could then create his own plastic fabrics by pouring them in pleasing patterns around the base of the pedestal, allowing it to catalize and harden into continuous containers to wear in new ways.

Let us discuss the chemically packaged lavatory which would rise to a comfortable height for the user, then slowly lower to provide the particular position that we have found to be best for total evacuation. Again the entire unit would rise through pressure and allow its occupant to comfortably withdraw from it, leaving the waste products to be chemically consumed and packaged, thus eliminating the needs for connective pipes. Having cut the umbilicus we find it possible to create the new house on any site in that it is chemically a complete organism in which to live, deriving strength from its surrounds. Houses such as this would grow to certain sizes, subdivide or fuse for larger functions. Great vaults would be produced with parabolic jets that catalize on contact with the air. Exploding patterns of an instantaneous architecture of transformations into desired densities, into known directions, for calculated durations. In the morning, suburbs might come together to create cities, and at night move like music to other moorings for cultural needs or to produce the socio-political patterns that the new life demands.

Noboru Kawazoe

From Metabolism to Metapolis— Proposal for a city of the future[30]

What should future cities and their components be like and what should be the attitude of architects in leading the way to future projects? In Japan, answers to these questions are being prominently sought by Professor Kenzo Tange of Tokyo University and the so-called 'metabolism' group of architects, planners, designers and one critic.
Professor Tange's 'Tokyo Plan-1960' is rather well known, but since then, he has not presented further new ideas. The 'Metabolism' group was established in 1960 and has been pursuing joint research since then. A basic proposal for a new urbanism was published under the title 'Metabolism 1960'. Since then, individual members have sporadically published their proposals, but a second combined report has not been published to date.
It is impossible to elaborate on all of these proposals. Therefore I would like to give a very brief introduction to the group's general thinking which is the basis of the individual proposals.
As is well known, metabolism is the series of processes which keep living organisms alive and growing through the balanced dynamics of assimilation and dissimilation, supplementary to and simultaneous with each other.
By assimilation, substances taken in from the outside are turned into living matter, and by dissimilation, living matter is broken up and energy is derived.
Of course, it would be too much to say that the functioning of society is identical to the biological operations, but it does seem to me that there is an analogy to the urbanization and industrialization now in rapid progress.
If this social phenomenon can be compared to metabolism, then, the task for 'metabolism' architects is to devise ways to cope with the problems of our rapidly-changing society and at the same

time to maintain stabilized human lives.
There are a number of methods to achieve these objectives, and some have already been proposed by members of the 'Metabolism' group.
The proposals, if implemented, would eliminate the confusion resulting from ruffled city 'metabolism' and in consequence would quicken transformation and growth. The development of city metabolism systems also means opening the way for the will of the masses to be reflected in city planning.
In an article for the 'Metabolism 1960', I stated that metabolism, as an architectural concept, is based on a belief in the vitality of life, namely a belief in the opinions of the masses. I termed it as an attitude bold and optimistic.
Acts of living creatures are fitting different purposes, but they are not necessarily the result of purposeful exertions. By the same token, metabolism, as architects see it, is a purely technical concept, and no questions are raised by them about the overall problems of current civilization, such as the direction in which it is heading, what significance it has for humans, and whether it is good or not.
The 'Metabolism' group has put up 'metamorphosis' as its theme since 1965. This was a declaration that the group has arrived at the stage where they can point the way to the future.
If metabolism is a principle calling for architects to execute their responsibility, trusting the will of the masses, 'metamorphosis' indicates the group's realization of their potential roles as intellectuals and spells out its aspiration to set targets in the path of civilization and clarify the processes to achieve them.
Civilization has been a system of cities ruling and controlling farming areas. Any living creature rules and controls the environment in which it lives. Consequently all phenomena of life are related closely to environment. In the same way, civilization also covers farming areas.

Nevertheless, life exists in living organisms and nowhere else. Just the same, civilization exists in cities and there has been no civilization not related to cities. At present, the distinction between cities and farming areas is gradually disappearing. This can be viewed as a transformation of civilization from cities to states. The metamorphosis process is believed to proceed until the whole world is organized into one unit. As an advance step for this, states are currently being turned into organic bodies.

In past civilizations, commerce ruled farming communities whereas currently industrial communities are ruled and controlled by bureaucracy and big enterprises operating on a national scale. Against these systems, a large number of middle-class people with time to spare are creating their own setups to fight back.

Past civilizations consisted of cities, namely the holders of power, dominating over nature through farmers. In future civilizations, human-beings will have the sway over nature through the medium of machinery.

This will not be achieved until at least whole continents are made into organic bodies. While states are being turned into organic bodies, domestic and foreign difficulties will persist, and consequently there will be many hurdles for mankind to clear. Still, the metamorphosis process is definitely moving toward universality. Such future civilizations will no longer be civilizations of cities as in the past. We, as members of the 'Metabolism' group, have decided to call the future mode of habitation a 'metapolis'. Mankind will have to go through various stages of development to attain the metapolis, and many paths to it are conceivable. Within the last several years, characteristic phenomena, entirely non-existent previously, have begun to occur in major Japanese cities.

One of these phenomena is the advent of multi-purpose buildings called 'Kaikan'. Many of these buildings are outwardly not distinguishable from normal 'office'

buildings. But, inside, they are full of such facilities as theatres, cinemas, shopping arcades, hotels, and offices. Moreover, in many cases—for instance, where a broadcasting station and a hotel share the same building—there is no inter-relation between the tenants. They are housed together on the ground that they all have 'city centre' functions. Another remarkable phenomenon is the appearance of underground shopping centres. They first came into existence in Nagoya, the only major city in Japan which was reconstructed after World War II under a modern city planning project covering the whole city area. Modern city planning has the character of renovating nineteenth-century commercial society into twentieth-century industrial society. In Nagoya, the whole city was cut into regular blocks with spacious roads.

As a result, shopping segments on which the citizens depended were driven to the brink of destruction and shop owners built underground shopping centres in an effort to seek a way out.

In other major Japanese cities, with surface roads occupied by motor traffic, more or less the same problem exists as in Nagoya City.

The solution exemplified in Nagoya found its way to various other parts of the country, and thus underground shopping centres, linking central train stations and city centres or connecting terminal stations and amusement centres, have been constructed in almost all major cities in Japan.

One cannot see an underground shopping centre on the ground, but stepping down a flight or two of stairs brings one into contact with a bustling shop complex where shopping can be done safely and freely and without being worried about the weather.

The underground shopping centre also links buildings standing apart from each other on the ground. The day will come when similar 'surface' links will be provided for buildings.

The above-mentioned 'Kaikan' has been

created in an attempt to fulfill varied needs of mass society at one location. But, of course, one structure is far from being sufficient for the purpose.

When one considers this problem and also 'surface' links for buildings, then it is just a matter of time for 'superstructures' covering a whole city centre area to appear.

Meanwhile, cities are expanding themselves into suburbs. But if citizens, living in far-off suburban districts, have to travel to enjoy urban life to their hearts' content, city confusion will become even worse.

To cope with the problem, it is necessary to construct 'super-structures' with city centre functions in the suburbs. But this is possible only where there is a dense population. Consequently, construction of residences which will result in a population concentration should be the first step to be taken.

A 'Pair City' plan, conceived by Kiyonori Kikutake, led to scheduled construction in a Tokyo suburb of a new town with city centre functions and including some multi-storey apartment buildings.

This is called a 'base development' method. In the 'development' area, various bases of smaller scale and with different contents are to be laid out with a communication network linking them. Bases lying in a selected section are to be put together and made into a new town. Consequently, this is also called a 'channel development' method.

It can be said that big cities, dubbed as megalopolis, are now in need of superstructures. The megalopolis has 'swallowed in' many cities in the past, and while it appears to be a compound of many cities, it actually is going through a process of city 'disintegration'.

The same can be said of super-structures which are combinations of many buildings. The process can be likened to the process of evolution of unicellular animals becoming multicellular through incessant cell division and differentiation.

Biology teaches us that multicellular animals create an inner environment by incorporating in their bodies certain features of their outer environment, thus achieving organic stability.

It may be interesting to note that a similar phenomenon occurs with super-structures.

That is to say super-structures in down-town areas must incorporate outer environmental factors such as roads and open spaces. Or sprawling residential areas may emerge around the super-structures to form an outer environment. In contrast, super-structures in suburban areas incorporate residential areas, hitherto treated as outer environmental factors.

After studying from various angles how roads and open spaces should be laid out in downtown areas to become part of the inner environment, Fumihiko Maki proposed that densely populated centres should become strategic points embody-ing their outer environment. And such population centres may be surrounded by sparsely-populated farming communities. Theoretically, through tightly-knit transportation and telecommunication networks, people in the countryside could then enjoy city life to the extent they desired.

A communication network linking these strategic high-density points will bring rural communities within the realm of the big city, thereby doing away with the traditional antagonism prevailing between urban and rural populations. Such a blueprint may become reality by transforming at least the entire Japanese archipelago or the whole Asian continent into an organic organism.

At this point, according to the principle of organisms, it would stop absorbing nourishment from the outside. It naturally follows that an archipelago or a continent will continue to exist as an organic body through the development of marine resources.

And this idea serves as the basis of Kikutake's theory on the 'Marine City'. But what we call 'metapolis' is different from Doxiadis' Ecumenopolis. We are not concerned with the size but with the quality of such a community. It is because such changes in our civilization would bring about a radical evolution in our mode of dwelling.

The recent qualitative changes in housing have been due largely to the populariza-tion of mass-produced electrical appliances.

In the beginning, man relied on tools, his 'personal' belongings, which subsequent-ly were changed into 'inhuman' machines.

But, the new mass-produced goods centred around electrical appliances reinjected the human touch into the machines.

Convinced that this was a chance to revive humanity in a mechanized civiliza-tion, industrial designer Kenji Ikuan designed a house with rooms functioning as tools. He treated a house in terms of a multi-tool complex, similar to the concept of the multi-structure complex in the field of architecture.

At the same time, Mr. Ekuan advocates the construction of 'Habita City', com-plete with groups of mass-produced prefabricated houses surrounding open spaces.

This may be likened to a sponge under-going a transition from a unicellular to a multicellular creature. It is important to discover a more modernized mode of housing to give full satisfaction to the inhabitants.

Inasmuch as the quality not the size of metapolis is our problem, super-struc-tures may not necessarily be a requisite. Plane architecture may also have to be taken into consideration.

With regards to recreational facilities, Noriaki Kurokawa unveiled a circular plan in which nature was introduced. He assumes that the circles will be linked linearly and he likens each circle to a cell.

In the Kurokawa-designed 'cell city', shopping districts will be completed with nature inside and form circles. Furthermore, housing areas will form a nucleus.

These houses will be developed and across the shopping districts, will be linked with each other.

This is a completely visionary plan, but the idea is being incorporated in the Seto New Town which will shortly be com-pleted in the suburbs of Nagoya City. Under this programme, housing areas will form circles and taking advantage of their hilly surroundings, will be grouped around small hills.

Public facilities and shopping districts will be utilized to link the circles to achieve development.

The 'Metabolism' group decided to explore the future of contemporary civilization on the theme of the meta-morphic force.

But we are yet to find an answer to the question as to what such civilization will mean to man. That most probably will be the theme for us in the period beginning in 1970.

We are planning to call this the theme of metempsychosis. This term has been chosen, because we believe that mankind has reached the stage of 'metapolis' following a variety of changes since primitive times, thereby achieving a historical regression toward the archetype mode of dwelling.

We often employ biological terms such as 'metabolism' and 'metamorphosis' because man has evolved from a living creature and what he creates in the form of cities or civilization should necessarily be linked to the principles of life. Tra-ditionally, this has been an idea charac-teristic of the Orient.

After 1970, we will begin to examine humanity itself on the basis of the Oriental philosophy of metempsychosis.

Kevin Lynch

Metropolitan Form[31]

The increasing size of our metropolitan areas and the speed with which we traverse them raise many new problems for perception. The metropolitan region is now the functional unit of our environment, and it is desirable that this functional unit should be identified and structured by its inhabitants. The new means of communication which allow us to live and work in such a large interdependent region, could also allow us to make our images commensurate with our experiences. Such jumps to new levels of attention have occurred in the past, as jumps were made in the functional organization of life.

Total imageability of an extensive area such as a metropolitan region would not mean an equal intensity of image at every point. There would be dominant figures and more extensive backgrounds, focal points, and connective tissue. But, whether intense or neutral, each part would presumably be clear, and clearly linked to the whole. We can speculate that metropolitan images could be formed of such elements as high-speed highways, transit lines or airways; large regions with coarse edges of water or open space; major shopping nodes; basic topographic features; perhaps massive, distant landmarks.

The problem is none the less difficult, however, when it comes to composing a pattern for such an entire area. There are two techniques with which we are familiar. First, the entire region may be composed as a static hierarchy. For example, it might be organized as a major district containing three sub-districts, which each contain three sub-sub-districts, and so on. Or as another example of hierarchy, any given part of the region might focus on a minor node, these minor nodes being satellite to a major node, while all the major nodes are arranged to culminate in a single primary node for the region.

The second technique is the use of one or two very large dominant elements, to which many smaller things may be related: the siting of settlement along a sea-coast, for example; or the design of a linear town depending on a basic communication spine. A large environment might even be radially related to a very powerful landmark, such as a central hill.

Both these techniques seem somewhat inadequate to the metropolitan problem. The hierarchical system, while congenial to some of our habits of abstract thinking, would seem to be a denial of the freedom and complexity of linkages in a metropolis. Every connection must be made in a roundabout, conceptual fashion: up to a generality and back to a particular, even though the bridging generality may have little to do with the real connection. It is the unity of a library, and libraries require the constant use of a bulky cross-referencing system. Dependence on a strong dominant element, while giving a much more immediate sense of relation and continuity, becomes more difficult as the environment increases in size, since a dominant element must be found that is big enough to be in scale with its task, and has enough 'surface area' so that all the minor elements can have some reasonably close relation to it. Thus one needs a big river, for example, that winds enough to allow all settlements to be fairly near its course.

Nevertheless, these are two possible methods, and it would be useful to investigate their success in unifying large environments. Air travel may simplify the problem again, since it is (in perceptual terms) a static rather than a dynamic experience, an opportunity to see a metropolitan area almost at a glance.

Considering our present way of experiencing a large urban area, however, one is drawn toward another kind of organization: that of sequence, or temporal pattern. This is a familiar idea in music, drama, literature, or dance. Therefore it is relatively easy to conceive of, and study, the form of a sequence of events along a line, such as the succession of elements that might greet a traveller on an urban highway. With some attention, and proper tools, this experience could be made meaningful and well shaped. It is also possible to handle the question of reversibility, i.e. the fact that most paths are traversed in both directions. The series of elements must have sequential form taken in either order, which might be accomplished by symmetry about the midpoint, or in more sophisticated ways. But the city problem continues to raise difficulties. Sequences are not only reversible, but are broken in upon at many points. A carefully constructed sequence, leading from introduction, first statement, and development to climax and conclusion, may fail utterly if a driver enters it directly at the climax point. Therefore it may be necessary to look for sequences which are interruptible as well as reversible, that is, sequences which still have sufficient imageability even when broken in upon at various points, much like a magazine serial. This might lead us from the classic start-climax-finish form to others which are more like the essentially endless, and yet continuous and variegated, patterns of jazz.

These considerations refer to organization along a single line of movement. An urban region might then be organized by a network of such organized sequences, any proposed form being tested to see if each major path, in each direction and from each entry point, was possessed of a formed sequence of elements. This is conceivable when the paths have some simple pattern such as radial convergence. It becomes more difficult to image where the network is a diffuse and intersecting one, as in a gridiron. Here the sequences work in four different directions throughout the map. Although on a much more sophisticated scale, this is akin to the problem of timing a progressive traffic-light system over a network.

It is even conceivable that one might compose in counterpoint along these lines, or from one line to another. One sequence of elements, or 'melody', might be played against a counter-sequence. Perhaps, however, such techniques would wait upon a time when there is a more attentive and critical audience.

Even this dynamic method, the organization of a network of formed sequences, does not yet seem ideal. The environment is still not being treated as a whole but rather as a collection of parts (the sequences) arranged so as not to interfere with each other. Intuitively, one could imagine that there might be a way of creating a whole pattern, a pattern that would only gradually be sensed and developed by sequential experiences, reversed and interrupted as they might be. Although felt as a whole, it would not need to be a highly unified pattern with a single centre or an isolating boundary. The principal quality would be sequential continuity in which each part flows from the next—a sense of interconnectedness at any level or in any direction. There would be particular zones that for any one individual might be more intensely felt or organized, but the region would be continuous, mentally traversable in any order. This possibility is a highly speculative one: no satisfactory concrete examples come to mind.

Perhaps this pattern of a whole cannot exist. In that case, the previously mentioned techniques remain as possibilities in the organization of large regions: the hierarchy, the dominant element of the network of sequences. Hopefully, these techniques would require no more than the metropolitan planning controls now sought for other reasons, but this also remains to be seen.

Eckhard Schulze-Fielitz

The Space City[32]

As a result of the machine's ability to multiply and the rapidly increasing population figures, our age has acquired a dynamic trend towards mass production; the need is quantity and quality with the minimum effort. But a raised standard of living through standardization seems dearly bought with the growing monotony of our industrially manufactured environment and restriction of freedom of decision. The ever-growing army of machines and automata will relieve man of an ever-increasing proportion of manual labour; electronic brains are taking over intellectual drudgery. But machines manufacture serial products, elements, and we shall have to tell them which elements; we shall have to test their capacity for combination. New materials will demand new systems of combination.

The systematization of space is a precondition for the spatial combination of standardized parts and hence a basic principle of prefabrication.

Despite rigid systematization, spatial modular co-ordination offers great freedom of choice and arrangement and hence a synthesis of the only apparently mutually exclusive tendencies of mass production and individual multiplicity. Interchangeability of spatially co-ordinated quanta offers flexibility and adaptation in dynamic developments. Serial building will be influenced by geometry, topology, group theory and the principles of combination.

The space structure is a macro-material capable of modulation, analogous to an intellectual model in physics, according to which the wealth of phenomena can be reduced to a few elementary particles. The physical material is a discontinuum of whole-number units, molecules, atoms, elementary particles. Their combinational possibilities determine the characteristics of the material.

It is modulation of the spatial structure

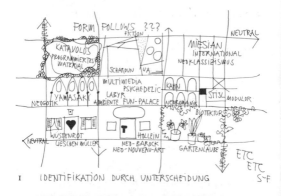

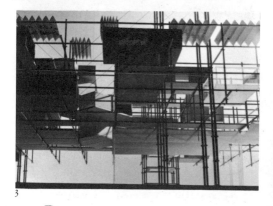

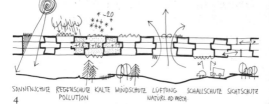

1. Eckhard Schulze-Fielitz, Sketch for the Space City. 'Although the Space City, will be based on a three-dimensional system of coordinates incorporating a spatial grid so as to facilitate organization and orientation, the end product will be so diversified that there will still be room for individuality and anarchy.'
2. Eckhard Schulze-Fielitz, Space City, 1960.
3, 4. Eckhard Schulze-Fielitz, later version of the Space City.

according to kind, size, material, and position that permits us to take the daring step of presenting it as a comprehensive means of town-planning. The space city is a discontinuous continuum, discontinuous through the demarcation between the part and the whole, continuous through the unalterable possibilities of alteration. In a free society the perfect planning of a city is neither possible nor desirable; it means fixation that impedes unpredictable developments.

The Space City, on the other hand, is an agglomeration of various spatial structures in pursuance of development; the ductus of the structure steers the unavoidable proliferation into ordered channels; freedom lies in the infinite possibilities of combination.

When the details are suitably designed, co-ordination of measurement permits the mutual interchange of all parts. This makes possible solution of the basic dilemma between the dynamic of urban life and the static of the built structure. Electronic calculating centres will examine the static and organizational conditions calling for change; automatic factories will produce the material substance of the city.

Multi-storey inhabited spatial carrying structures will bridge over great spans by their static height. In the centres of density the city will rise up from the ground, leaving the latter to mechanical transport. The possibility of greater density, building over traffic areas and watercourses, keeping whole stretches free for flowing or stationary traffic, the strict segregation of types of traffic, make possible solution of the problems of circulation in centres of traffic concentration. The smallest possible number of obstacles stand in the way of traffic and its unforeseeable development, thereby avoiding from the outset the majority of the problems we face today. On the other hand, the space city creates a continuous, three-dimensional public space which was lost when the motorcar perverted streets and squares

into motorways and parking lots. A three-dimensional system of coordinates identical with a spatial grid will facilitate organization and orientation in the space city, yet the multiplicity of the possible material forms it can take leaves room for individuality and anarchy. Thanks to the ordering of space, the architectural substance is adaptable to every topographical datum, absorbing, altering, levelling, or raising it.

The Space City accompanies the profile of the landscape as a crystalline layer; it is itself a landscape, comparable to geological formations with peaks and valleys, ravines and plateaux, comparable to the leafy area of the forest with its branches. To regenerate existing cities, structures will stretch above their degenerate sections and cause them to fall into disuse.

Consistency of these ideas demands that property or exploitation rights shall no longer—in pursuance of the agricultural tradition—be related to the surface area (as the medium of agricultural production) but to utilizable space. The compact city offers possibilities of an improved heating economy, a self-air-conditioning; in the future it will even permit a controlled internal climate of the city, which could radically reduce the cost of insulating the individual building. The space city is the structural, systematized, prefabricated, growing or shrinking, adaptable, air-conditioned, multipurpose space labyrinth that can be fitted together or taken apart at will.

Paolo Soleri

Arcology[33]

Architecture is in the process of becoming the physical definition of a multilevel, human ecology. It will be arc-ology. Arcology, instrumented by science and technology, will be an aestheto-compassionate phenomenon. Its advent will be the implosion of the flat megalopolis of today into an urban solid of superdense and human vitality.

1. Arcology, or Ecological Architecture
This is the definition of urban structures so 'dense' as to host life, work, education, culture, leisure, and health for hundreds of thousands of people per square mile. The weak veneer of life ridden with blight and stillness, which megalopolis and suburbia are, is thus transformed and miniaturized into a metropolitan solid, saturated with flux and liveliness.

2. Arcology and Man
Man, a creature of culture, is given such instrumentality as to have his reach greatly incremented. Education, culture, production, service, health, play, and an untouched countryside are at his fingertips. He can walk to them from his home, the place where he is master and the place he can define and construct by himself if he so pleases.

3. Arcology and Change
As for the cities we have, we will live with them. We cannot live for them. Thus, while effort will go into improving what we have, great and persistent effort must go into the development, parallel to the condemned patterns, of new systems coherent with man's needs. Arcology is, in short, an efficient plumbing system for contemporary society.

4. Arcology and Dimension
The squandering in land, time, energy, and the wealth of megalopolis and

suburbia, now well entangled in their increasing contradictions, is rejected as obsolete. With arcology there are two conditions: (1) immense nature: extensive, kind, and brutal, the reservoir of life; and (2) the man-made: dense, organized, powerful, and serving man well. With the third dimension, the vertical, no longer a limitless sea of housing in a choked system of dim vitality, man is reinstated as the measure of things and primarily as the compassionate measure of himself and nature.

5. Arcology and Scale
Scale is that characterization that makes the performance effort congruous with the aim.

The configuration that makes it impossible for the hungry man to sit at the bountiful table is a configuration that is not human. Dimension, proportions, and visual grasp are subordinate categories made human or inhuman by the amount of real reaching power they offer to the individual. A building or a city are out of scale with the people they serve when the function they promise is put out of the realm of the possible. Arcology is both dimensionally (one cubic kilometre as against four hundred square miles) and functionally on the human scale without loss of its awesome force, indeed almost because of it.

6. Arcology and Distance
Distance is a tax on reaching power. By the aberration of the car, such a tax is starving our culture. The car is dividing things more and more by scattering them all over. Then one finds that it becomes more and more difficult to reach them one by one, impossible to reach them all in one. Acceleration-deceleration, natural sluggishness, and the antiswiftness inherent to scatterization make high speed urban transportation a perpetual illusion.
In arcology, distances are measured again by walks and in minutes. Within it the car is nonsensical. It has nowhere to go.

7. Arcology and Land Conservation
The compactness of arcology gives back to farming and to land conservation ninety per cent or more of the land that megalopolis and suburbia are engulfing in their sprawl. To be a city dweller and a country man at one and the same time, to be able to partake fully of both city and country life, will make the arcology a place in which man will want to live. The creation of truly lovable cities is the only lasting solution for land conservation.

8. Arcology and Natural Resources
The reserves of ores and fuels are not infinite. The squandering of such collective capital wealth, while proclaiming the sacredness of exclusive and personal possession, is irrational, to say the least. Chemistry and biochemistry might find a magnificent future for such resources. By then most of these will be reduced to the second-rate pockets that will have escaped man's greed. The frugal character of arcology moves consumption toward the use of the earth's income rather than the exhaustion of its capital.

9. Arcology and Industry
The destructive bite of the car on the U.S. economy and life will not last another fifteen years, nor will the Pentagon's ravenous hunger for war hardware. The car will follow the horse to the pastures of sport and eccentricity. War hardware will destroy us or will be destroyed by us.
There is the colossal and challenging task of punctuating the earth's landscape with a humane, beautiful 'culturescape'. Each arcology will be an industry in itself with its original standardizations, its automated systems, a cybernetic organism growing of its own volition. It will be an industry turned forward instead of backward.

10. Arcology and Pollution
We are concerned with the immediate menaces of pollution, but the long-term consequences escape us. These may well reach into our genetic structure as well as into the total geophysical and biochemical balance of the planet.
In arcology the ratio of efficiency to energy becomes many times greater, thus pollution will be manyfold smaller. Pollution is a direct function of wastefulness. The elimination of wastefulness is the elimination of pollution.

11. Arcology and Climate
For both extremes of heat and cold, as for any intermediate condition, the compactness of arcology makes it a most workable system. Instead of sealing the outside out, conditioning will extend to the ground, space, and the air enveloping the structure. The climate of the arcology, not a sealed cell but an open city, will be a tamed facsimile of the regional climate.

12. Arcology and Waste
As a sprawled-out man twenty square feet in area and three inches tall can work only on paper, if at all, so possibly can our megalopoly and suburbias work only on paper. They will never truly and substantially work for real. They are not real. They are utopian. Arcology can be a congruous system and, as such, an optimum system for the full and complex logistics of individual and social life.

13. Arcology and Cost
The initial cost of research and experimentation is by necessity high. A radical turn is never inexpensive. The actual planning and production cost of an arcology would be a fraction of the cost of our gigantic dwarfs for equal population, but not equal fullness, of life.

14. Arcology and Obsolescence
Flexibility and dynamism cannot be found where there is built-in obsolescence (a downgraded system is by nature inflexible). These are to be found where the full flow of life runs throughout a structure. If the tempo of obsolescence

has the same beat as individual growth—childhood, youth, maturity, age—the individual himself is obsolete. The precariousness of his significance will destroy him. Arcology is a mirror of man's identity and a support to his doings.

15. Arcology and Underdeveloped Countries
With arcology comes the possibility of leaping beyond the mechanical age into the cybernetic culture and thus the chance of avoiding the robotization of men, the blight of the environment, the slavery of the car, the starvation of culture, all scourges of our Western success story.

16. Arcology and Leisure
A cybernetic system of immediate feedback with information, communication, transportation, and transfer quickened by shrunken distances, is an organism for true leisure.
For many, if not most, of the citizens such leisure will be voluntary work at the enrichment of the city, starting from one's own home and reaching throughout the infrastructure of the whole city. This will be a totally new challenge for artists, performers, craftsmen, and the engaged citizenry.

17. Arcology and Segregation
Segregation concerns not only ethnics and religions. It concerns activities and all age levels as well as it concerns, and stills, life itself. A social pattern is influenced, if not directed, by the physical pattern that shelters it. In a one-container system are the best premises for a non-segregated culture. The care for oneself will tend to be care for the whole.

18. Arcology, Aggression, and Guilt
Aggression and guilt are in good proportion a bridge of a sort connecting meaninglessness to meaningfulness. Therefore a better bridge must be found. If man is really in need of risk and violence, if frustration and guilt are really tearing society asunder, then the awesomeness of arcology and the complexity of its construction are positive alternatives to war, social strife, and squalor.

19. Arcology and Medical Care
In arcology there is interchangeability and diffusion of functions because the obstacles of time and space are minimized, miniaturized. As all of arcology can be called a market-place, all of it a learning organism, all of it a productive mechanism and a playground, so in a true sense arcology can be considered a total medical-care system. Home nursing becomes as feasible and as professional as hospital care, but far less costly and far more personal. Nurses and doctors move from home to home, as from ward to ward, making the family doctor real again. Infirmaries, clinics, and hospitals are always at walking distance, leaving no pockets of indifference (if not those maliciously wanted) that might be maliciously ignored.

20. Arcology and Survival
To pinpoint an orbital warhead on a square mile or so is a feat for the not-too-distant future. Evacuation in arcology can be almost instantaneous; its vast underground structure for foundations, anchorages, and automated industries will be good emergency systems. Arcology is the coherent expression of a faith in man, and as such it is beyond the survival platform.

21. Arcology and the Underground
Man must refute underground living. He is a biological animal of sun, air, light, and seasons. He is an aesthetic animal, and his senses are more and more oriented toward a usefulness of purely aesthetic worth.
The underground is ideal for automated production in need of technologically sophisticated environment: pressure, vacuum, radiation, heat, cold, rare atmospheres, and so forth. (It is also ideal for sense-less and senseless man.)

22. Arcology and Spaces
Man has been experiencing what one might call flat spaces. It is congruous with the space age itself that man acquaints himself and lives with the deep spaces an arcology creates.
As man lives intensely on the horizontal, the density of his societies can only be achieved vertically.

23. Arcology and Space
If we are destined to a 'space' life of some sort, this life will be miniaturized by necessity. In arcology are the elements of interiorization, living inside instead of on top, and of compactness. In this sense arcology is a space architecture as much as it is a land and sea architecture.

24. Arcology and the Sacred
Limitless energies in limitless spaces for limitless time are the scattered ingredients by which nature works. For man to succeed, he must make tight bundles of that minimal portion of them allowed to him so that his own infinity—the infinite complexity of his compassionate and aesthetic universe—can blossom. Life is literally in the thick of things. Its sacramentality is in the awesome power concealed in its 'densified' fragility.

25. Arcology and Geriatrics
One of the ravages of 'mobility', or at least directly accountable to it, is the institutionalized ghetto for the elderly. Following the generalized scattering of things and thoughts, the family has broken down into four main fragments: the young, the parents, the grandparents, and the anonymous relative. Aging being common to all (the lucky ones), all will have a taste of the tragic segregation of the aged; the insurance company and social security will not do, lest men become or remain marketable goods.
The implications of 'arcological life' are the most favourable for reintegration of the different age groups and thus for the knitting of family strands.

26. Arcology and Play

The playground is the act of condescending to playfulness in a habitat where grimness, ugliness, and danger are endemic and offer the last measure of unconcern in an adult world gone sour. The playground is segregative. The absence of children in the so-called respectable public places is disheartening. The child has reason to become irresponsible and destructive, caged, as he is, away from the 'other world.' Arcology is an 'environmental toy'. As a miniaturized universe it offers unending elements for surprise and stimulation. There will not be fenced-in playgrounds. The whole city is the place where the child is acting out the learning process, one aspect of which is play.

27. Arcology and Youth

The rift between youth and the holders of power, from the home up to the nation's policy-makers, parallels the schism that exists between the preaching and the doing of the elders. The flow of hypocrisy is constant and perhaps irresistible. The revolt is at times blind, at times cynical, but it is a matter of survival within the limits of self-respect. If mere survival is to be dislodged by hopefulness, a form of things to come has to be suggested that will not drift away in the sea of the faceless, the irrelevant, and the expedient. As the god of the past 'illserves' imperfect man and technology may yet cancel his humaneness, a step toward realism at the expense of powerful but conservative, if not reactionary, 'practicality' is what the young may need most.
Arcology is a container where ideas and vision can meet man in his quest for a structure for living and not just an amorphous container for depersonalized survival.

28. Arcology, the Practical and the Real

The function of the practical is to instrumentalize the real. The function of the real is to dictate why, what, where, and when the practical is to operate. This antimaterialistic tenet is lost in the feverish idolatry of the feasible and the license of 'free' enterprise. Most of what is feasible is irrelevant or unreal. It is not real because it does not converge with the aims of free man. The practical is no longer the specially tempered tip of a willfully driven utensil but is instead a vain, aimless, and squalid façade imposed upon the well burdened train of the real. The real is to be sought by the skill of the practical. The practical is a subskill whenever it is enthroned on the idol's chair. Arcology rejects as totally unreal the practicality of such a bigoted position.

29. Arcology and Identification

The capacity of suburbia and megalopolis for unending sprawl, the amorphism caused by the lack of structuralization, the blurring of everything into the countless makes the identification of the individual as difficult as the identification of the environment. What one reflects in, one is or one tends to become. Arcology is physical identification. The whole of it is at grasp and unmistakable, while the detail in its secretiveness can be unlimited and ever changing.

30. Arcology and Culture

To be exposed early in life to the complex workings of the individual and of society, to have a substantial reach for all those things and institutions that make metropolitan life rewarding, to be able at the same time to seek and be in the midst of nature, to enjoy the limitless and meaningful variety the life of society may produce for itself and the individual are all built-in characteristics of arcology. Arcology is the largest cultural whole physically available to men day in and day out.

31. Arcology and Aesthetics

The beauty of nature is achieved in the awesome reservoirs of space and time where things are hammered out in the order that probability dictates, justly, rationally, impassionately. The genesis of man-made beauty, the aesthetic, is of a different nature. It is not incidental to man's action but is the very essence of man himself. By necessity it has to be frugal. It does away with probability and predictability. It is synthetic and transfigurative. It is never irrational because it is always superrational. It cannot simply be just, because it must also be compassionate.
With the aesthetogenesis of nature, man reaches into the structure of reality and forms a new universe in his own image. Arcology can be one of these forms. Arcology is essentially an aesthetocompassionate phenomenon.

32. Arcology and Politics

The long involvements of the generations that have produced today's cities constitute such tightly interwoven interests that the hopes are very dim for a really purposeful renewal.
What has been the living cause has become very much that which takes life away. Too many things in our cities are spent cartridges, too little is of a nonbrittle nature. Even doodling around any of the city's many problems tends to weaken this or that interest or this or that group. And doodling seems to be what at best we do with them. An urban culture is per se the nth power of complexity. The burden of a not-too-glorious past may be just the amount of ballast that will not allow the take-off.

33. Arcology and Miniaturization

In its evolution from matter to mind, the real has been submitted to numerous phases of miniaturization so as to fit more things into smaller spaces in shorter times. This process, from haphazardness and dislocation to coordination and fitness, has been mandatory because each successive form of reality carried in itself a greater degree of complexity. Any higher organism contains more performances than a chunk of the unlimited universe light years thick, and it ticks on a time clock immensely swifter. This miniaturization process may well be one of the fundamental rules of evolution. Now that the inquietude of man is turned to the construction of the superorganism, which society is, a new phase of miniaturization is imperative. Arcology is a step toward it. Arcological miniaturization will cause the scale of the earth to 'expand' and will also make feasible the migration of man to the seas and orbital lands. The orbital lands will also function as transformers of the earth's climate. The population explosion will then have different meanings. Both terrestrial and extra-terrestrial towns and cities will be arcological.

34. Arcology and Symmetry

There are, among others, the following three kinds of symmetry: structural symmetry, functional symmetry, and formal symmetry. Structural symmetry is probably observed throughout the universe. It is the necessary balancing of stresses that finds its patterns around points, lines, planes, and spaces of symmetry.

Functional symmetry is observed very clearly in any organism, be it monocellular or highly composite. Functional symmetry is the direct solution to the constant wavering of the energy balances composing the living organism and its non-symmetrical behaviour. Without such symmetry the organism would be constantly lopsided, that is to say, unfit for life. Formal symmetry might well be the imprint of all other kinds of symmetry into the mind and the sensitivity of man. Even if the impositions of structure and function were lifted, impositions that result in formal symmetry, there would still linger in man the need for a visual and in general sensorial symmetry.

The greater the symmetry, the greater the vitality of the performance. Arcology is not an exception, especially when one considers the enormous structural and functional complexity involved. It is never symmetrical for the individual user. In other words, the individual user is always eccentric to the whole: symmetry in the whole, singularity in the parts.

35. Arcology and Mobility

Structure defines a certain configuration suited to a particular set of performances. Urban planning supposedly defines that structure which channels, contains, and swiftens the performances of society. Mobility in society does not reside in migratory waves but in the minute and perpetual shifting of bodies, functions, relationships, and mental processes of the body-social. To suppose that lack of structure favours mobility is tantamount to saying that a disintegrating corpse can function as a living body. To suppose furthermore that tenuity can favour mobility is like saying that nature was foolish in inventing almost exclusively three-dimensional organisms.

The explicit structurality of arcology and its three-dimensional congruence are, at least potentially, the basis for full and pragmatic mobility. In arcology coercive mobility is unnecessary—the kind of mobility, commuting for instance, that orders and pushes people and things around. (The penalty for non-cooperation is the loss of man's source of livelihood.) Unburdened of coercive mobility, free and functional mobility obtains the necessary elbow room for the full display of its dynamics.

36. Arcology and the Biological

An animal is an organism of one mind. The city is an organism of one thousand minds. This is the most significant difference between a biological organism and the city. Furthermore, those one thousand minds do not stay put. They are eminently peripatetic, but in clusters of three or four or so (the family) they tend to define a territoriality that is more static (the home). What confronts the planner is the organization of the body to the satisfaction of the thousand minds. One may say that while an inner centre, the brain, is the centre to which the body renders service biologically, urbanistically the epidermis made up of a thousand brains is the 'centre' to which the body is dedicated.

The mental processes of the biological entity are centralized and interiorized; the mental processes of the city are diffuse and epidermal. While the skin is prevalently a defensive and containing device for the animal body, for the city it is eminently a casual, ontological structure. The miniaturizing implosion of the social body is thus accompanied by a micro-explosion of the thousand brains toward the periphery of the miniaturized organism. The mental, installed within its biological receptacle (the individual), places itself in the skin where its senses can capture both the natural vastness of the outer and the man-made miniaturization of the inner. This is a description of arcology.

37. Arcology and Cybernation

The urban organism has a new tool on hand. It can delegate to a non-biological brain some of its labours. This non-biological brain can be collectivized and can be interiorized because it does not belong to a body, to any body. Then the parallel between the biological and the urban is modified. In the biological, the brain and the body are single and almost certainly spatially coincidental. In the urban organism, the brain may be imagined as split: one part is the group of the single brains, each belonging to individuals; the other part is the collectivized non-biological brain ideally centred in the organism.

In the urban organism, the mind remains in independent but correlated parcels divided spatially and coincidental with the parcelled brains, the whole forming the mental or thinking skin of the city. In the function of the urban organism the implosion of the whole performance is paralleled by the parcelling of the mind-brain toward the skin, leaving in the 'cranial box' a shadow brain which is mechanically and chemically composed and not biologically developed. Such a centralized brain cares for the collective and instrumental functions while individual minds govern the pluralism inherent in the whole organism. Arcology is such an organism.

Notes

1 Arno Plack, Article in: *Die Weltwoche* (Zürich), 12 September 1969.

2 *Project METRAN—An Integrated, Evolutionary Transportation System for Urban Areas,* Cambridge, Mass. 1966 (M.I.T. Report, 8).

3 Hans Paul Bahrdt, *Die moderne Großstadt—Soziologische Überlegungen zum Städtebau,* Hamburg 1969.

4 Hans Paul Bahrdt, *op. cit.*

5 Pierre Bertaux, *Mutation der Menschheit—Zukunft und Lebenssinn,* Munich n. d.

6 Wolf Schneider, *Überall ist Babylon,* Düsseldorf 1960.

7 Jane Jacobs, *Death and Life of Great American Cities,* New York 1961.

8 Georgy Kepes, 'The Lost Pageantry of Nature', *artscanada,* 124–127.

9 Kevin Lynch, *The Image of the City,* Cambridge, Mass. 1960.

10 Alexander Tzonis, 'Transformations of the Initial Structure', *Perspecta* (New Haven), 12.

11 Henry van Lier, *Architecture Synergique,* Brussels n. d. (*Cahiers du Centre d' Etudes Architecturales,* 4).

12 Richard Buckminster Fuller, *Die Aussichten der Menschheit 1965–1985 (The Prospect for Humanity),* Frankfurt/M. and Berlin, 1968 (German original).

13 Alexander Mitscherlich (Ed.), *Das beschädigte Leben,* Munich 1969.

14 Reyner Banham, 'A Clip-on Architecture', *Architectural Design* (London), 1965, 11.

15 Richard Buckminster Fuller, *op. cit.*

16 Günther Feuerstein, 'Hantierung und Manipulation', *TRANSPARENT* (Vienna), 1970, 1.

17 Holger Lueder, 'Neue Mittel und Wege zu einer biologisch angemessenen und wirtschaftlichen Klimatisierung von Gebäuden', *Elektrizitätsverwertung,* 1969, 3/4.

18 Christopher Alexander, 'A City is not a Tree', *Design* (London), 1967, 7.

19 Hans Paul Bahrdt, *op. cit.*

20 David Georges Emmerich, *Exercices de géométrie constructive—Travaux d'étudiants,* Paris 1970.

21 Quoted from: *Architectural Design* (London), 1967, 3.

22 Paolo Soleri, *The City in the Image of Man,* Cambridge, Mass. and London 1969.

23 Manifesto, 1960; quoted from: Ulrich Conrads (Ed.), *Programmes and Manifestoes on Twentieth-Century Architecture,* London and Cambridge, Mass. 1970.

24 Paper given to the 'Environment and Architecture' Conference, London, October 1969.

25 Comments to the project 'Kiryat Ono'.

26 Condensed version prepared by the author of a lecture given at the Max-Planck-Institut, Munich, in November 1970 entitled 'Arch-a-itektur und Architektur / Biologie und Bauen'.

27 Slightly condensed text of 5 September 1970.

28 Extract from a lecture held in Tel-Aviv in December 1967 entitled 'Design Science-Engineering, an Economic Success of all Humanity'.

29 Quoted from: Ulrich Conrads (Ed.), *op. cit.* and *Quadrat-Prints*.

30 Manuscript.

31 Kevin Lynch, *op. cit.*

32 Manifesto, 1960; quoted from: Ulrich Conrads (Ed.), *op. cit.*

33 Paolo Soleri, *op. cit.*

Bibliography

Christopher Alexander, 'A City is not a Tree', *Design* (London), 1967, 7.

Hans Paul Bahrdt, *Die moderne Großstadt—Soziologische Überlegungen zum Städtebau,* Hamburg 1969.

Reyner Banham, 'A Clip-on Architecture', *Architectural Design* (London), 1965, 11.

Pierre Bertaux, *Mutation der Menschheit—Zukunft und Lebenssinn,* Munich n. d.

Robert Boguslaw, *The New Utopians—A Study of Design and Social Change,* Englewood, N. J. 1963.

Cahiers du Centre d'Etudes Architecturales, Brussels.

Serge Chermayeff and Christopher Alexander, *Community and Privacy—Towards a New Architecture of Humanism,* New York 1963.

Ulrich Conrads (Ed.), *Programmes and Manifestoes on Twentieth-Century Architecture,* Cambridge, Mass. and London 1970.

Peter Cook, *Architecture: Action and Plan,* London and New York 1967.

Peter Cook, *Experimental Architecture,* London 1970.

David Georges Emmerich, *Exercices de géométrie constructive—Travaux d'étudiants,* Paris 1970.

Günther Feuerstein, 'Hantierung und Manipulation', *TRANSPARENT* (Vienna), 1970, 1.

Richard Buckminster Fuller, *Die Aussichten der Menschheit 1965–1985 (The Prospect for Humanity),* Frankfurt/M. and Berlin 1968 (German original).

Herbert J. Gans, *The Levittowners—Ways of Life and Politics in a New Suburban Community,* New York 1967.

Jane Jacobs, *Death and Life of Great American Cities,* New York 1961.

Georgy Kepes, 'The Lost Pageantry of Nature', *artscanada,* 124–127.

Kevin Lynch, *The Image of the City,* Cambridge, Mass. 1960.

Project METRAN—An Integrated, Evolutionary Transportation System for Urban Areas, Cambridge, Mass. 1966 (*M.I.T. Report,* 8).

Alexander Mitscherlich (Ed.), *Das beschädigte Leben,* Munich 1969.

Sibyl Moholy-Nagy, *Matrix of Man—An Illustrated History of Urban Environment,* New York and London 1968.

Georg Picht, *Mut zur Utopie—Die großen Zukunftsaufgaben—12 Vorträge,* Munich 1970.

Michel Ragon, *La Cité de l'an 2000,* Tournai 1968.

Michel Ragon, *Où vivrons-nous demain?,* Paris 1963.

Norbert Schmidt-Relenberg, *Soziologie und Städtebau—Versuch einer systematischen Grundlegung,* Stuttgart 1969.

Wolf Schneider, *Überall ist Babylon,* Düsseldorf 1960.

Arnold Toynbee (Ed.), *Cities on the Move,* Oxford 1970.

Alexander Tzonis, 'Transformations of the Initial Structure', *Perspecta* (New Haven), 12.

Bernard Willms, *Planungsideologie und revolutionäre Utopie—Die zweifache Flucht in die Zukunft,* Stuttgart 1969.

Selected Texts on Individual Architects

Susumi Abukawa
Architectural Design (London), 1967, 5. *Deutsche Bauzeitung* (Stuttgart), 1968, 10. *The Japan Architect* (Tokyo), 127 (1967, 1/2).

Katsuhiko Akimitsu
Deutsche Bauzeitung (Stuttgart), 1968, 10. *The Japan Architect* (Tokyo), 137 (1967, 12).

Tetsuya Akiyama
Architectural Design (London), 1967, 5. *Deutsche Bauzeitung* (Stuttgart), 1968, 10. *The Japan Architect* (Tokyo), 127 (1967, 1/2).

Yoshitaka Akui
Architectural Design (London), 1964, 10. *L'architecture d'aujourd'hui* (Boulogne), 98 (1961, 10).

Edouard Albert
l'architecture d'aujourd'hui (Boulogne), 131 (1967, 4/5).

Tadaaki Anzai
Deutsche Bauzeitung (Stuttgart), 1968, 10. *The Japan Architect* (Tokyo), 137 (1967, 12).

Archigram
ARCHIGRAM (London). *The Architect's Journal* (London), Vol. 152, No. 35 (2 September 1970). *Architectural Design* (London), 1965, 11; 1967, 3; 1968, 5; 1969, 5; 1971, 8. *l'architecture d'aujourd'hui* (Boulogne), 139 (1968, 9). *Bauen + Wohnen* (Munich and Zürich), 1967, 5. Peter Cook, *Experimental Architecture,* London 1970. *Hogar y Arquitectura* (Madrid), 72 (1967, 9/10).

André Birò
Architecture Formes Fonctions (Lausanne), 12 (1965/6). *l'architettura* (Milan), 167 (1969, 9).

Alan Boutwell
l'architecture d'aujourd'hui (Boulogne), 148 (1970, 2/3).

Fabrizio Carola
domus (Milan), 447 (1967, 2).

Warren Chalk
ARCHIGRAM (London), 6. *Architectural Design* (London), 1965, 11. *Bauen + Wohnen* (Munich and Zürich), 1967, 5. Peter Cook, *Experimental Architecture,* London 1970. *Hogar y Arquitectura* (Madrid), 72 (1967, 9/10). See also: Archigram.

Chanéac
l'architettura (Milan), 167 (1969, 9). *Bauen + Wohnen* (Munich and Zürich), 1967, 5.

Constant
l'architecture d'aujourd'hui (Boulogne), 102 (1962, 6/7). Ulrich Conrads (Ed.), *Programmes and Manifestoes on Twentieth-century Architecture,* Cambridge, Mass. and London, 1970. *werk* (Winterthur), 1963, 2.

Peter Cook
ARCHIGRAM (London), 5. *Architectural Design* (London), 1965, 11. *Bauen + Wohnen* (Munich and Zürich), 1967, 5. Peter Cook, *Experimental Architecture,* London 1970. *Hogar y Arquitectura* (Madrid), 72 (1967, 9/10). See also: Archigram.

Adrien Courtois
Michel Ragon, *La Cité de l'an 2000,* Tournai 1968.

Jacques Cousteau
l'architecture d'aujourd'hui, 131 (1967, 4/5).

Justus Dahinden
ARCH + (Stuttgart), 3. *l'architecture d'aujourd'hui* (Boulogne), 148 (1970, 2/3). *Architecture Formes Fonctions* (Lausanne), 14 (1968); 16 (1971). *Bauen + Wohnen* (Munich and Zürich), 1971, 7. *Baumeister* (Munich), 1968, 4. Justus Dahinden, *Structures Urbaines,* Brussels (*Cahiers du Centre d'Etudes Architecturales,* in preparation). Justus Dahinden, *Centres Flottants,* Brussels (*Cahiers du Centre d'Etudes Architecturales,* in preparation). *Deutsche Bauzeitschrift* (Gütersloh), 1969, 6. *Kunst und Kirche* (Linz), 1971, 4. W. Meyer-Bohe, *Vorfertigung—Atlas der Systeme,* Essen 1967. *TRANSPARENT* (Vienna), 1971, 7/8.

Dale Dashiell
l'architecture d'aujourd'hui (Boulogne), 148 (1970, 2/3). *Bauen + Wohnen* (Munich and Zürich), 1970, 11. *domus* (Milan), 476 (1969, 7).

Rudolf Doernach
Architectural Design (London), 1966, 2. *möbel interior design* (Stuttgart), 1971, 1.

Günther Domenig
l'architecture d'aujourd'hui (Boulogne), 148 (1970, 2/3). *l'architettura* (Milan), 167 (1969, 9). *Bauen + Wohnen* (Munich and Zürich), 1967, 5. Peter Cook, *Experimental Architecture,* London 1970.

Wolfgang Döring
l'architecture d'aujourd'hui (Boulogne), 148 (1970, 2/3). Peter Cook, *Experimental Architecture,* London 1970. *domus* (Milan), 467 (1968, 10).

David Georges Emmerich
Architectural Design (London), 1964, 10; 1968, 1. *l'architecture d'aujourd'hui* (Boulogne), 110 (1963, 10/11); 141 (1968, 12 / 1969, 1). David Georges Emmerich, *Exercices de géométrie constructive— Travaux d'étudiants,* Paris 1970.

Franz Fehringer
l'architecture d'aujourd'hui (Boulogne), 148 (1970, 2/3).

Jean-Jacques Fernier
Architecture Formes Fonctions (Lausanne), 12 (1965/6). *l'architettura* (Milan), 167 (1969, 9).

Yona Friedman
l'architecture d'aujourd'hui (Boulogne), 102 (1962, 6/7). Ulrich Conrads (Ed.), *Programmes and Manifestoes on Twentieth-century Architecture,* Cambridge, Mass. and London 1970. Peter Cook, *Experimental Architecture,* London 1970. Yona Friedman, *L'Architecture Mobile,* Brussels n.d. (*Cahiers du Centre d'Etudes Architecturales,* 3, 1). Yona Friedman, *Les Mécanismes Urbains,* Brussels n.d. (*Cahiers du Centre d'Etudes Architecturales,* 3, 2). Yona Friedman, *La Planification Urbaine,* Brussels n.d. (*Cahiers du Centre d'Etudes Architecturales,* 6). *werk* (Winterthur), 1963, 2.

Richard Buckminster Fuller
Deutsche Bauzeitung (Stuttgart), 1967, 8. Peter Cook, *Experimental Architecture,* London 1970. Richard Buckminster Fuller, *Die Aussichten der Menschheit 1965–1985,* Frankfurt/M. and Berlin 1968. Robert W. Marks, *The Dymaxion World of Buckminster Fuller,* New York 1960. *Playboy* (Chicago), 1968, 1. *Zodiac* (Milan), 19.

David Greene
Architectural Design (London), 1966, 11. Peter Cook, *Experimental Architecture,* London 1970. See also: Archigram.

Yoshiyuki Haruta
Deutsche Bauzeitung (Stuttgart), 1968, 9. *The Japan Architect* (Tokyo), 137 (1967, 12).

Claude Häusermann
Architecture Formes Fonctions (Lausanne), 12 (1965/6). *l'architettura* (Milan), 167 (1969, 9). Peter Cook, *Experimental Architecture,* London 1970.

Pascal Häusermann
See: Claude Häusermann.

Hausrucker-Co.
Architectural Design (London), 1970, 2. Peter Cook, *Experimental Architecture,* London 1970. *domus* (Milan), 1969, 6. *Neue Architektur in Österreich 1945–1970,* Vienna 1969.

Kunihiko Hayakawa
Deutsche Bauzeitung (Stuttgart), 1968, 10. *The Japan Architect* (Tokyo), 137 (1967, 12).

Zvi Hecker
Zodiac (Milan), 19.

Ron Herron
Architectural Design (London), 1965, 11. Peter Cook, *Experimental Architecture,* London 1970. *Hogar y Arquitectura* (Madrid), 72 (1967, 9/10). See also: Archigram.

Yoichiro Hosaka
l'architecture d'aujourd'hui (Boulogne), 127 (1966, 9).

Hakuji Hoshino
Deutsche Bauzeitung (Stuttgart), 1968, 10. *The Japan Architect* (Tokyo), 137 (1967, 12).

Eilfried Huth
l'architecture d'aujourd'hui (Boulogne), 148 (1970, 2/3). *l'architettura* (Milan), 167 (1969, 9). *Bauen + Wohnen* (Munich and Zürich), 1967, 5. Peter Cook, *Experimental Architecture,* London 1970.

Hiroshi Inagaki
Deutsche Bauzeitung (Stuttgart), 1968, 10. *The Japan Architect* (Tokyo), 137 (1967, 12).

Fumie Innan
Deutsche Bauzeitung (Stuttgart), 1968, 10. *The Japan Architect* (Tokyo), 137 (1967, 12).

Arata Isozaki
Architectural Design (London), 1964, 10. Peter Cook, *Experimental Architecture,* London 1970. *Deutsche Bauzeitung* (Stuttgart), 1968, 10.

Walter Jonas
Architecture Formes Fonctions (Lausanne), 9 (1962).

Jean-Paul Jungmann
Architectural Design (London), 1968, 6. Peter Cook, *Experimental Architecture,* London 1970. *domus* (Milan), 457 (1967, 12).

V. Kalinine
Architecture Formes Fonctions (Lausanne), 14 (1968).

Yan Karczewski
See: Equipe MIASTO.

William Katavolos
l'architecture d'aujourd'hui (Boulogne), 102 (1962, 6/7). *casabella* (Milan), 311 (1966, 11/12).

Yaeko Kawabe
Deutsche Bauzeitung (Stuttgart), 1968, 10. *The Japan Architect* (Tokyo), 137 (1967, 12).

Iwao Kawakami
Architectural Design (London), 1967, 5. *Deutsche Bauzeitung* (Stuttgart), 1968, 10. *The Japan Architect* (Tokyo), 127 (1967, 1/2).

Kikuo Kawasumi
Architectural Design (London), 1967, 5. *Deutsche Bauzeitung* (Stuttgart), 1968, 10. *The Japan Architect* (Tokyo), 127 (1967, 1/2).

Kiyonori Kikutake
Architectural Design (London), 1964, 10; 1967, 5. *Bauen + Wohnen* (Munich and Zürich), 1967, 7. Peter Cook, *Experimental Architecture,* London 1970.
See also: The Metabolists.

Tsutomu Kimura
Deutsche Bauzeitung (Stuttgart), 1968, 10. *The Japan Architect* (Tokyo), 137 (1967, 12).

Yoshiaki Koyama
Architectural Design (London), 1967, 5. *Deutsche Bauzeitung* (Stuttgart), 1968, 10. *The Japan Architect* (Tokyo), 127 (1967, 1/2).

Noriaki Kurokawa
Architectural Design (London), 1964, 10; 1965, 5. *l'architecture d'aujourd'hui* (Boulogne), 101 (1962, 4/5); 148 (1970, 2/3). *casabella* (Milan), 327 (1968, 8). Peter Cook, *Experimental Architecture,* London 1970. *Deutsche Bauzeitung* (Stuttgart), 1968, 10. See also: The Metabolists.

Pierre Lajus
Michel Ragon, *La Cité de l'an 2000,* Tournai 1968.

Michel Lefebvre
See: Equipe MIASTO.

A. J. Lumsden
Deutsche Bauzeitung (Stuttgart), 1967, 9. *Progressive Architecture* (New York), 1966, 1.

Merete Mattern
l'architettura (Milan), 167 (1969, 9). *aujourd'hui* (Boulogne), 57/58 (1967, 10). *Bauwelt* (Berlin), 1967, 1/2.

Paul Maymont
l'architecture d'aujourd'hui (Boulogne), 131 (1967, 4/5). *Architecture Formes Fonctions* (Lausanne), 10 (1963); 12 (1965/6). Peter Cook, *Experimental Architecture,* London 1970.

The Metabolists
Architectural Design (London), 1964, 10; 1967, 5. *Bauen + Wohnen* (Munich and Zürich), 1967, 5. Peter Cook, *Experimental Architecture,* London 1970. *Deutsche Bauzeitung* (Stuttgart), 1968, 10.

Equipe MIASTO
l'architecture d'aujourd'hui (Boulogne), 135 (1967, 12 / 1968, 1). *l'architettura* (Milan), 167 (1969, 9).

Lionel Mirabaud
l'architecture d'aujourd'hui (Boulogne), 102 (1962, 6/7). *Architecture Formes Fonctions* (Lausanne), 9 (1962).

Munehisa Miyazaki
Deutsche Bauzeitung (Stuttgart), 1968, 10. *The Japan Architect* (Tokyo), 137 (1967, 12).

Hal Moggridge
Progressive Architecture (New York), 1968, 7.

Kinji Nakamura
Architectural Design (London), 1967, 5. *Deutsche Bauzeitung* (Stuttgart), 1968, 10. *The Japan Architect* (Tokyo), 127 (1967, 1/2).

Alfred Neumann
Zodiac (Milan), 19.

Manfredi Nicoletti
l'architecture d'aujourd'hui (Boulogne), 148 (1970, 2/3). *Progressive Architecture* (New York), 1968, 7. Michel Ragon, *La Cité de l'an 2000,* Tournai 1968.

Shokyo Nishihara
Deutsche Bauzeitung (Stuttgart), 1968, 10. *The Japan Architect* (Tokyo), 137 (1967, 12).

So Nishikawa
Deutsche Bauzeitung (Stuttgart), 1968, 10. *The Japan Architect* (Tokyo), 137 (1967, 12).

Masakatsu Nishio
Deutsche Bauzeitung (Stuttgart), 1968, 10. *The Japan Architect* (Tokyo), 137 (1967, 12).

T. Nozawa
Architectural Design (London), 1964, 10. *l'architecture d'aujourd'hui* (Boulogne), 98 (1961, 10).

Kazunori Odahara
Architectural Design (London), 1967, 5. *Deutsche Bauzeitung* (Stuttgart) 1968, 10. *The Japan Architect* (Tokyo), 127 (1967, 1/2).

Masao Otani
Deutsche Bauzeitung (Stuttgart), 1968, 10. *The Japan Architect* (Tokyo), 137 (1967, 12).

Erich Ott
l'architecture d'aujourd'hui (Boulogne), 148 (1970, 2/3).

Frei Otto
Architectural Design (London), 1971, 3. *l'architecture d'aujourd'hui* (Boulogne), 102 (1962, 6/7). Peter Cook, *Experimental Architecture,* London 1970. Frei Otto (Ed.), *Tensile Structures* (2 Vols.), Cambridge, Mass. 1967 (Vol. 1) and 1969 (Vol. 2). Conrad Roland, *Frei Otto—Structures,* London and New York 1971.

Claude Parent
l'architecture d'aujourd'hui (Boulogne), 102 (1962, 6/7). *Architecture Formes Fonctions* (Lausanne), 9 (1962).

Cesar Pelli
Deutsche Bauzeitung (Stuttgart), 1967, 9. *Progressive Architecture* (New York), 1966, 1.

Herbert Prader
l'architecture d'aujourd'hui (Boulogne), 148 (1970, 2/3).

Arthur Quarmby
Peter Cook, *Experimental Architecture,* London 1970. *L'ŒIL* (Paris), 99 (1963, 3).

Shoji Sadao
Zodiac (Milan), 19.

Moshe Safdie
Architectural Design (London), 1967, 3. *l'architecture d'aujourd'hui* (Boulogne), 139 (1968, 9). *Bauen + Wohnen* (Munich and Zürich), 1969, 5. *Deutsche Bauzeitung* (Stuttgart), 1967, 8. *Zodiac* (Milan), 19.

Yves Salier
Michel Ragon, *La Cité de l'an 2000,* Tournai 1968.

Norio Sato
Architectural Design (London), 1967, 5. *Deutsche Bauzeitung* (Stuttgart), 1968, 10. *The Japan Architect* (Tokyo), 127 (1967, 1/2).

A. Schipkov
l'architecture d'aujourd'hui (Boulogne), 134 (1967, 10/11).

E. Schipkova
See: A. Schipkov.

Helmut C. Schulitz
l'architecture d'aujourd'hui (Boulogne), 148 (1970, 2/3). *Bauen + Wohnen* (Munich and Zürich), 1970, 11. *domus* (Milan), 476 (1969, 7).

Eckhard Schulze-Fielitz
l'architecture d'aujourd'hui (Boulogne), 102 (1962, 6/7). Peter Cook, *Experimental Architecture,* London 1970. Eckhard Schulze-Fielitz, *Stadtbausystem,* Stuttgart (in preparation).

Akira Shibuya
Architectural Design (London), 1967, 5. *Deutsche Bauzeitung* (Stuttgart), 1968, 10. *The Japan Architect* (Tokyo), 127 (1967, 1/2).

Hiroshi Shimamura
Deutsche Bauzeitung (Stuttgart) 1968, 10. *The Japan Architect* (Tokyo), 137 (1967, 12).

Hideo Shimizu
Architectural Design (London), 1967, 5. *Deutsche Bauzeitung* (Stuttgart), 1968, 10. *The Japan Architect* (Tokyo), 127 (1967, 1/2).

Yuji Shiraishi
Architectural Design (London), 1967, 5. *Deutsche Bauzeitung* (Stuttgart), 1968, 10. *The Japan Architect* (Tokyo), 127 (1967, 1/2).

Paolo Soleri
Architectural Forum (New York), Vol. 114, No. 3 (1961, 3). *l'architecture d'aujourd'hui* (Boulogne), 102 (1962, 6/7); 139 (1968, 9); 146 (1969, 10/11). *Architecture Formes Fonctions* (Lausanne), 9 (1962). Paolo Soleri, *The City in the Image of Man,* Cambridge, Mass. and London 1969.

A. Stinco
Peter Cook, *Experimental Architecture,* London 1970.

Kuniaki Suda
Deutsche Bauzeitung (Stuttgart), 1968, 9. *The Japan Architect* (Tokyo), 137 (1967, 12).

Mikiro Takaki
Deutsche Bauzeitung (Stuttgart), 1968, 10. *The Japan Architect* (Tokyo), 137 (1967, 12).

Shingo Takamizawa
Deutsche Bauzeitung (Stuttgart), 1968, 10. *The Japan Architect* (Tokyo), 137 (1967, 12).

Kunitsugu Takuri
Deutsche Bauzeitung (Stuttgart), 1968, 10. *The Japan Architect* (Tokyo), 137 (1967, 12).

Kenzo Tange
l'architecture d'aujourd'hui (Boulogne), 98 (1961, 10/11). *Architecture Formes Fonctions* (Lausanne), 9 (1962). *Bauen + Wohnen* (Munich and Zürich), 1964, 1. Peter Cook, *Experimental Architecture,* London 1970. *The Japan Architect* (Tokyo), 130 (1967, 5). Udo Kultermann (Ed.), *Kenzo Tange 1946–1969,* London and New York 1970. Egon Tempel, *New Japanese Architecture,* New York and London 1970.

Stanley Tigerman
l'architecture d'aujourd'hui (Boulogne), 128 (1966, 10/11); 134 (1967, 10/11). *casabella* (Milan), 306 (1966, 6). *Progressive Architecture* (New York), 1968, 7.

Hiroshi Toyomura
Deutsche Bauzeitung (Stuttgart), 1968, 10. *The Japan Architect* (Tokyo), 137 (1967, 12).

Mitsunobu Ueno
Deutsche Bauzeitung (Stuttgart), 1968, 10. *The Japan Architect* (Tokyo), 137 (1967, 12).

Yoshio Yamamori
Architectural Design (London), 1967, 5. *Deutsche Bauzeitung* (Stuttgart), 1968, 10. *The Japan Architect* (Tokyo), 127 (1967, 1/2).

Kenzo Yoshikawa
Deutsche Bauzeitung (Stuttgart), 1968, 10. *The Japan Architect* (Tokyo), 137 (1967, 12).

Witold Zandvos
See: Equipe MIASTO

Engelbert Zobl
l'architecture d'aujourd'hui (Boulogne), 148 (1970, 2/3). *Bauen + Wohnen* (Munich and Zürich), 1970, 11. *domus* (Milan) 476 (1969, 7).

Acknowledgements

AMAG, Zürich 25 (18)
Archigram, London 22 (9), 30 (33–35), 34 (48), 69 (1–4), 70 (1, 2), 71 (3–5), 110 (1), 111 (2, 3), 112 (1, 2), 113 (3–5), 114 (1, 2), 115 (3)
Harald Boering 20 (1)
Henry Brandt, Geneva 14 (18)
F. Bruckmann KG., Bildarchiv, Munich 14 (17)
Burdin, Mérignac, France 88 (1), 89 (2)
Orlando R. Cabanban, Oak Park, Illinois 132 (1)
Comet, Zürich 8 (1)
Deutsche Presse-Agentur GmbH., Frankfurt/M. 12 (10, 11)
Presse-Agentur L. Dukas 28 (29)
Dwain Faubion, San Francisco 142 (1)
Alex Fellner, Zürich 49 (2)
Georg Gerster, Zürich 16 (26)
Monica Hennig-Schefold, Berlin 35 (51)
Etienne Hubert, Paris 58 (1), 59 (2, 5), 128 (1, 2), 129 (3, 4)
H. Hutter 43 (6)
Institut für leichte Flächentragwerke, Stuttgart 31 (36, 37), 116 (1, 2, 4), 117 (2), 118 (3, 4)
Jens Jansen, Stuttgart 33 (44), 35 (50), 45 (4, 5, 8)
Kawasumi Architectural Photograph Office, Tokyo 124 (1)
Balthazar Korab, Troy, Michigan 158 (1)
Heinz Lohoff, Bochum 12 (12)
André Martin 38 (64)
McDonnell Douglas Corporation 25 (17)
MERO, Würzburg 27 (25)
Osamu Murai, Tokyo 22 (8), 72 (2), 73 (3), 100 (1), 101 (3, 4), 102 (7), 157 (3, 4)
Sigrid Neubert, Munich 186 (7)
Niedersächsisches Landesinstitut für Marschen- und Wurtenforschung, Wilhelmshaven 10 (5)
Victor E. Nieuwenhuys, Amsterdam 188 (1–3)
Photopress, Grenoble 62 (1)
The Port of New York Authority, New York 14 (19)
Eduard Probst, Zürich 11 (8)
Christoph-Albrecht Kühn zu Reineck, Hamburg 35 (53)
Eckart Schuster, Wettmannstätten, Austria 104 (1), 105 (3)
K. Schweizer, Tages-Anzeiger, Zürich 37 (62)
Terence Shaw, Weston, Ontario 31 (39), 44 (1), 120 (2)
Shokokusha, Tokyo 98 (2), 99 (3, 4)
E. Torihata 127 (7)
Klaus Uhlig, Cologne 35 (52)
Gerhard Ullmann, Berlin 10 (3, 4), 12 (9)
Otto Umbehr, Hanover 26 (20)
USIS Photos, Bonn-Bad Godesberg 32 (43)
Werbe- und Verkehrsamt, Münster/Westf. 16 (25)
Michael Wolgensinger, Zürich 13 (16), 18 (30), 50 (2), 170 (8), 171 (9, 10), 172 (11–13), 173 (14–17), 174 (18), 175 (19, 20), 191–193
Ursula Zeidler, Munich Jacket (portrait of Justus Dahinden)

Archiv Günter Nitschke, Princeton, N. J. 22 (8), 72 (2), 73 (3), 74 (1), 76 (2), 92 (1), 96 (1), 122 (2), 130 (1)

Architectural Design (London) 20 (4), 75 (5, 6), 90 (1–5), 91 (6), 108 (2, 3), 109 (5–7)

l'architecture d'aujourd'hui (Boulogne) 24 (16), 74 (2), 75 (3, 4), 130 (2, 3), 160 (1, 2), 161 (3, 4)
Architecture Formes Fonctions (Lausanne) 60 (2), 61 (3), 82/83 (1, 2), 144 (1–3), 145 (4, 5), 150 (3), 151 (5–7)
Bauen + Wohnen (Munich and Zürich) 125 (2, 3), 126 (4, 5)
Deutsche Bauzeitung (Stuttgart) 22 (10), 31 (39), 44 (1), 120 (2)
The Japan Architect (Tokyo) 76 (1), 77 (3–7), 78 (1–4), 79 (5–7), 80 (1–3), 81 (4–8), 93 (2), 94 (3–7), 95 (1–3), 97 (2, 3), 100 (2), 101 (5, 6)
Kenchiku Bunka (Tokyo) 157 (3–5)
Kinder sehen ihre Siedlung (Children view their settlements), Exhibition catalogue of the Städtebauinstitut Nürnberg e.V. 15 (24)
Udo Kultermann (Ed.), _Kenzo Tange 1946–1969_, Verlag für Architektur, Zürich 100 (1), 101 (3, 4), 102 (7), 124 (1), 127 (6)
S. Lissitzky-Küppers, _El Lissitzky_, VEB Verlag der Kunst, Dresden 26 (20)
Mondlandung, Chr. Belser Verlag, Stuttgart 32 (43)
Fr. Pootman, _Nach der Hochzeit kommt der Tod_, Süddeutscher Verlag, Munich 20 (1)
Charles-Albert Reichen, _Histoire de la Chimie_, Editions Rencontre, Lausanne 20 (5)
Siedler/Niggemeyer/Angreß, _Die gemordete Stadt_, F. A. Herbig Verlagsbuchhandlung, Berlin 11 (7)
Paolo Soleri, _The City in the Image of Man_, Cambridge, Mass. 39 (67), 178–183
werk (Winterthur) 35 (51)